The Russian Discoveries

William Coxe

The Russian Discoveries
Between Asia and America

by William Coxe

READEX MICROPRINT

Foreword

Account of the Russian Discoveries Between Asia and America...By William Coxe, printed in London in 1780, gave to the English public its first clear report of the Russian discoveries in Alaska since 1745. Russian expeditions before 1745 were covered in *Voyages from Asia to America, for Completing the Discoveries of the North West Coast of America,* translated from the German of G. F. Müller, official historiographer of the Russian Empire, and published in 1761.

William Coxe, designated on the title page as "Fellow of King's College, Cambridge, and Chaplain to His Grace the Duke of Marlborough," had visited Russia in 1778 as tutor to Lord Herbert, son of the Earl of Pembroke. There he met scholars in Moscow and in St. Petersburg and collected oral and manuscript accounts of the Russian discoveries in the northern Pacific.

The first part of the *Account* consists of an almost complete translation of an anonymous German treatise, published in Hamburg in 1776, which summarizes twenty-four voyages of Russian hunters and merchants to Bering and Copper Islands, and to the Aleutian Islands and Kodiak, with facts concerning the identity of the islands, their natural history, and the natives. Since the furs brought back from the newly discovered islands were sold to the Chinese, Coxe gives in the second part of the book a short account of "The Conquest of Siberia, and the History of the Transactions and Commerce Between Russia and China." The folding plate illustrating this section shows the Chinese frontier town Maimatschin, where commerce between the two countries was transacted. Of this town Coxe notes: "It is a remarkable circumstance, that there is not one woman in Maimatschin. This restriction arises from the policy of the Chinese government, which totally prohibits the women from having the slightest intercourse with foreigners." Part three of the *Account* includes an abstract of the journals of Krenitsin and Levashev, previously unknown even to Russian readers, and a number of other documents with Coxe's explanatory and corroborative appendices. The volume contains four folding maps engraved by Thomas Kitchin.

When the first edition of Coxe's *Account* was published in 1780, the survivors of Cook's last voyage had not yet arrived in England. In 1787 Coxe published, as a supplement, *A Comparative View of the Russian Discoveries with those Made by Captains Cook and Clerke,* which is appended to this volume.

Coxe's work made available to English readers a large accession of geographic knowledge that was entirely new to them. There were four editions published in London between 1780 and 1803, and the work was translated into French and German. A discussion of Coxe's *Account,* the sources he used, and the place his work occupies among other accounts of Russian discoveries in the general area of Alaska is included in *Bering's Successors 1745-1780* by Peter S. Pallas (Seattle, 1948), pp. 10-11 and 50-53.

The Russian Discoveries

ACCOUNT

OF THE

RUSSIAN DISCOVERIES

BETWEEN

ASIA AND AMERICA.

TO WHICH ARE ADDED,

THE CONQUEST OF SIBERIA,

AND

THE HISTORY OF THE TRANSACTIONS AND COMMERCE BETWEEN RUSSIA AND CHINA.

BY WILLIAM COXE, A.M.

Fellow of King's College, Cambridge, and Chaplain to his Grace the Duke of MARLBOROUGH.

THE SECOND EDITION, REVISED AND CORRECTED.

LONDON,

PRINTED BY J. NICHOLS,

FOR T. CADELL, IN THE STRAND.

MDCCLXXX.

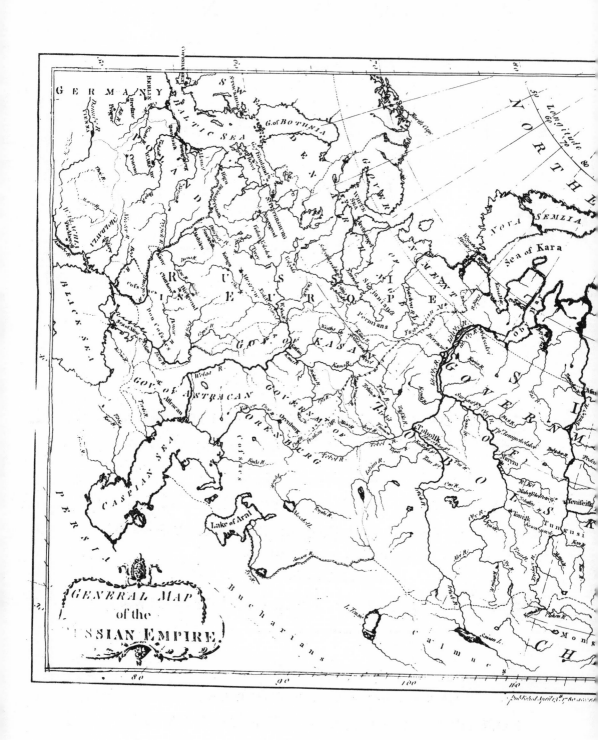

GERMANY

BALTIC SEA

G. of BOTHNIA

NORTH

NOVA SEMLIA

Sea of Kara

Longitude

BLACK SEA

R U S

E I R

O P E

GOVERNMENT

Permians

CASPIAN SEA

GOV. OF KASA

GOV. OF ASTRACAN

GOVERNATOR of ORENBOURG

Tobolk

GOVERNMENT OF TOBOLSKOI

Narym

Jenissei

Tomsk

Tungusi

PERSIA

Lake of Aral

Bucharians

Calmues

Mongal

CHI

GENERAL MAP
of the
RUSSIAN EMPIRE.

80   90   100   110

Published April 13th 1780 ......

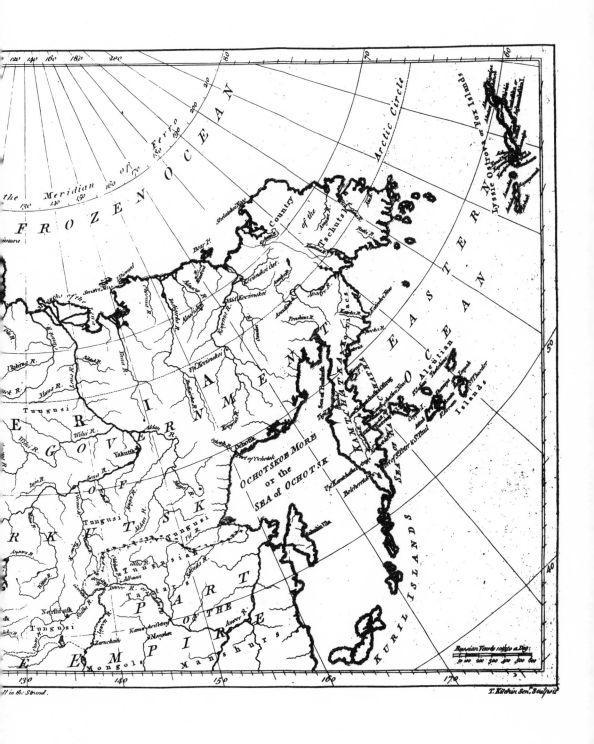

TO

JACOB BRYANT, ESQ.

AS A PUBLIC TESTIMONY

OF

THE HIGHEST RESPECT FOR

HIS DISTINGUISHED LITERARY ABILITIES,

THE TRUEST ESTEEM FOR

HIS PRIVATE VIRTUES,

AND THE MOST GRATEFUL SENSE OF

MANY PERSONAL FAVOURS,

THE FOLLOWING PAGES ARE INSCRIBED,

BY

HIS FAITHFUL AND AFFECTIONATE

HUMBLE SERVANT,

WILLIAM COXE.

Cambridge,
March 27, 1780.

P R E F A C E.

THE late Ruffian Difcoveries between Afia and America have, for fome time, engaged the attention of the curious; more efpecially fince Dr. Robertfon's admirable Hiftory of America has been in the hands of the public. In that valuable performance the elegant and ingenious author has communicated to the world, with an accuracy and judgement which fo eminently diftinguifh all his writings, the moft exact information at that time to be obtained, concerning thofe important difcoveries. During my ftay at Peterfburg, my inquiries were particularly directed to this interefting fubject, in order to learn if any new light had been thrown on an article of knowledge of fuch confequence to the hiftory of mankind. For this purpofe I endeavoured to collect the refpective journals of the feveral voyages fubfequent to the expedition of Beering and Tfchirikoff in 1741, with which the celebrated Muller concludes his account of the firft Ruffian navigations.

During

During the courfe of my refearches I was informed, that a treatife in the German language, publifhed at Hamburg and Leipfic in 1776, contained a full and exact narrative of the Ruffian voyages, from 1745 to 1770 *.

As the author has not prefixed his name, I fhould have paid little attention to an anonymous publication, if I had not been affured, from very good authority, that the work in queftion was compiled from the original journals. Not refting however upon this intelligence, I took the liberty of applying to Mr. Muller himfelf, who, by order of the Emprefs, had arranged the fame journals, from which the anonymous author is faid to have drawn his materials. Previous to my application, Mr. Muller had compared the treatife with the original papers ; and he favoured me with the following ftrong teftimony to its exactnefs and authenticity :
" Vous ferès bien de traduire pour l'ufage de vos com-
" patriotes le petit livre fur les ifles fituées entre le Kamt-
" chatka et l'Amerique. Il n'y a point de doute, que
" l'auteur n'ait eté pourvu de bons memoirs, et qu'il ne
" s'en foit fervi fidelement. J'ai confronté le livre avec

* The title of the book is, Neue Nachrichten von denen Neuendeckten Infuln in der See zwifchen Afia und Amerika aus mitgetheilten Urkunden und Aufzuegen verfaffet von J. L. S.

" les

" les originaux." Supported therefore by this very re-
fpectable authority, I confidered this treatife as a performance of the higheft credit, and well worthy of being
more generally known and perufed.   I have accordingly,
in the firft part of the prefent publication, fubmitted a
tranflation of it to the reader's candour ; and added occafional notes to fuch paffages as feemed to require an explanation.   The original is divided into fections without any
references.   But as it feemed to be more convenient to
divide it into chapters ; and to accompany each chapter
with a fummary of the contents, and marginal references;
I have moulded it into that form, without making however any alteration in the order of the journals.

The additional intelligence which I procured at Petersburg, is thrown into an appendix : It confifts of
fome new information, and of three journals *, never
before given to the public.   Amongft thefe I muft
particularly mention that of Krenitzin and Levafheff,
which, together with the chart of their voyage, was
communicated to Dr. Robertfon, by order of the
Emprefs of Ruffia; and which that juftly admired
hiftorian has, in the politeft and moft obliging manner,

---

* The journal of Krenitzin and Levafheff, the fhort account of Synd's
voyage, and the narrative of Shalauroff's expedition, Nº I. IX. XI.

permitted

permitted me to make ufe of in this collection. This voyage, which redounds greatly to the honour of the fovereign who planned it, confirms in general the authenticity of the treatife above-mentioned; and afcertains the reality of the difcoveries made by the private merchants.

As a farther illuftration of this fubject, I collected the beft charts which could be procured at Petersburg, and of which a lift will be given in the following advertifement. From all thefe circumftances, I may venture, perhaps, to hope that the curious and inquifitive reader will not only find in the following pages the moft authentic and circumftantial account of the progrefs and extent of the Ruffian difcoveries, which has hitherto appeared in any language; but be enabled hereafter to compare them with thofe more lately made by that great and much to be regretted navigator, Captain Cooke, when his journal fhall be communicated to the public.

As all the furs which are brought from the New-difcovered Iflands are fold to the Chinefe, I was naturally led to make enquiries concerning the commerce between Ruffia and China; and finding this branch of traffic much more important than is commonly imagined, I thought that a general fketch of its prefent ftate,

together

together with a fuccinct view of the tranfactions between the two nations, would not be unacceptable.

The conqueft of Siberia, as it firft opened a communication with China, and paved the way to all the interefting difcoveries related in the prefent attempt, will not appear unconnected, I truft, with its principal defign.

The materials of this fecond part, as alfo of the preliminary obfervations concerning Kamtchatka, and the commerce to the New-difcovered Iflands, are drawn from books of eftablifhed and undoubted reputation. Mr. Muller and Mr. Pallas, from whofe interefting works thefe hiftorical and commercial fubjects are chiefly compiled, are too well known in the literary world to require any other vouchers for their judgment, exactnefs, and fidelity, than the bare mentioning of their names. I have only farther to apprize the reader, that, befides the intelligence extracted from thefe publications, he will find fome additional circumftances relative to the Ruffian commerce with China, which I collected during my continuance in Ruffia.

I CAN-

I CANNOT clofe this addrefs to the reader without embracing with peculiar fatisfaction the juft occafion, which the enfuing treatifes upon the Ruffian difcoveries and commerce afford me, of joining with every friend of fcience in the warmeft admiration of that enlarged and liberal fpirit, which fo ftrikingly marks the character of the prefent Emprefs of Ruffia. Since her acceffion to the throne, the inveftigation and difcovery of ufeful knowledge has been the conftant object of her generous encouragement. The authentic records of the Ruffian hiftory have, by her exprefs orders, been properly arranged; and permiffion is readily granted of infpecting them. The moft diftant parts of her vaft dominions have, at her expence, been explored and defcribed by perfons of great abilities and extenfive learning; by which means new and important lights have been thrown upon the geography and natural hiftory of thofe remote regions. In a word, this truly great princefs has contributed more, in the compafs of only a few years, towards civilizing and informing the minds of her fubjects, than had been effected by all the fovereigns her predeceffors fince the glorious æra of Peter the Great.

In

In order to prevent the frequent mention of the full title of the books referred to in the courſe of this performance, the following catalogue is ſubjoined, with the abbreviations.

Müller's Samlung Ruſſiſcher Geſchichte, IX volumes, 8vo. printed at St. Peterſburg in 1732, and the following years; it is referred to in the following manner: S. R. G. with the volume and page annexed.

From this excellent collection I have made uſe of the following treatiſes:

vol. II. p. 293, &c. Geſchichte der Gegenden an dem Fluſſe Amur.

There is a French tranſlation of this treatiſe, called Hiſtoire du Fleuve Amur, 12mo, Amſterdam, 1766.

vol. III. p. 1, &c. Nachrichten von See Reiſen, &c.

There is an Engliſh and a French tranſlation of this work; the former is called "Voyages from Aſia to America for completing the Diſcoveries of the North Weſt Coaſt of America," 4to, London, 1764. The title of the latter is "Voyages et Decouvertes faites par les Ruſſes," &c. 12mo, Amſterdam, 1766. p. 413. Nachrichten Von der Handlung in Sibirien.

Vol. VI. p. 109, Sibiriſche Geſhichte.

Vol. VIII. p. 504, Nachricht Von der Ruſſiſchen Handlung nach China.

Pallas Reiſe durch verchiedene Provinzen des Ruſſiſchen Reichs, in Three Parts, 4to, St. Peterſburg, 1771, 1773, and 1776, thus cited, Pallas Reiſe.

Georgi Bemerkungen einer Reiſe im Ruſſiſchen Reich in Jahre, 1772, III volumes, 4to, St. Petersburg, 1775, cited Georgi Reiſe.

Fiſcher Sibiriſche Geſchichte, 2 volumes, 8vo, St. Petersburg, cited Fiſ. Sib. Geſ.

Gmelin Reiſe durch Sibirien, Tome IV. 8vo, Gottingen, 1752, cited Gmelin Reiſe.

There

There is a French tranflation of this work, called " Voyage en Siberie," &c. par Gmelin. Paris, 1767.

Neuefte Nachrichten von Kamtchatka aufgefetft im Junius des 1773ften Yahren von dem dafigen Befehls-haber Herrn Kapitain Smalew. Aus dem abhandlungen der freyen Ruffifchen Gefellfchaft Mofkau.

In the journal of St. Petersburg, April, 1776,—cited Journal of St. Pet.

Explanation of fome Ruffian words made ufe of in the following work.

Baidar, a fmall boat.

Guba, a bay.

Kamen, a rock.

Kotche, a veffel.

Krepoft, a regular fortrefs.

Nofs, a cape.

Oftrog, a fortrefs furrounded with palifadoes.

Oftroff, an ifland.

Oftrova, iflands.

Quafs, a fort of fermented liquor.

Reka, a river.

The Ruffians, in their proper names of perfons, make ufe of patronymics; thefe patronymics are formed in fome cafes by adding *Vitch* to the chriftian name of the father; in others *Off* or *Eff:* the former termination is applied only to perfons of condition; the latter to thofe of an inferior rank. As, for inftance,

Among perfons of condition——*Ivan Ivanovitch,*
        of inferior rank, *Ivan Ivanoff,* } Ivan the fon of Ivan.

             Michael Alexievitch, } Michael the fon
             Michael Alexeeff, }   of Alexèy.

Sometimes a furname is added, *Ivan Ivanovitch Romanoff.*

Table

Table of Ruſſian Weights, Meaſures of Length, and Value of Money.

WEIGHT.

A pood weighs 40 Ruſſian pounds = 36 Engliſh.

MEASURES OF LENGTH.

16 verſhocks = an arſheen.

An arſheen = 28 inches.

Three arſheens, or ſeven feet, = a fathom *, or ſazſhen.

500 ſazſhens = a verſt.

A degree of longitude compriſes 104 ½ verſts = 69 ½ Engliſh miles. A mile is therefore 1,515 parts of a verſt ; two miles may then be eſtimated equal to three verſts, omitting a ſmall fraction.

VALUE OF RUSSIAN MONEY.

A rouble = 100 copecs: Its value varies according to the exchange from 3 s. 8 d. to 4 s. 2 d. Upon an average, however, the value of a rouble is reckoned at four ſhillings.

---

* The fathom for meaſuring the depth of water is the ſame as the Engliſh fathom, = 6 feet.

ADVER-

ADVERTISEMENT

A S no aftronomical obfervations have been taken in the voyages related in this collection, the longitude and latitude afcribed to the New-difcovered Iflands in the journals and upon the charts cannot be abfolutely depended upon. Indeed the reader will perceive, that the pofition * of the Fóx Iflands upon the general map of Ruffia is materially different from that affigned to them upon the chart of Krenitzin and Levafheff. Without endeavouring to clear up any difficulties which may arife from this uncertainty, I thought it would be moft fatisfactory to have the beft charts engraved: the reader will then be able to compare them with each other, and with the feveral journals. Which reprefentation of the New-difcovered Iflands deferves the preference, will probably be afcertained upon the return of captain Clerke from his prefent expedition.

* See p. 286.

Lift

Lift of the CHARTS, and Directions for placing them.

CON-

C O N T E N T S.

P A R T I.

c   Account

Umnak

P A R T   II.

Chap.

PART III.

N.° II

4

PART

P A R T I.

CONTAINING

I. PRELIMINARY OBSERVATIONS CONCERNING KAMTCHATKA.

AND

II. ACCOUNT OF THE NEW DISCOVERIES MADE BY THE RUSSIANS.

B

PRELIMINARY OBSERVATIONS

CONCERNING

KAMTCHATKA, &c.

CHAP. I.

Diſcovery and Conqueſt of Kamtchatka—Preſent ſtate of that Peninſula—Population—Tribute—Productions, &c.

THE Peninſula of Kamtchatka was not diſcovered by the Ruſſians before the latter end of the laſt century. The firſt expedition towards thoſe parts was made in 1696, by ſixteen Coſſacs, under the command of Lucas Semænoff Moroſko, who was ſent againſt the Koriacks of the river Opooka by Volodimir Atlaſſoff commander of Anadirſk. Moroſko continued his march until he came within four days journey of the river Kamtchatka, and having rendered a Kamtchadal village tributary, he returned to Anadirſk *.

Firſt Diſcovery of Kamtchat-ka.

* S. R. G. V. III. p. 72.

The

The following year Atlaſſoff himſelf at the head of a larger body of troops penetrated into the Peninſula, took poſſeſſion of the river Kamtchatka by erecting a croſs upon its banks; and built ſome huts upon the ſpot, where Upper Kamtchatkoi Oſtrog now ſtands.

That Peninſula conquered and coloniſed by the Ruſſians.

Theſe expeditions were continued during the following years: Upper and Lower Kamtchatkoi Oſtrogs and Bolcheretſk were built; the Southern diſtrict conquered and coloniſed; and in 1711 the whole Peninſula was finally reduced under the dominion of the Ruſſians.

During ſome years the poſſeſſion of Kamtchatka brought very little advantage to the crown, excepting the ſmall tribute of furs exacted from the inhabitants. The Ruſſians indeed occaſionally hunted in that Peninſula foxes, wolves, ermines, ſables, and other animals, whoſe valuable ſkins form an extenſive article of commerce among the Eaſtern nations. But the fur trade carried on from thence was inconſiderable; until the Ruſſians diſcovered the iſlands ſituated between Aſia and America, in a ſeries of voyages, the journals of which will be exhibited in the ſubſequent tranſlation. Since theſe diſcoveries, the variety of rich furs, which are procured from thoſe Iſlands, has greatly encreaſed the trade of Kamtchatka, and rendered it a very important branch of the Ruſſian commerce.

The

The Peninſula of Kamtchatka lies between 51 and 62 degrees of North latitude, and 173 and 182 of longitude from the Iſle of Fero. It is bounded on the Eaſt and South by the Sea of Kamtchatka, on the Weſt by the Seas of Ochotſk and Penſhinſk, and on the North by the country of the Koriacs.

It is divided into four diſtricts, Bolcherefk, Tigilſkaia Preſent State of Kamtchat- Krepoſt, Verchnei or Upper Kamtchatkoi Oſtrog, and ka. Niſhnei or Lower Kamtchatkoi Oſtrog. The govern- Government. ment is veſted in the chancery of Bolcherefk, which depends upon and is ſubject to the inſpection of the chancery of Ochotſk. The whole Ruſſian force ſtationed in the Peninſula conſiſts of no more than three hundred men *.

The preſent population of Kamtchatka is very ſmall, Population. amounting to ſcarce four thouſand ſouls. Formerly the inhabitants were more numerous; but in 1768, that country was greatly depopulated by the ravages of the ſmall-pox, by which diſorder five thouſand three hundred and ſixty-eight perſons were carried off. There are now only ſeven hundred and ſix males in the whole Peninſula who are tributary, and an hundred and fourteen in the Kuril Iſles, which are ſubject to Ruſſia.

* Journal of St. Peterſburg for April 1777.

The

Tribute.   The fixed annual tribute confifts in 279 fables, 464 red foxes, 50 fea-otters with a dam, and 38 cub fea-otters. All furs exported from Kamtchatka pay a duty of 10 per cent. to the crown; the tenth of the cargoes brought from the new difcovered iflands is alfo delivered into the cuftoms.

Volcanos.   Many traces of Volcanos have been obferved in this Peninfula; and there are fome mountains, which are at prefent in a burning ftate. The moft confiderable of thefe Volcanos is fituated near the Lower Oftrog. In 1762 a great noife was heard iffuing from the infide of that mountain, and flames of fire were feen to burft from different parts. Thefe flames were immediately fucceeded by a large ftream of melted fnow-water, which flowed into the neighbouring valley, and drowned two Kamtchadals, who were at that time upon an hunting party. The afhes, and other combuftible matter, thrown from the mountain, fpread to the circumference of three hundred verfts. In 1767 there was another difcharge, but lefs confiderable. Every night flames of fire were obferved ftreaming from the mountain; and the eruption, which attended them, did no fmall damage to the inhabitants of the Lower Oftrog. Since that year no flames have been feen; but the mountain emits a conftant fmoke. The fame phænomenon is alfo obferved upon another mountain, called Tabaetfhinfkian.

The

The face of the country throughout the Peninſula _{Productions.} is chiefly mountainous. It produces in ſome parts birch, poplars, alders, willows, underwood, and berries of dif-ferent ſorts. Greens and other vegetables are raiſed with great facility; ſuch as white cabbage, turneps, radiſhes, beetroot, carrots, and ſome cucumbers. Agriculture is in a very low ſtate, which is chiefly owing to the nature of the ſoil and the ſevere hoar froſts: for though ſome trials have been made with reſpect to the cultivation of oats, barley, and rye; yet no crop has ever. been pro-cured ſufficient in quantity or quality to anſwer the pains and expence of raiſing it. Hemp however has of late years been cultivated. with great ſucceſs *.

Every year a veſſel, belonging to the crown, ſails from Ochotſk to Kamtchatka laden with ſalt, provi-ſions, corn, and Ruſſian manufactures; and returns in June or July of the following years with ſkins and. furs.

* Journal of St. Peterſburg.

C H A P.   II.

General idea of the commerce carried on to the New Dif-
covered Iflands.——Equipment of the veffels.——Rifks of the
trade, profits, &c.

SINCE the conclufion of Beering's Voyage, which
was made at the expence of the crown, the profecution of the New Difcoveries begun by him has been
almoft entirely carried on by individuals. Thefe perfons
were principally merchants of Irkutfk, Yakutfk, and
other natives of Siberia, who formed themfelves into
fmall trading companies, and fitted out veffels at their
joint expence.

Equipment of
he Veffels.

Moft of the veffels which are equipped for thefe expeditions are two-mafted: they are commonly built without iron, and in general fo badly conftructed, that it is
wonderful how they can weather fo ftormy a fea. They
are called in Ruffian Skitiki or fewed veffels, becaufe the
planks are fewed together with thongs of leather. Some
few are built in the river of Kamtchatka; but they are
for the moft part conftructed at the haven of Ochotfk.
The largeft of thefe veffels are manned with feventy men,
and the fmalleft with forty. The crew generally confifts
of an equal number of Ruffians and Kamtchadals. The
latter

latter occafion a confiderable faving, as their pay is fmall; they alfo refift, more eafily than the former, the attacks of the fcurvy. But Ruffian mariners are more enterprifing and more to be depended upon in time of danger than the others; fome therefore are unavoidably neceffary.

The expences of building and fitting out the veffels are very confiderable: for there is nothing at Ochotfk but timber for their conftruction. Accordingly cordage, fails, and fome provifions, muft be brought from Ya-kutfk upon horfes. The dearnefs of corn and flour, which muft be tranfported from the diftricts lying about the river Lena, renders it impoffible to lay-in any large quantity for the fubfiftence of the crew during a voyage, which commonly lafts three or four years. For this reafon no more is provided, than is neceffary to fupply the Ruffian mariners with quafs and other fermented liquors.

Expences at-tending this Trade.

From the exceffive fcarcity of cattle both at Ochotfk and * Kamtchatka very little provifion is laid in at either of thofe places: but the crew provide themfelves

* In 1772 there were only 570 head of cattle upon the whole Penin fula. A cow fold from 50 to 60 roubles, an ox from 60 to 100. A pound of frefh beef fold upon an average for $12\frac{1}{2}$ copecs. The exeef-five dearnefs of this price will be eafily conceived, when it is known, that at Mofcow a pound of beef fells for about three copecs. Journ. St. Peterfb.

C   with

with a large ftore of the flefh of fea animals, which
are caught and cured upon Beering's Ifland, where the
veffels for the moft part winter.

After all expences are paid, the equipment of each
veffel ordinarily cofts from 15,000 to 20,000 roubles:
and fometimes the expences amount to 30,000.   Every
veffel is divided into a certain number of fhares, generally from thirty to fifty; and each fhare is worth
from 300 to 500 roubles.

Profits.

The rifk of the trade is very great, as fhipwrecks are
common in the fea of Kamtchatka, which is full of rocks
and very tempeftuous. Befides, the crews are frequently
furprifed and killed by the iflanders, and the veffels
deftroyed.   In return the profits arifing from thefe
voyages are very confiderable, and compenfate the in-
conveniencies and dangers attending them.   For if a
fhip comes back after having made a profitable voyage,
the gain at the moft moderate computation amounts
to cent. per cent. and frequently to as much more.
Should the veffel be capable of performing a fecond
expedition, the expences are of courfe confiderably
leffened, and the fhares are at a lower price.

Some notion of the general profits arifing from
this trade (when the voyage is fuccefsful), may be
deduced from the fale of a rich cargo of furs, brought

to

to Kamtchatka, on the 2d of June, 1772, from the New-difcovered iflands, in a veffel belonging to Ivan Popoff.

The tenth part of the fkins being delivered to the cuftoms, the remainder was diftributed in fifty-five fhares.   Each fhare confifted of twenty fea-otters, fixteen black and brown foxes, ten red foxes, three fea-otter tails ; and fuch a portion was fold upon the fpot from 800 to 1000 roubles :   fo that according to this price the whole lading was worth about 50,000 roubles *.

* Georgi Reife Tom. I. p. 23, & feq. Journal of St. Peterfburg.

C H A P.   III.

Furs and skins procured from Kamtchatka *and the New Discovered Islands.*

Furs and Skins
brought from
Kamtchatka
and the New
Discovered
Islands.

THE principal furs and skins procured from the Peninsula of Kamtchatka and the New Discovered Islands are sea-otters, foxes, sables, ermines, wolves, bears, &c.——These furs are transported to Ochotsk by sea, and from thence carried to *Kiachta upon the frontiers of Siberia; where the greatest part of them are sold to the Chinese at a very considerable profit.

Sea-Otters.

Of all these furs the skins of the sea-otters are the richest and most valuable. Those animals resort in great numbers to the Aleütian and Fox Islands: they are called by the Russians Bobri Morski or sea-beavers, and sometimes Kamtchadal beavers, on account of the re-semblance of their fur to that of the common beaver. From these circumstances several authors have been led into a mistake, and have supposed that this animal is of the beaver species; whereas it is the true sea-otter †.

* See Part II. Chap. III.

† S. R. G. III. p. 530.   For a description of the sea-otter, Lutra Marina, called by Linnæus Mustela Lutris, see Nov. Comm. Pet. Vol. II. p. 367, &c.

The

The female are called Matka or dams; and the cubs till five months old Medviedki or little bears, becaufe their coat refembles that of a bear; they lofe that coat after five months, and then are called Kofchloki.

The fur of the fineft fort is thick and long, of a dark colour, and a fine gloffy hue. The methods of taking thefe fea-otters are, by ftriking them with harpoons as they are fleeping upon their backs in the fea; by hunting them down in boats; by furprifing them in caverns; or taking them in nets.

Their fkins bear different prices according to their quality.

At Kamtchatka * the beft fell for
        per fkin from   —— ——   30 to 40 roubles.
                Middle fort 20 to 30
                Worft fort 15 to 25

At Kiachta† the old and middle-
        aged fea-otter fkins are fold
        to the Chinefe per fkin from 80 to 140
                The worft fort 30 to   40

* Journal St. Peterfburg.
† Pallas Reife. Part III. p. 137.

As

As thefe furs are fold at fo great a price to the Chinefe, they are feldom brought into Ruffia for fale: and feveral, which have been carried to Mofcow as a tribute, were purchafed for 30 roubles per fkin; and fent from thence to the Chinefe frontiers, where they were difpofed of at a very high intereft *.

Different Species of Foxes.

There are feveral fpecies of Foxes, whofe fkins are fent from Kamtchatka into Siberia and Ruffia. Of thefe the principal are the black foxes, the Petfi or Arctic foxes, the red and ftone foxes.

The fineft black foxes are caught in different parts of Siberia, and more commonly in the Northern regions between the Rivers Lena, Indigirka, and Kovyma: the black foxes found upon the remoteft Eaftern iflands difcovered by the Ruffians, or the Lyffie Oftrova, are not fo valuable. They are very black and large; but the coat for the moft part is as coarfe as that of a wolf. The great difference in the finenefs of the fur, between thefe foxes and thofe of Siberia, arifes probably from the following circumftances. In thofe iflands the cold is not fo fevere as in Siberia; and as there is no wood, the foxes live in holes and caverns of the rocks; whereas in the abovementioned parts of Siberia, there are large tracts of forefts in which they find fhelter. Some black foxes how-

* S. R. G. V. III. Pallas Reife.

ever

ever are occasionally caught in the remoteft Eaftern
Iflands, not wholly deftitute of wood, and thefe are
of great value. In general the Chinefe, who pay the
deareft for black furs, do not give more for the black
foxes of the New-difcovered iflands than from 20 to
30 roubles per fkin.

The Arctic or ice foxes are very common upon fome of
the New-difcovered Iflands. They are called Petfi by the
Ruffians, and by the Germans blue foxes. Their natural $^{Pennant's}_{Synopfis.}$
colour is of a bluifh grey or afh colour; but they change
their coat at different ages, and in different feafons of
the year. In general they are born brown, are white in
winter, and brown in fummer; and in fpring and autumn,
as the hair gradually falls off, the coat is marked with
different fpecks and croffes.

At Kiachta* all the feveral varieties fell upon an average to the Chinefe per fkin from 50

copecs to — — — —	$2\frac{2}{3}$ roubles.	
Stone foxes at Kamtchatka per fkin from — — — —	1 to $2\frac{1}{2}$	
Red foxes from 80 copecs to —		1 80 copecs.
At Kiachta from 80 copecs to —	9	
Common wolves fkins at per fkin	2	
Beft fort per fkin from —	8 to 16	
Sables per ditto — — —	$2\frac{1}{2}$ to 10	

* Pallas Reife.

A pood

A pood of the beſt ſea-horſe teeth * ſells

At Yakutſk for - - - -	10 roubles.
Of the middling - - - -	8
Inferior ditto - - -	from 5 to 7.

Four, five, or ſix teeth generally weigh a pood, and ſometimes, but very rarely, three.   They are ſold to the Chineſe, Monguls, and Calmucs.

* S. R. G. V. III.

CHAP.

ACCOUNT

OF THE

NEW DISCOVERIES

MADE BY THE

RUSSIANS

IN THE EASTERN OCEAN,

BETWEEN KAMTCHATKA AND AMERICA.

TRANSLATED FROM THE GERMAN.
WITH NOTES BY THE TRANSLATOR.

D

A C C O U N T

O F T H E

RUSSIAN DISCOVERIES.

C H A P. I.

Commencement and progress of the Ruffian *Difcoveries in the fea of* Kamtchatka—*General divifion of the New Difcovered Iflands.*

A Thirft after riches was the chief motive which excited the Spaniards to the difcovery of America; and which turned the attention of other maritime nations to that quarter. The fame paffion for riches occafioned, about the middle of the fixteenth century, the difcovery and conqueft of Northern Afia, a country, before that time unknown to the Europeans. The firft foundation of this ^{Conqueft of Siberia.} conqueft was laid by the celebrated Yermac *, at the head of a band of adventurers, lefs civilized, but at the fame time not fo inhuman as the conquerors of America. By the acceffion of this vaft territory, now known by the name of Siberia, the Ruffians have acquired an extent of empire never before attained by any other nation.

* The reader will find an account of this conqueft by Yermac in Part II. Chap. I.

D 2   The

The firſt project * for making diſcoveries in that tempeſtuous ſea, which lies between Kamtchatka and America, was conceived and planned by Peter I. the greateſt
ſovereign who ever ſat upon the Ruſſian throne, until
it was adorned by the preſent empreſs.   The mature and
completion of this project under his immediate ſuccef-
ſors are well known to the public from the relation of
the celebrated Muller.   No ſooner had † Beering and

* There ſeems a want of connection in this place, which will be cleared
up by confidering, that, by the conqueſt of Siberia, the Ruſſians advanced to the ſhores of the Eaſtern Ocean, the ſcene of the diſcoveries
here alluded to.

† Beering had already made ſeveral expeditions in the ſea of Kamtchatka, by orders of the crown, before he undertook the voyage mentioned in the text.
    In 1728, he departed from the mouth of the Kamtchatka river, in
company with Tſchirikoff. The object of this voyage was to afcertain, whether the two Continents of Afia and America were ſeparated ;
and Peter I. a ſhort time before his death, had drawn up inſtructions
with his own hand for that purpofe. Beering coaſted the Eaſtern ſhore
of Siberia as high as latitude 67° 18′ ; but made no diſcovery of the
oppoſite Continent.
    In 1729, he ſet ſail again for the profecution of the ſame deſign ; but
this ſecond attempt equally failed of ſuccefs.
    In 1741, Beering and Tſchirikoff went out upon the celebrated expe-
dition (alluded to in the text, and which is ſo often mentioned in the
courfe of this work) towards the coaſts of America. This expedition led
the way to all the important diſcoveries ſince made by the Ruſſians.
    Beering's veſſel was wrecked in December of the ſame year ; and
Tſchirikoff landed at Kamtchatka on the 9th of October, 1742.
    S. R. G. III. Nachrichten von See Reiſen, &c. and Robertſon's Hif-
tory of America, Vol. I. p. 273, & ſeq.

5   Tſchirikoff,

Tfchirikoff, in the profecution of this plan, opened their way to iflands abounding in valuable furs, than private merchants immediately engaged with ardour in fimilar expeditions; and, within a period of ten years, more im- Their Pro-
portant difcoveries were made by thefe individuals, at grefs.
their own private coft, than had been hitherto effected by all the expenfive efforts of the crown.

Soon after the return of Beering's crew from the ifland where he was fhip-wrecked and died, and which is called after his name, the inhabitants of Kamtchatka ventured over to that ifland, to which the fea-otters and other fea-animals were accuftomed to refort in great numbers. Mednoi Oftroff, or Copper Ifland, which takes that appellation from large maffes of native copper found upon the beach, and which lies full in fight of Beering's Ifle, was an eafy and fpeedy difcovery.

Thefe two fmall uninhabited fpots were for fome time the only iflands that were known; until a fcarcity of land and fea-animals, whofe numbers were greatly diminifhed by the Ruffian hunters, occafioned other expeditions. Several of the veffels which were fent out upon thefe voyages were driven by ftormy weather to the South-eaft; by which means the Aleütian Ifles, fituated about the 195th * degree of longitude, and but moderately peopled, were difcovered.

From

* The author reckons, throughout this treatife, the longitude from
the

From the year 1745, when it seems these islands were first visited, until 1750, when the first tribute of furs was brought from thence to Ochotsk, the government appears not to have been fully informed of their discovery. In the last mentioned year, one Lebedeff was commander of Kamtchatka. From 1755 to 1760, Captain Tsheredoff and Lieutenant Kashkareff were his successors. In 1760, Feodor Ivanovitch Soimonoff, governor of Tobolsk, turned his attention to the abovementioned islands; and, the same year, Captain Rtiftsheff, at Ochotsk, instructed Lieutenant Shmaleff, the same who was afterwards commander in Kamtchatka, to promote and favour all expeditions in those seas. Until this time, all the discoveries subsequent to Beering's voyage were made, without the interposition of the court, by private merchants in small vessels fitted out at their own expence.

The Empress promotes all Attempts towards New Discoveries.

The present Empress (to whom every circumstance which contributes to aggrandize the Russian empire is an object of attention) has given new life to these discoveries. The merchants who engaged in them have been animated by recompences. The importance and true position of the

the first meridian of the isle of Fero. The longitude and latitude, which he gives to the Fox Islands, corresponds exactly with those in which they are laid down upon the General Map of Russia. The longitude of Beering's, Copper Island, and of the Aleütian Isles, are somewhat different. See Advertisement relating to the Charts, and also Appendix L N° IV. p. 286.

Russian

Ruffian iflands have been afcertained by an expenfive
voyage *, made by order of the crown; and much additional information will be derived from the journals
and charts of the officers employed in that expedition,
whenever they fhall be publifhed.

Meanwhile, we may reft affured, that feveral modern
geographers have erred in advancing America too much
to the Weft, and in queftioning the extent of Siberia Eaftwards, as laid down by the Ruffians.- It appears, indeed,
evident,, that the accounts and even conjectures of the
celebrated Muller, concerning the pofition of thofe diftant
regions, are more and more confirmed by facts; in the
fame manner as the juftnefs of his fuppofition concerning the form of the coaft of the fea of Ochotfk † has
been lately eftablifhed.- With refpect to the extent of
Siberia, it appears almoft beyond a doubt from the moft
recent obfervations, that its Eaftern extremity is fituated
beyond‡ 200 degrees of longitude. In regard to the
Weftern coaft of America, all the navigations to the
New Difcovered Iflands evidently fhew, that between 50

* The author here alludes to the fecret expedition of Captain Krenitzin and Levaheff, whofe journal and chart were fent, by order of the
Emprefs of Ruffia, to Dr. Robertfon. See Robertfon's Hiftory of America, Vol. I. p. 276 and 460. See Appendix I. Nº II.

† Mr. Muller formerly conjectured, that the coaft of the fea of
Ochotfk ftretched South-weft towards the river Ud; and from thence to
the mouth of the Amoor South-eaft: and the truth of this conjecture
had been fince confirmed by a coafting voyage made by Captain Synd.

‡ Appendix I. Nº I.

and

and 60 degrees of latitude, that Continent advances no where nearer to Afia than the * coafts touched at by Beering and Tfchirikoff, or about 236 degrees of longitude.

As to the New Difcovered Iflands, no credit muft be given to a chart publifhed in the Geographical Calendar of St. Peterfburg for 1774; in which they are inaccurately laid down. Nor is the antient chart of the New Difcoveries, publifhed by the Imperial Academy, and which feems to have been drawn up from mere reports, more deferving of attention †.

Pofition of the New Difcovered Iflands.

The late navigators give a far different defcription of the Northern Archipelago. From their accounts we learn, that Beering's Ifland is fituated due Eaft from Kamtchatkoi Nofs, in the 185th degree of longitude. Near it is Copper Ifland; and, at fome diftance from them, Eaft-fouth-eaft, there are three fmall iflands, named by their inhabitants, Attak, Semitfhi, and Shemiya: thefe are properly the Aleütian Ifles; they ftretch from Weft-north-weft towards Eaft-fouth-eaft, in the fame direction as Beering's and Copper Iflands, in the longitude of 195, and latitude 54

* Appendix I. Nº III.
† Appendix I. Nº IV.

To the North-eaſt of theſe, at the diſtance of 600 or 800 verſts, lies another group of ſix or more iſlands, known by the name of the Andreanoffſkie Oſtrova.

South-eaſt, or Eaſt-ſouth, of theſe, at the diſtance of about fifteen degrees, and North by Eaſt of the Aleütian, begins the chain of Lyſſie Oſtrova, or Fox Iſlands: this chain of rocks and iſles ſtretches Eaſt-north-eaſt between 56 and 61 degrees of North latitude*, from 211 degrees of longitude moſt probably to the Continent of America; and in a line of direction, which croſſes with that in which the Aleütian iſles lie. The largeſt and moſt remarkable of theſe iſlands are Umnak, Aghunalaſhka, or, as it is commonly ſhortened, Unalaſhka, Kadyak, and Alagſhak.

Of theſe and the Aleütian Iſles, the diſtance and poſition are tolerably well aſcertained by ſhips reckonings, and latitudes taken by pilots. But the ſituation of the Andreanoffsky Iſles † is ſtill ſomewhat doubtful, though probably their direction is Eaſt and Weſt; and ſome of them may unite with that part of the Fox Iſlands which are moſt contiguous to the oppoſite Continent.

---

* See p. 286.

† Theſe are the ſame iſlands which are called, by Mr. Staehlin, Anadirſky Iſlands, from their ſuppoſed vicinity to the river Anadyr. See Appendix I. N° V. p. 289.

E   The

The main land of America has not been touched at by any of the veffels in the late expeditions; though poffibly the time is not far diftant when fome of the Ruffian adventurers will fall in with that coaft *. More to the North perhaps, at leaft as high as 70 degrees latitude, the Continent of America may ftretch out nearer to the coaft of the Tfchutfki; and form a large promontory, accompanied with iflands, which have no connection with any of the preceding ones. That fuch a promontory really exifts, and advances to within a very fmall diftance from Tfchukotfkoi Nofs, can hardly be doubted; at leaft it feems to be confirmed by all the lateft accounts which have been procured from thofe parts †. That prolongation, therefore, of America, which by Delifle is made to extend Weftward, and is laid down juft oppofite to Kamtchatka, between 50 and 60 degrees latitude, muft be entirely removed; for many of the voyages related in this collection lay through that part of the ocean, where this imaginary Continent was marked down.

It is even more than probable, that the Aleütian, and fome of the Fox Iflands, now well known, are the very fame which Beering fell-in with upon his return; though from the unfteadinefs of his courfe, their true pofition

* Appendix I. Nº VI.
† Appendix I. Nº VII.

could

could not be exactly laid down in the chart of that expedition *.

As the fea of Kamtchatka is now fo much frequented, thefe conjectures cannot remain long undecided; and it is only to be wifhed, that fome expeditions were to be made North-eaft, in order to difcover the neareft coafts of America. For there is no reafon to expect a fuccefsful voyage by taking any other direction; as all the veffels, which have fteered a more foutherly courfe, have failed through an open fea, without meeting with any figns of land.

A very full and judicious account of all the difcoveries hitherto made in the Eaftern ocean may be expected from the celebrated Mr. Muller †. Meanwhile, I hope the following account, extracted from the original papers, and procured from the beft intelligence, will be the more acceptable to the public; as it may prove an inducement to the Ruffians to publifh fuller and more circumftantial

* This error is however fo fmall, and particularly with refpect to the more Eaftern coafts and iflands, as laid down in Beering's chart, fuch as Cape Hermogenes, Toomanoi, Shumaghin's Ifland, and mountain of St. Dolmat, that if they were to be placed upon the general map of Ruffia, which is prefixed to this work, they would coincide with the very chain of the Fox Iflands.

† Mr. Muller has already arranged and put in order feveral of the journals, and fent them to the board of admiralty at St. Peterfburg, where they are at prefent kept, together with the charts of the refpective voyages.

E 2   relations.

relations.   Befides, the reader will find here a narrative more authentic and accurate, than what has been pub- lifhed in the abovementioned calendar*; and feveral miftakes in that memoir are here corrected.

* A German copy of the treatife alluded to in the text, was fent, by its author, Mr. Stæhlin Counfellor of State to the Emprefs of Ruffia, to the late Dr. Maty; and it is mentioned, in the Philofophical Tranfactions for 1774, under the following title: " A New Map and Preliminary " Defcription of the New Archipelago in the North, difcovered a few " Years ago by the Ruffians in the N. E. beyond Kamtchatka." A tranflation of this treatife was publifhed the fame year by Heydinger.

C H A P.

C H A P. II.

Voyages in 1745.——*Firſt diſcovery of the* Aleütian Iſles *by* Michael Nevodtſikoff.

A Voyage made in the year 1745 by Emilian Baſſoff is ſcarce worth mentioning; as he only reached Beering's Iſland; and two ſmaller ones, which lie South of the former, and returned on the 31ſt of July, 1746.

The firſt voyage which is in any wiſe remarkable, was undertaken in the year 1745. The veſſel was a Shitik named Eudokia, fitted out at the expence of Aphanaſſei Tſebaefskoi, Jacob Tſiuproff and others; ſhe ſailed from the Kamtchatka river Sept. 19, under the command of Michael Nevodtſikoff a native of Tobolſk. Having diſcovered three unknown iſlands, they wintered upon one of them, in order to kill ſea-otters, of which there was a large quantity. Theſe iſlands were undoubtedly the neareſt * Aleütian Iſlands: the language of the inhabi-

Voyage of Nevodtſikoff in 1745.

Diſcovers the Aleütian Iſlands.

---

* The ſmall group of iſlands lying S. E. of Beering's Iſland, are the real Aleütian iſles: they are ſometimes called the Neareſt Aleütian Iſlands; and the Fox Iſlands the Furtheſt Aleütian Iſles.

tants

tants was not underftood by an interpreter, whom they had brought with them from Kamtchatka. For the purpofe therefore of learning this language, they carried back with them one of the Iflanders; and prefented him to the chancery of Bolcheretſk, with a falfe account of their proceedings. This iflander was examined as foon as he had acquired a flight knowledge of the Ruffian language; and as it is faid, gave the following report. He was called Temnac, and the name of the ifland of which he was a native was Att. At fome diftance from thence lies a great ifland called Sabya, of which the in-habitants are denominated Kogii: thefe inhabitants, as the Ruffians underftood or thought they underftood him, made croffes, had books and fire arms, and navigated in baidars or leathern canoes. At no great diftance from the ifland where they wintered, there were two well-inhabited iflands: the firft lying E. S. E. and S. E. by South, the fecond Eaft and Eaft by South. The above-mentioned Iflander was baptifed under the name of Paul, and fent to Ochotfk.

As the mifconduct of the fhip's crew towards the na-tives was fufpected, partly from the lofs of feveral men, and partly from the report of thofe Ruffians, who were not concerned in the diforderly conduct of their compa-nions, a ftrict enquiry was inftituted; in confequence of which the following circumftances relating to the voyage were brought to light.

4

According

According to the account of fome of the crew, and particularly of the commander, after fix days failing they came in fight of the firft ifland on the 24th of September, at mid-day. They paffed it, and towards evening they difcovered the fecond ifland; where they lay at anchor until the next morning.

The 25th feveral inhabitants appeared on the coaft, and the pilot was making towards fhore in the fmall boat, with an intention of landing; but obferving their numbers increafe to about an hundred, he was afraid of venturing among them, although they beckoned to him. He contented himfelf therefore with flinging fome needles amongft them: the iflanders in return threw into the boat fome fea-fowl of the cormorant kind. He endeavoured to hold a converfation with them by means of the interpreters, but no one could underftand their language. And now the crew attempted to row the veffel out to fea; but the wind being contrary, they were driven to the other fide of the fame ifland, where they caft anchor.

The 26th, Tfiuproff having landed with fome of the crew in order to look for water, met feveral inhabitants: he gave them fome tobacco and fmall Chinefe pipes; and received in return a prefent of a ftick, upon which the head of a feal was carved. They endeavoured to wreft his

hunting

hunting gun from him; but upon his refusing to part
with it and retiring to the small boat, the islanders ran
after him; and seized the rope by which the boat was
made fast to shore. This violent attack obliged Tsiuproff
to fire; and having wounded one person in the hand,
they all let go their hold; and he rowed off to the ship.
The Savages no sooner saw that their companion was
hurt, than they threw off their cloaths, carried the
wounded person naked into the sea, and washed him.
In consequence of this encounter the ship's crew would
not venture to winter at this place, but rowed back again
to the other island, where they came to an anchor.

The next morning Tsiuproff and one Shaffyrin landed
with a more considerable party: they observed several
traces of inhabitants; but meeting none they returned
to the ship, and coasted along the island. The following day the Cossac Shekurdin went on shore, accompanied by five sailors: two of whom he sent back with a
supply of water; and remained himself with the others
in order to hunt sea-otters. At night they came to some
dwellings inhabited by five families: upon their approach
the natives abandoned their huts with precipitation, and
hid themselves among the rocks. Shekurdin no sooner
returned to the ship, than he was again sent on shore
with a larger company, in order to look out for a
proper place to lay up the vessel during winter: In their
way they observed fifteen islanders upon an height;
                                                        and

and threw them fome fragments of dried fifh in order to entice them to approach nearer. But as this overture did not fucceed, Tfiuproff, who was one of the party, ordered fome of the crew to mount the height, and to feize one of the inhabitants, for the purpofe of learning their language : this order was accordingly executed, notwithftanding the refiftance which the iflanders made with their bone fpears ; and the Ruffians immediately returned with their prifoner to the fhip. They were foon afterwards driven to fea by a violent ftorm, and beat about from the 2d to the 9th of October, during which time they loft their anchor and boat ; at length they came back to the fame ifland, where they paffed the winter.

Soon after their landing they found in an adjacent hut the dead bodies of two of the inhabitants, who had probably been killed in the laft encounter. In their way the Ruffians were met by an old woman, who had been taken prifoner, and fet at liberty. She was accompanied with thirty-four iflanders of both fexes, who all came dancing to the found of a drum; and brought with them a prefent of coloured earth. Pieces of cloth, thimbles, and needles, were diftributed among them in return ; and they parted amicably. Before the end of October, the fame perfons, together with the old woman and feveral children, returned dancing as before, and brought birds, fifh, and other provifion. Having paffed the night with

F the

the Ruffians, they took their leave.   Soon after their departure, Tfiuproff, Shaffyrin, and Nevodtfikoff, accompanied
with feven of the crew, went after them, and found them
among the rocks.   In this interview the natives behaved
in the moft friendly manner, and exchanged a baidar and
fome fkins for two fhirts.   They were obferved to have
hatchets of fharpened ftone, and needles made of bone :
they lived upon the flefh of fea-otters, feals, and fea-
lions, which they killed with clubs and bone lances.

So early as the 24th of October, Tfiuproff had fent
ten perfons, under the command of Larion Belayeff, upon
a reconnoitring party.   The latter treated the inhabitants
in an hoftile manner; upon which they defended themfelves as well as they could with their bone lances.   This
refiftance gave him a pretext for firing; and accordingly
he fhot the whole number, amounting to fifteen men,
in order to feize their wives.

Shekurdin, fhocked at thefe cruel proceedings, retired unperceived to the fhip, and brought an account of
all that had paffed.   Tfiuproff, inftead of punifhing thefe
cruelties as they deferved, was fecretly pleafed with them;
for he himfelf was affronted at the iflanders for having
refufed to give him an iron bolt, which he faw in their
poffeffion.   He had, in confequence of their refufal,
committed feveral acts of hoftilities againft them; and
had even formed the horrid defign of poifoning
them with a mixture of corrofive fublimate.   In order
                                                    however

however to preferve appearances, he difpatched Shekurdin and Nevodtfikoff to reproach Belayeff for his diforderly
conduct; but fent him at the fame time, by the above-
mentioned perfons, more powder and ball.

The Ruffians continued upon this ifland, where they
caught a large quantity of fea otters, until the 14th
of September, 1746; when, no longer thinking themfelves fecure, they put to fea with an intention of looking
out for fome uninhabited iflands. Being however overtaken by a violent ftorm, they were driven about until
the 30th of October, when their veffel ftruck upon a
rocky fhore, and was fhipwrecked, with the lofs of almoft all the tackle, and the greateft part of the furs.
Worn out at length with cold and fatigue, they ventured,
the firft of November, to penetrate into the interior
part of the country, which they found rocky and un-
even. Upon their coming to fome huts, they were informed, that they were caft away upon the ifland of
Karaga, the inhabitants of which were tributary to Ruffia,
and of the Koraki tribe. The iflanders behaved to them
with great kindnefs, until Belayeff had the imprudence
to make propofals to the wife of the chief. The woman
gave immediate intelligence to her hufband; and the
natives were incenfed to fuch a degree, that they threatened the whole crew with immediate death : but means
were found to pacify them, and they continued to live
with the Ruffians upon the fame good terms as before.

The

The 30th of May, 1747, a party of Olotorians made a descent upon the island in three baidars, and attacked the natives; but, after some loss on both sides, they went away. They returned soon after with a larger force, and were again compelled to retire. But as they threatened to come again in a short time, and to destroy all the inhabitants who paid tribute, the latter advised the Russians to retire from the island, and assisted them in building two baidars. With these they put to sea the 27th of June, and landed the 21st of July at Kamtchatka, with the rest of their cargo, consisting of 320 sea-otters, of which they paid the tenth into the customs. During this expedition twelve men were lost.

CHAP. III.

Succeſſive voyages, from 1747 *to* 1753, *to* Beering's *and* Copper Iſland, *and to the* Aleütian Iſles.——*Some account of the inhabitants.*

IN the year 1747 * two veſſels ſailed from the Kamtchatka river, according to a permiſſion granted by the chancery of Bolckeretſk for hunting ſea-otters. One was fitted out by Andrew Wſevidoff, and carried forty-ſix men, beſides eight Coſſacs: the other belonged to Feodor Cholodiloff, Andrew Tolſtyk, and company; and had on board a crew, conſiſting of forty-one Ruſſians and Kamtchadals, with ſix Coſſacs.

The latter veſſel ſailed the 20th of October, and was forced, by ſtreſs of weather and other accidents, to winter at Beering's Iſland. From thence they departed May the 31ſt, 1748, and touched at another ſmall iſland, in order to provide themſelves with water and other neceſſaries. They then ſteered S. E. for a conſiderable way without

* It may be neceſſary to inform the reader, that, in this and the two following chapters, ſome circumſtances are occaſionally omitted, which are to be found in the original. Theſe omiſſions relate chiefly to the names of ſome of the partners engaged in the equipments, and to a detail of immaterial occurrences prior to the actual departure of the veſſels.

diſcovering

difcovering any new iflands ; and, being in great want
of provifions, returned into Kamtchatka River, Auguft
14, with a cargo of 250 old fea-otter-fkins, above 100
young ones, and 148 petfi or arctic fox-fkins, which were
all killed upon Beering's Ifland.

We have no fufficient account of Wfevidoff's voyage.
All that is known amounts only to this, that he returned
the 25th of July, 1749, after having probably touched
upon one of the neareft Aleütian Ifles which was uninhabited : his cargo confifted of the fkins of 1040 fea-
otters, and 2000 arctic foxes.

Voyage of
Emilian Yu-
goff.

    Emilian Yugoff, a merchant of Yakutfk, obtained from
the fenate of St. Peterfburg the permiffion of fitting out
four veffels for himfelf and his affociates.   He procured, at
the fame time, the exclufive privilege of hunting fea-
otters upon Beering's and Copper Ifland during thefe
expeditions ; and for this monopoly he agreed to deliver
to the cuftoms the third part of the furs.

October 6, 1750, he put to fea from Bolcherefk, in
the floop John, manned with twenty-five Ruffians and
Kamtchadals, and two Coffacs : he was foon overtaken
by a ftorm, and the veffel driven on fhore between the
mouths of the rivers Kronotfk and Tfchafminfk.

October 1751, he again fet fail.   He had been commanded to take on board fome officers of the Ruffian

navy ;

navy; and, as he difobeyed this injunction, the chancery
of Irkutfk iffued an order to confifcate his fhip and cargo
upon his return. The fhip returned on the 22d of July,
1754, to New Kamtchatkoi Oftrog, laden with the fkins
of 755 old fea-otters, of 35 cub fea-otters, of 447 cubs
of fea-bears, and of 7044 arctic fox-fkins: of the
latter 2000 were white, and 1765 black. Thefe furs
were procured upon Beering's and Copper Ifland. Yu-
koff himfelf died upon the laft-mentioned ifland. The
cargo of the fhip was, according to the above-mentioned
order, fealed and properly fecured. But as it appeared
that certain perfons had depofited money in Yugoff's
hand, for the purpofe of equipping a fecond veffel, the
crown delivered up the confifcated cargo, after referving
the third part according to the original ftipulation.

This kind of charter-company, if it may be fo called,
being foon diffolved for mifconduct and want of fufficient
ftock, other merchants were allowed the privilege of fitting out veffels, even before the return of Yugoff's fhip;
and thefe perfons were more fortunate in making new
difcoveries than the above-mentioned monopolift.

Nikiphor Trapefnikoff, a merchant of Irkutfk, obtained the permiffion of fending out a fhip, called the
Boris and Glebb, upon the condition of paying, befides
the tribute which might be exacted, the tenth of all the
furs. The Coffac Sila Sheffyrin went on board this

Voyage of the Boris and Glebb.

                                                            veffel

veffel for the purpofe of collecting the tribute. They failed
in Auguft, 1749, from the Kamtchatka river; and re-
entered it the 16th of the fame month, 1753, with a
large cargo of furs. In the fpring of the fame year,
they had touched upon an unknown ifland, probably one
of the Aleütians, where feveral of the inhabitants were
prevailed upon to pay a tribute of fea-otter fkins. The
names of the iflanders who had been made tributary,
were Igya, Oeknu, Ogogoektack, Shabukiauck, Alak,
Tutun, Ononufhan, Rotogèi, Tfchinitu, Vatfch, Afhagat,
Avyjanifhaga, Unafhayupu, Lak, Yanfhugalik, Umgali-
kan, Shati, Kyipago, and Olofhkot*; another Aleütian
had contributed three fea-otters. They brought with
them 320 of the beft fea-otter fkins, 480 of the fecond,
and 400 of the third fort, 500 female and middle aged,
and 220 medwedki or young ones.

Voyage of An-
drew Tolftyk
to the Aleütian
Ifles, 1749.   Andrew Tolftyk, a merchant of Selenginfk, having
obtained permiffion from the chancery of Bolfheretfk,
refitted the fame fhip which had made a former voyage;
he failed from Kamtchatka Auguft the 19th, 1749, and
returned July the 3d, 1752.

According to the commander's account, the fhip lay
at anchor from the 6th of September, 1749, to the 20th

* The author here remarks in a note, that the proper names of the
iflanders mentioned in this place, and in other parts, bear a furprifing
refemblance, both in their found and termination, to thofe of the Greenlanders.

                                                        of

of May, 1750, before Beering's Island, where they caught only 47 sea-otters. From thence they made to those Aleütian Islands, which were * first discovered by Nevodtsikoff, and slew there 1662 old and middle-aged sea-otters, and 119 cubs; besides which, their cargo consisted of the skins of 720 blue foxes, and of 840 young sea-bears.

The inhabitants of these islands appeared to have never before paid tribute; and seemed to be a-kin to the Tschutski tribe, their women being ornamented with different figures sewed into the skin in the manner of that people, and of the Tungusians of Siberia. They differed however from them, by having two small holes cut through the bottom of their under-lips, through each of which they pass a bit of the sea-horse tush, worked into the form of a tooth, with a small button at one end to keep it within the mouth when it is placed in the hole. They had killed, without being provoked, two of the Kamtchadales who belonged to the ship. Upon the third Island some inhabitants had payed tribute; their names were reported to be Anitin, Altakukor, and Aleshkut, with his son Atschelap. The weapons of the whole island consisted of no more than twelve spears pointed with flint, and one dart of bone pointed with the same; and the Russians observed in the possession of the natives two figures, carved out of wood, resembling sea-lions.

* See Chap. II.

G　　　　　　　　August

Voyage of
Vorobieff,
1750.

Auguſt 3, 1750, the veſſel Simeon and John, fitted
out by the above-mentioned Wſevidoff, agent for the
Ruſſian merchant R. Rybenſkoi, and manned with fourteen Ruſſians (who were partly merchants and partly
hunters) and thirty Kamtchadals, failed out for the
diſcovery of new iſlands, under the command of the
Coſſac Vorobieff. They were driven by a violent current
and tempeſtuous weather to a ſmall deſert iſland, the
poſition whereof is not determined ; but which was probably one of thoſe that lie near Beering's Iſland. The ſhip
being ſo ſhattered by the ſtorm, that it was no longer in a
condition to keep the ſea, Vorobieff built another ſmall
veſſel with drift-wood, which he called Jeremiah ; in
which he arrived at Kamtchatka in autumn, 1752.

Upon the above-mentioned iſland were caught 700
old and 120 cub ſea-otters, 1900 blue foxes, 5700 black
ſea-bears, and 1310 Kotiki, or cub ſea-bears.

A voyage made about this time from Anadyrſk deſerves to be mentioned.

Voyage of
Novikoff and
Bacchoff from
Anadyrſk.

Auguſt 24, 1749, Simeon Novikoff of Yakutſk, and
Ivan Bacchoff of Uſtyug, agents for Ivan Shilkin, ſailed
from Anadyrſk into the mouth of the Kamtchatka river.
They aſſigned the inſecurity of the roads as their reaſon
for coming from Anadyrſk to Kamtchatka by ſea ; on
this account, having determined to riſk all the dangers

of

of a sea voyage, they built a vessel one hundred and thirty versts above Anadyr, after having employed two years and five months in its construction.

The narrative of their expedition is as follows. In 1748, they sailed down the river Anadyr, and through two bays, called Kopeikina and Onemenskaya, where they found many sand banks, but passed round them without difficulty. From thence they steered into the exterior gulph, and waited for a favourable wind. Here they saw several Tschutski, who appeared upon the heights singly and not in bodies, as if to reconnoitre; which made them cautious. They had descended the river and its bays in nine days. In passing the large opening of the exterior bay, they steered between the beach, that lies to the left, and a rock near it; where, at about an hundred and twenty yards from the rock, the depth of water is from three to four fathoms. From the opening they steered E. S. E. about 50 versts, in about four fathom water; then doubled a sandy point, which runs out directly against the Tschutski coast, and thus reached the open sea.

From the 10th of July to the 30th, they were driven about by tempestuous winds, at no great distance from the mouth of the Anadyr; and ran up the small river Katirka, upon whose banks dwell the Koriacs, a people

G 2

tributary

tributary to Ruſſia. The mouth of the river is from sixty to eighty yards broad, from three to four fathoms deep, and abounds in fiſh. From thence they put again to ſea, and after having beat about for ſome time, they at length reached Beering's Iſland. Here they lay at anchor from the 15th of September to the 30th of October, when a violent ſtorm blowing right from the ſea, drove the veſſel upon the rocks, and daſhed her to pieces. The crew however were ſaved: and now they looked out for the remains of Beering's wreck, in order to employ the materials for the conſtructing of a boat. They found indeed ſome remaining materials, but almoſt entirely rotten, and the iron-work corroded with ruſt. Having ſelected however the beſt cables, and what iron-work was immediately neceſſary, and collected drift-wood during the winter, they built with great difficulty a ſmall boat, whoſe keel was only ſeventeen Ruſſian ells and an half long, and which they named Capiton. In this they put to ſea, and ſailed in ſearch of an unknown iſland, which they thought they ſaw lying North-eaſt; but finding themſelves miſtaken, they tacked about, and ſtood for Copper Iſland: from thence they ſailed to Kamtchatka, where they arrived at the time above-mentioned.

The new conſtructed veſſel was granted in property to Ivan Shilkin as ſome compenſation for his loſſes, and with the privilege of employing it in a future expedition

to

Shipwreck upon Beering's Iſland.

to the New Difcovered Iflands. Accordingly he failed therein on the 7th of October, 1757, with a crew of twenty Ruffians, and the fame number of Kamtchadals : he was accompanied by Studentzoff a Coffac, who was fent to collect the tribute for the crown. An account of this expedition will be given hereafter *.

August, 1754, Nikiphor Trapefnikoff fitted out the Shitik St. Nicholas, which failed from Kamtchatka under the command of the Coffac Kodion Durneff. He firft touched at two of the Aleütian Ifles, and afterwards upon a third, which had not been yet difcovered. He returned to Kamtchatka in 1757. His cargo confifted of the fkins of 1220 fea-otters, of 410 female, and 665 cubs; befides which, the crew had obtained in barter from the iflanders the fkins of 652 fea-otters, of 30 female ditto, and 50 cubs. *Voyage of Durneff, in the St. Nicholas, 1754.*

From an account delivered in the 3d of May, 1758, by Durneff and Sheffyrin, who was fent as collector of the tributes, it appears that they failed in ten days as far as Ataku, one of the Aleütian Iflands; that they remained there until the year 1757, and lived upon amicable terms with the natives. *Narrative of the Voyage.*

The fecond ifland, which is neareft to Ataku, and which contains the greateft number of inhabitants, is *Defcription of the Aleütian Ifles.*

* See Chap. V.

called

called Agataku; and the third Shemya: they lie from forty to fifty verfts afunder. Upon all the three iflands there are (exclufive of children) but fixty males, whom they Account of
Inhabitants. made tributary. The inhabitants live upon roots which grow wild, and fea animals: they do not employ themfelves in catching fifh, although the rivers abound with all kinds of falmon, and the fea with turbot. Their cloaths are made of the fkins of birds and of fea-otters. The Toigon or chief of the firft ifland informed them, by means of a boy who underftood the Ruffian language, that Eaft-ward there are three large and well-peopled iflands, Ibiya, Kickfa, and Olas, whofe inhabitants fpeak a dif-ferent language. Sheffyrin and Durneff found upon the ifland three round copper plates, with fome letters en-graved upon them, and ornamented with foliage, which the waves had caft upon the fhore: they brought them, together with other trifling curiofities, which they had procured from the natives, to New Kamtchatkoi Oftrog.

Another fhip built of larchwood by the fame Trapef-nikoff, which failed in 1752 under the conduct of Alexei Drufinin a merchant of Kurfk, had been wrecked at Beer-ing's Ifland, where the crew conftructed another veffel out of the wreck, which they named Abraham. In this veffel they bore away for the more diftant iflands; but being forced back by contrary winds to the fame ifland, and meeting with the St. Nicholas upon the point of failing for the Aleütian Ifles, they embarked on that fhip, after having left the new conftructed veffel under the care of

four

four of their own failors. The crew had flain upon Beering's Ifland five fea-otters, 1222 arctic foxes, and 2500 fea-bears: their fhare of the furs, during their expedition in the St. Nicholas, amounted to the fkins of 500 fea-otters, and of 300 cubs, exclufive of 200 fea-otters-fkins, which they procured by barter.

CHAP.

CHAP. IV.

Voyages from 1753 *to* 1756.

Some of the further Aleütian *or* Fox Iſlands *touched at by* Serebranikoff's *veſſel.—Some account of the Natives.*

THREE veſſels were fitted out for the iſlands in 1753, one by Cholodiloff, a ſecond by Serebrani-koff agent for the merchant Rybenſkoy, and the third by Ivan Kraſſilnikoff a merchant of Kamtchatka.

Cholodiloff's Ship ſails from Kamtchatka, 1753.

Cholodiloff's ſhip ſailed from Kamtchatka the 19th of Auguſt, the crew whereof conſiſted of thirty-four per-ſons; and anchored the 28th before Beering's Iſland, where they propoſed to winter, in order to lay-in a ſtock of proviſions: as they were attempting to land, the boat overſet, and nine of the crew were drowned.

June 30, 1754, they ſtood out to ſea in queſt of new diſcoveries: the weather however proving ſtormy and foggy, and the ſhip ſpringing a leak, they were all in danger of periſhing: in this ſituation they unexpectedly reached one of the Aleütian Iſlands, where they lay from the 15th of September until the 9th of July, 1755. In

the

the autumn of 1754 they were joined by a Kamtchadal, and a Koriac: thefe perfons, together with four others, had deferted from Trapefnikoff's crew; and had remained upon the ifland in order to catch fea-otters for their own profit. Four of thefe deferters were killed by the iflanders for having debauched their wives: but as the two perfons above-mentioned were not guilty of the fame diforderly conduct, the inhabitants fupplied them with women, and lived with them upon the beft terms. The crew killed upon this ifland above 1600 fea-otters, and came back fafe to Kamtchatka in autumn 1755.

Serebranikoff's veffel failed in July 1753, manned alfo with thirty-four Ruffians and Kamtchadals: they difcovered feveral new iflands, which were probably fome of the more diftant ones; but were not fo fortunate in hunting fea-otters as Cholodiloff's crew. They fteered S. E. and on the 17th of Auguft anchored under an unknown ifland; whofe inhabitants fpoke a language they did not underftand. Here they propofed looking out for a fafe harbour; but were prevented by the coming on of a fudden ftorm, which carried away their anchor. The fhip being toft about for feveral days towards the Eaft, they difcovered not far from the firft ifland four others: ftill more to the Eaft three other iflands appeared in fight; but on neither of thefe were they able to land. The veffel continued driving until the 2d of September, and was confiderably fhattered, when they fortunately came

Departure of Serebranikoff's Veffel.

Shipwrecked
upon one of
the more dif-
tant Iflands.
near an ifland and caft anchor before it; they were however again forced from this ftation, the veffel wrecked
upon the coaft, and the crew with difficulty reached the
fhore.

This ifland feemed to be oppofite to Katyrfkoi Nofs
in the peninfula of Kamtchatka, and near it they faw
three others. Towards the end of September Demitri
Trophin, accompanied with nine men, went out in
the boat upon an hunting and reconnoitring party:
they were attacked by a large body of inhabitants, who
hurled darts from a fmall wooden engine, and wounded
one of the company. The firft fire however drove them
back; and although they returned feveral times to the
attack in numerous bodies, yet they were always repulfed without difficulty.

Account of the
Inhabitants.
Thefe favages mark and colour their faces like the
Iflanders above-mentioned; and alfo thruft pieces of
bone through holes made in their under-lips.

Soon afterwards the Ruffians were joined in a friendly
manner by ten iflanders, who brought the flefh of fea-
animals and of fea-otters; this prefent was the more
welcome, as they had lived for fome time upon nothing
but fmall fhell-fifh and roots; and had fuffered greatly
from hunger. Several toys were in return diftributed

ed among the favages. The Ruffians remained until
June, 1754, upon this ifland: at that time they departed in a fmall veffel, conftructed from the remains of
the wreck, and called the St. Peter and Paul: in this they
landed at Katyrfkoi Nofs; where having collected 140
fea-horfe teeth, they got fafe to the mouth of the Kamtchatka river.

During this voyage twelve Kamtchadals deferted;
of whom fix were flain, together with a female in-
habitant, upon one of the moft diftant iflands. The
remainder, upon their return to Kamtchatka, were
examined; and from them the following circumftances
were collected. The ifland, where the fhip was wrecked,
is about 70 verfts long, and 20 broad. Around it lie
twelve other iflands of different fizes, from five to ten
verfts diftant from each other. Eight of them appear
to be no more than five verfts long. All thefe iflands
contain about a thoufand fouls. The dwellings of the
inhabitants are provided with no other furniture than
benches, and mats of platted grafs*. Their drefs confifts
of a kind of fhirt made of bird-fkins, and of an upper
garment of inteftines ftitched together; they wear wood-
en caps, ornamented with a fmall piece of board projecting forwards, as it feemed, for a defence againft the
arrows. They are all provided with ftone knives, and a

* Matten aus einem geviffen Krautgeflochten.

H 2　　　　　　　　　few

few of them poffefs iron ones: their only weapons are arrows with points of bone or flint, which they fhoot from a wooden inftrument. There are no trees upon the ifland: it produces however the cow-parfnip*, which grows at Kamtchatka. The climate is by no means fevere, for the fnow does not lie upon the ground above a month in the year.

Departure of
Kraffilnikoff's
Veffel. Kraffilnikoff's veffel failed in 1754, and anchored on the 18th of October before Beering's Ifland; where all the fhips which make to the New Difcovered Iflands are accuftomed to winter, in order to procure a flock of falted provifions from the fea-cows and other amphibious animals, that are found in great abundance. Here they refitted the veffel, which had been damaged by driving upon her anchor; and having laid in a fufficient ftore of all neceffaries, weighed the 1ft of Auguft, 1754. The 10th they were in fight of an ifland, the coaft whereof was lined with fuch a number of inhabitants, that they durft not venture afhore. Accordingly they ftood out to fea, and being overtaken by a ftorm, they were reduced to great diftrefs for want of water; at length they were driven upon Copper Ifland, where they landed; and having taken in wood and water, they again Shipwrecked
upon Copper
Ifland. fet fail. They were beat back however by contrary winds, and dropped both their anchors near the fhore; but the ftorm increafing at night, both the cables were broken, and the fhip dafhed to pieces upon the coaft.

* Heracleum.

All

All the crew were fortunately faved; and means were found to get afhore the fhip's tackle, ammunition, guns, and the remains of the wreck; the provifions, however, were moftly fpoiled. Here they were expofed to a variety of misfortunes; three of them were drowned on the 15th of October, as they were going to hunt; others almoft perifhed with hunger, having no nourifhment but fmall fhell-fifh and roots. On the 29th of December great part of the fhip's tackle, and all the wood, which they had collected from the wreck, was wafhed away during an high fea. Notwithftanding their diftreffes, they continued their hunting parties, and caught 103 fea-otters, together with 1390 blue foxes.

In fpring they put to fea for Beering's Ifland in two baidars, carrying with them all the ammunition, fire-arms, and remaining tackle. Having reached that ifland, they found the fmall veffel Abraham, under the care of the four failors who had been left afhore by the crew of Trapefnikoff's fhip*: but as that veffel was not large enough to contain the whole number, together with their cargo of furs, they ftaid until Serebranikoff's and Tolftyk's veffels arrived. Thefe took in eleven of the crew, with their part of the furs. Twelve remained at Beering's Ifland, where they killed great numbers of arctic foxes, and returned to Kamtchatka in the Abraham, excepting two, who joined Shilkin's crew.

The Crew reach Beering's Ifland in two Baidars.

* See the preceding chapter.

C H A P.

CHAP. V.

Voyages from 1756 *to* 1758.

SEPTEMBER 17, 1756, the veffel Andrean and
Natalia, fitted out by Andrean Tolftyk, merchant
of Selenginfk, and manned with thirty-eight Ruffians
and Kamtchadals, failed from the mouth of the Kamtchatka river. The autumnal ftorms coming on, and
a fcarcity of provifions enfuing, they made to Beering's
Ifland, where they continued until the 14th of June,
1757. As no fea-otters came on fhore that winter, they
killed nothing but feals, fea-lions, and fea-cows; whofe
flefh ferved them for provifion, and their fkins for the
coverings of baidars.

June 13, 1757, they weighed anchor, and after
eleven days failing came to Ataku, one of the Aleütian
ifles difcovered by Nevodtfikoff. Here they found the
inhabitants, as well of that as of the other two iflands,
affembled; thefe iflanders had juft taken leave of the
crew of Trapefnikoff's veffel, which had failed for
Kamtchatka. The Ruffians feized this opportunity of
perfuading them to pay tribute; with this view they
beckoned

5

beckoned the Toigon, whofe name was Tunulgafen : the latter recollected one of the crew, a Koriac, who had formerly been left upon thefe iflands, and who knew fomewhat of their language. A copper kettle, a fur and cloth coat, a pair of breeches, ftockings and boots, were beftowed upon this chief, who was prevailed upon by thefe prefents to pay tribute. Upon his departure for his own ifland, he left behind him three women and a boy, in order to be taught the Ruffian language, which the latter very foon learned.

The Ruffians wintered upon this ifland, and divided themfelves, as ufual, into different hunting parties : they were compelled, by ftormy weather, to remain there until the 17th of June, 1758 : before they went away, the above-mentioned chief returned with his family, and paid a year's tribute.

This veffel brought to Kamtchatka the moft circum-ftantial account of the Aleütian ifles which had been yet received.

The two largeft contained at that time about fifty Account of those Iflands. males, with whom the Ruffians had lived in great har-mony. They heard of a fourth ifland, lying at fome diftance from the third, called by the natives Iviya, but which they did not reach on account of the tempeftuous weather.

The

The firſt iſland is about an hundred verſts long and from five to twenty broad. They eſtimated the diſtance from the firſt to the ſecond, which lies Eaſt by South, to be about thirty verſts, and about forty from the latter to the third, which ſtands South Eaſt. The original dreſs of the iſlanders was made of the ſkins of birds, ſea-otters and ſeals, which were tanned; but the greateſt part had procured from the Ruſſians dog-ſkin coats, and under-garments of ſheep-ſkin, which they were very fond of. They are repreſented as naturally talkative, quick of ap-prehenſion, and much attached to the Ruſſians. Their dwellings are hollowed in the ground, and covered with wooden roofs reſembling the huts in the peninſula of Kamtchatka. Their principal food is the fleſh of ſea animals, which they harpoon with their bone lances; they alſo feed upon ſeveral ſpecies of roots and berries: namely * cloud-berries, crake-berries, bilberries, and ſer-vices. The rivulets abound with ſalmon, and other fiſh of the trout kind ſimilar to thoſe of Kamtchatka; and the ſea with turbot, which are caught with bone hooks.

Theſe iſlands produce quantities of ſmall oſiers and underwood, but no large trees: the ſea however drives aſhore fir and larch, ſufficient for the conſtruction of

* Rubus Chamæmorus—Empetrum—Myrtillus—Sorbus.

their

their huts. There are a great number of arctic foxes upon the firft ifland, as well as fea-otters; and the fhores, during ftormy weather, are covered with wild geefe and ducks.

The Ruffians, according to the order of the chancery of Bolcheretfk, endeavoured to perfuade the Toigon of thefe iflands to accompany them to Kamtchatka, but without fuccefs: upon their departure they diftributed among the iflanders fome linen, and, thirteen nets for the purpofe of catching fea-otters, which were very thankfully received. This veffel brought to Kamtchatka the fkins of 5030 old and young fea-otters, of 1040 old and young arctic foxes, and of 330 Medwedki or cubs of fea-otters.

In the year 1757, Ivan Nikiphoroff, a merchant of Mofcow, fitted out a veffel: but we have no further account of this voyage, than that fhe failed to the Fox Iflands, at leaft as far as Umnak.

The fmall veffel Capiton, the fame that was built Voyage of Ivan Shilkin in upon Beering's Ifland, and which was given to the mer- the Capiton chant * Ivan Shilkin, put to fea September 26, 1757, 1757. carrying on board the Coffac Ignatius Studentfoff, who has given the following account of the voyage.

* See chap. III.

I   They

They had not long failed, before they were driven back to the fhore of Kamtchatka by ftrefs of weather, and the veffel ftranded; by which accident they loft the rudder and one of the crew. This misfortune prevented them from putting to fea again until the following year, with thirty-nine of the original crew, feveral perfons being left behind on account of ficknefs. They made directly to Beering's Ifland, where they took up two of Krafilnikoff's crew *, who had been fhipwrecked. They again fet fail in Auguft of the fame year, and touched at the neareft Aleütian Ifles, after fuffering greatly from ftorms. They then continued their courfe to the remoter iflands lying between Eaft and South Eaft; and having paffed by the firft, they anchored before the fecond. A boat being immediately fent out towards the fhore, the crew was attacked by a numerous body of Iflanders in fo fudden a manner, that they had fcarcely time to fecure themfelves by returning to the veffel. They had no fooner got aboard, than a violent gale of wind blowing from the fhore broke the cable, and drove them out to fea. The weather became fuddenly thick and foggy; and under thefe circumftances the veffel was forced upon a fmall ifland at no great diftance from the other, and fhipwrecked. The crew got to fhore with difficulty, and were able to fave nothing but the fire arms and ammunition.

Shipwrecked upon one of the Fox Iflands.

* See chap. IV.

They

They had scarcely got to land, before they were beset by a number of savages, rowing in baidars from the Western point of the island. This attack was the more to be dreaded, because several of the Russians were disabled by cold and wet; and there remained only fifteen capable of defending themselves. They advanced however without hesitation to the islanders; and one Nicholas Tsiuproff (who had a slight knowledge of their language) accosted and endeavoured to sooth them, but without success. For upon their approach the savages gave a sudden shout, and saluting them at the same time with a volley of darts, wounded one person in the hand. Upon this the Russians fired, killed two of the assailants, and forced the remainder to retire; and although a fresh body appeared in sight, as if they were coming to the assistance of their companions, yet no new attack was made. Soon afterwards the savages left the island, and rowed across the strait.

From the 6th of September to the 23d of April, they underwent all the extremities of famine: during that period their best fare was shell-fish and roots; and they were even at times reduced to still the cravings of their appetite with the leather, which the waves washed ashore from the wreck. Seventeen died of hunger, and the rest would soon have followed their companions, if they had not fortunately discovered a dead whale, which the sea had

I 2

had caft afhore. They remained upon this ifland another winter, where they killed 230 fea-otters; and having built a fmall veffel out of the remains of the wreck, they put to fea in the beginning of fummer 1760. They had fcarcely reached one of the Aleütian iflands, where Serebranikoff's veffel lay at anchor, when they were again fhipwrecked, and loft all the remaining tackle and furs. Only thirteen of the crew now remained, who returned on board the above-mentioned veffel to Kamtchatka July 1751.

CHAP.

C H A P. VI.

Voyages in 1758, 1759, *and* 1760——*to the* Fox Iflands——
in the St. Vladimir, *fitted out by* Trapefnikoff——*and in*
the Gabriel, *by* Betfhevin——*The latter under the command*
of Pufhkareff *fails to* Alakfu *or* Alachíkak, *one of the*
remoteft Eaftern Iflands hitherto vifited——Some account
of its inhabitants, and productions, which latter are dif-
ferent from thofe of the more Weftern Iflands.

SEPTEMBER 1758, the merchant Simeon Krafilnikoff and Nikiphor Trapefnikoff fitted out two veffels for the purpofe of catching fea-otters. One of thefe
veffels, called the St. Vladimir, failed the 28th under the
command of Demetri Paikoff, carrying on board the Coffac Sila Shaffyrin as collector of the tribute, and a crew
of forty-five men. In twenty-four hours they reached
Beering's Ifland, where they wintered. July 16, 1759,
they fteered towards the South in order to difcover land;
but being difappointed, they bore away to the North for
the Aleütian Ifles: being prevented however by contrary
winds from reaching them, they failed ftreight towards
the diftant iflands, which are known at prefent under
the name of Lyffie Oftrova or the Fox Iflands. September 1, they reached the firft of thefe, called by the natives
Atchu, and by the Ruffians Goreloi or the Burnt Ifland:

but

Voyage of the
St. Vladimir,
commanded by
Paikoff, 1758.

Arrival at the
Fox Ifland.

but as the coasts were very steep and craggy, they made
to Amlak, lying at a small distance, where they determined to pass the winter. They divided themselves accordingly into three parties; the first, at the head of
which was Alexey Drusinin, went over to a small island
called in the journal Sitkin; the Cossac Shaffyrin led the
second, consisting of ten persons, to the island Atach;
and Simeon Polevoi remained aboard with the rest of the
crew.   All these islands were well peopled; the men had
bones thrust through their ears, under lips, and gristle
of their noses; and the faces of the women were marked
with blackish streaks made with a needle and thread in
the skin, in the same manner as a Cossac one of the crew
had observed before upon some of the Tschutski. The
inhabitants had no iron; the points of their darts and
lances were tipped with bone and flint.

They at first imagined, that Amlak was uninhabited;
but in one of their hunting parties they found a boy of
eight years old, whom they brought with them: they
gave him the name of Hermolai, and taught him the
Russian language, that he might serve as an interpreter.
After penetrating further they discovered an hut, wherein
were two women, four men, and as many boys, whom
they treated kindly, and employed in hunting, fishing,
and in digging roots. This kind behaviour encouraged
others to pay frequent visits, and to exchange fish and
flesh for goats hair, horses manes, and glass beads.

I   They

They procured alſo four other iſlanders with their wives, who dug roots for them: and thus the winter paſſed away without any diſturbance.

In the ſpring the hunting parties returned; during theſe excurſions one man alone was killed upon the iſland Atach, and his fire-arms taken away by the natives. June 1760, the ſame parties were ſent again to the ſame iſlands. Shaffyrin, who headed one of the parties, was ſoon afterwards killed, with eleven men, by the inhabitants of Atach, but for what reaſon is not known.— Druſinin received the firſt information of this maſſacre from ſome inhabitants of Sitkin, where he then was; and immediately ſet out with the remaining hunters to join their companions, who were left on board. Although he ſucceeded in regaining the veſſel, their number was by this time ſo conſiderably reduced that their ſituation appeared very dangerous: he was ſoon however relieved from his apprehenſions by the arrival of the merchant Betſhevin's veſſel at the iſland of Atchu*. The two crews entered into partnerſhip: the St. Vladimir received twenty-two men, and transferred eleven of her own to the other veſſel. The former wintered at Amlak, and the latter continued at anchor before Atchu.

* Atach and Atchu are two names for the ſame iſland, called alſo by the Ruſſians Goreloi or Burnt Iſland. This iſland and Amlak are probably two of the Andreanoffsky Iſles. See p. 289.

This

Voyage of
.Puſhkareff,
1760.

This veſſel, fitted out at the expence of Betſhevin, a merchant of Irkutſk, was called Gabriel; and put to ſea from the mouth of the Bolſhaia Reka July 31ſt, 1760. She was manned with forty Ruſſians and twenty Kamtchadals, and carried on board Gabriel Puſhkareff, of the garriſon of Ochotſk, Andrew Shdanoff, Jacob Sharypoff, Prokopèi Lobaſhkoff, together with Nikiphor Golodoff, and Aphanaſſèi Oſkoloff, Betſhevin's agents.

Having ſailed through the ſecond ſtrait of the Kurill Iſles, they reached the Aleütian Iſles on the 24th of Auguſt. They ſtood out from thence in order to make new diſcoveries among thoſe more remote iſlands, which lie in one continued chain to the extent of 15 degrees of longitude.

Reaches At-
chu, one of
the Fox Iſlands.

September 25 they reached Atchu, or Burnt Iſland, and found the above-mentioned ſhip, the St. Vladimir, lying twenty verſts from that iſland, before Amlak, in danger of being attacked by the iſlanders. They immediately joined crews in order to enable the enfeebled company of the St. Vladimir to continue hunting; and, as it is uſual in ſuch caſes, entered into a contract for the diviſion of the profit. During that winter the two crews killed partly upon Siguyam, about 800 ſea otters of different ſizes, about 100 medwedki or cubs, ſome river otters,

above

above 400 red, greyiſh, and black foxes, and collected twelve pood of ſea-horſe teeth.

In June, of the following year, the two crews were diſtributed equally on board the two veſſels: Kraſſilni-koff's remained at Amlak, with an intention of returning to Kamtchatka; and Betſhevin's put to ſea from Atchu in queſt of other iſlands. They touched firſt at Umnak, Departs from thence. where they met Nikiphoroff's veſſel. Here they took in wood and water, and repaired their ſails: they then ſailed to the moſt remote iſland Alakſu*, or Alachſhak, Winters upon Alakſu. where, having laid up the ſhip in a bay, they built huts, and made preparations for wintering. This iſland was very well inhabited, and the natives behaved at firſt in a very friendly manner, for they trafficked with the Ruſ-ſians, and even delivered up nine of their children as hoſtages; but ſuch was the lawleſs and irregular beha-viour of the crew, that the iſlanders were ſoon irritated and provoked to hoſtilities.

In January 1762, Golodoff and Puſhkareff went with a party of twenty men along the ſhore; and, as they were attempting to violate ſome girls upon the iſland Uny-umga, were ſurpriſed by a numerous body of the na-tives: Golodoff and another Ruſſian were killed, and three were wounded. Not long afterwards the watch of

* This is probably the ſame iſland which is laid down in Krenitzin's chart under the name of Alaxa.

K

the

the crew was fuddenly attacked by the iflanders; four
men were flain upon the fpot, as many wounded, and
the huts reduced to afhes.

May 3, Lobafchkoff and another Ruffian were killed,
as they were going to bathe in the warm fprings, which
lie about five verfts from the haven: upon which feven
of the hoftages were put to death. The fame month the
natives attempted to furprife the Ruffians in their huts;
but being fortunately difcovered in time were repulfed by
means of the fire arms. At length the Ruffians, finding
themfelves in continual danger from thefe attempts,
weighed anchor, and failed for Umnak, where they took
up two inhabitants with their wives and children, in
order to fhew them other iflands. They were prevented
however by tempeftuous weather from reaching them;
and were driven out to fea Weftward with fuch violence,
that all their fails were carried away: at length on the
23d of September they ftruck againft land, which they
took for the peninfula of Kamtchatka; and they found
it to be the diftrict of Stobolfkoi Oftrog. Six men were
immediately difpatched in the fmall boat and two baidars
to land: they carried with them feveral girls (who had
been brought from the New-difcovered iflands) in order
to gather berries. Mean while the crew endeavoured to
ply the fhip to the windward. When the boat returned,
thofe on board were fcarcely able, on account of the
ftorm, to row to the fhip, and to catch hold of a rope,

4   which

which was flung out to them. Two men remained with the baidars, and were afterwards carried by fome Kamtchadals to New Kamtchatkoi Oftrog. The fhip without one fail remaining was driven along the coaft of Kamtchatka towards Avatcha, and about feventy verfts from that harbour ran into the bay of Kalatzoff on the 25th of September. Their cargo confifted of the fkins of 900 old and young fea-otters, and of 350 foxes.

Pufhkareff and his crew had during this voyage behaved with fuch inhumanity towards the iflanders, that they were brought to trial in the year 1764; and the above-mentioned account is taken from the concurring evidence of feveral witneffes. It appears alfo, that they brought away from Atchu and Amleg two Aleütian men and three boys, Ivan an Aleütian interpreter, and above twenty women and girls whom they debauched. Ivan, and one of the boys whom they called Mofes, were the only perfons who arrived at Kamtchatka. Upon their firft approach to that coaft, fourteen women were fent afhore to dig roots and to gather berries. Of thefe, two ran away, and a third was killed, as they were returning to the fhip by one Gorelin: upon this the others in a fit of defpair leaped into the fea and were drowned. All the remaining Aleütians, excepting the two perfons abovementioned, were immediately thrown overboard by Pufhkareff's order. The account which follows, although it is found in the depofitions, does not deferve to be entirely credited in all particulars.

K 2 The

The natives of the above-mentioned iflands are very tall and ftrongly made. They make their cloaths of the fkins of birds; and thruft bones through their under-lips by way of ornament. They were faid to ftrike their nofes until they bled, in order to fuck the blood; but we are informed from fubfequent accounts, that the blood thus drawn from themfelves was intended for other purpofes *. They were accufed even of murdering their own children in order to drink their blood; but this is undoubtedly an invention of the criminals, who reprefented the iflanders in the moft hideous colours, in order to excufe their own cruelties. Their dwellings under-ground are fimilar to thofe of the Kamtchadals; and have feveral openings on the fides, through which they make their efcape when the principal entrance is befet by an enemy. Their weapons confift of arrows, and lances pointed with bone, which they dart at a confiderable diftance.

Animals.   The ifland Alakfu is faid to contain rein-deer, bears, wild boars, wolves, otters, and a fpecies of dogs with long ears, which are very fierce and wild. And as the greateft part of thefe animals are not found upon thofe Fox Iflands which lie nearer to the weft, this circum-

---

* It appears in the laft chapter of this tranflation, that the iflanders are accuftomed to glue on the point of their darts with blood; and that this was the real motive to the practice mentioned in the text.

ftance

ftance feems to prove that Alakfu is fituated at no great diftance from the Continent of America. As to red, black, and grey foxes, there is fo large a quantity, that they are feen in herds of ten or twenty at a time. Wood is driven upon the coaft in great abundance. The ifland produces no large trees, having only fome under-wood, and a great variety of bulbs, roots, and berries. The coafts are frequented by large flocks of fea-birds, the fame which are obferved upon the fhore of the fea of Penfhinfk.

Auguft 4, 1759, the Peter and Paul, fitted out at the expence of the merchant Rybenfkoi by his agent Andrew Serebranikoff, and manned with thirty-three perfons, fet fail from the mouth of the Kamtchatka river. They fteered fouthwards until the 20th of September without feeing any land, when they ftood for the Aleütian Ifles, one of which they reached the 27th of September. They remained there until the 24th of June, 1761; during which time they killed upon this and the two other iflands 1900 old and young fea-otters, and obtained 450 more by bartering with the iflanders. The Coffac Minyachin, who was on board as collector of the tribute, calls in his account the firft ifland by the Ruffian name of Krugloi, or Round Ifland, which he fuppofes to be about fixty verfts in circumference : the largeft ifland lies thirty verfts from thence, and is about an hundred and fifty round: the fmalleft is about thirty verfts.

Voyage of the Peter and Paul to the Aleütian Iflands, 1759.

verſts from the latter, and is forty in circumference. Theſe three iſlands contain ſeveral high rocky mountains. The number of inhabitants were computed to be about forty-two men, without reckoning women and children.

CHAP. VII.

Voyage of Andrean Tolſtyk *in the* St. Andrean *and* Natalia—*Diſcovery of ſome New Iſlands called* Andreanoffſkye Oſtrova—*Deſcription of ſix of thoſe Iſlands.*

THE moſt remarkable voyage hitherto made is that of the St. Andrean and Natalia, of which the following extract is drawn from the Journals of the two Coſſacs, Peter Waſyutinſkoi and Maxim Laſaroff. This veſſel, fitted out by the above-mentioned merchant Andrean Tolſtyk, weighed from the mouth of the Kamtchatka river September 27, 1760; ſhe ſtood out to ſea right Eaſtwards, and on the 29th reached Beering's Iſland. There ſhe lay at anchor in a bay, from whence the crew brought all the tackle and lading aſhore. Soon afterwards they were driven upon the ſhore by a violent autumnal ſtorm, without any other damage than the loſs of an anchor. Here they paſſed the winter; and, having refitted their veſſel, put to ſea June 24, 1761: they paſſed by Copper Iſland, which lies about an hundred and fifty verſts from the former, and ſteered S. E. towards the Aleütian Iſles, which they did not reach before the 6th of Auguſt. They caſt anchor in an open bay near Attak, in order to procure an interpreter from the Toigon

Voyage of Andrean Tolſtyk in the St. Andrean and Natalia, 1760.

Toigon Tunulgafen; but the latter being dead, they fent prefents to the Toigon Bakutun. As there were already three ſhips lying at anchor before this iſland, on the 19th they again ſtood out to fea in queſt of the more diſtant iſlands, for the purpoſe of exacting a tribute. They carried on board a relation of the Toigon Bakutun, who had a ſlight knowledge of the Ruſſian language. They ſteered N. E. and N. E. by E. and were driven, on the 28th, by a high gale of wind towards an iſland, before which they immediately caſt anchor. The following morning the two Coſſacs with a party of eight perſons went aſhore to reconnoitre the iſland; they ſaw no inhabitants. Auguſt 30, the veſſel was brought into a fafe bay. The next day ſome of the crew were ſent aſhore to procure wood, that the ſhip might be refitted; but there were no large trees to be met with upon the whole

Reaches Ayagh, one of the Andrea- noffikye Iſlands. iſland. Lafaroff, who was one of the party, had been there before in Serebranikoff's veſſel: he called the iſland Ayagh or Kayachu; and another, which lay about the diſtance of twenty verſts, Kanaga. As they were returning to the ſhip, they ſaw two iſlanders rowing in ſmall canoes towards Kanaga, one of whom had ſerved as an interpreter, and was known to Lafaroff. The latter accordingly made them a preſent of ſome freſh proviſion, which the others gratefully accepted, and then continued their courſe acroſs the ſtrait to Kanaga. Soon afterwards Lafaroff and eight men rowed over to that iſland; and having invited the Toigon, who was a rela-

tion

tion of the above-mentioned interpreter, to pay them a
vifit at Kayachu, they immediately returned to the ſhip.

Near the place where they lay at anchor, a rivulet
falls into the bay; it flows from a lake that is about
two or three verſts in circumference, and which is formed
from a number of ſmall ſprings. Its courſe is about
eight verſts long; and in ſummer ſeveral ſpecies of ſalmon and other fiſh, ſimilar to thoſe which are found at
Kamtchatka, aſcend the ſtream as far as the lake.

Lafaroff was employed in fiſhing in this rivulet, when
the Toigon of Kanaga, accompanied with a confiderable
number of the natives in fifteen baidars, arrived at the
ſhip: he was hoſpitably entertained, and received ſeveral
preſents. The Ruſſians ſeized this opportunity of per-
ſuading the iſlanders to acknowledge themſelves ſubject
to the Empreſs, and to pay a regular tribute; to which
they made no great objection. By means of the interpreter, the following information was obtained from the
Toigon. The natives chiefly ſubſiſt upon dried fiſh and
other ſea animals. They catch * turbot of a very large
ſize, and take ſeals by means of harpoons, to which they
faſten bladders. They fiſh for cod with bone hooks,
and lines made of a long and tough ſpecies of ſea-weed,

* The author adds, that theſe turbot [paltus] weigh occaſionally ſeven
or eight pood.

L

which

which they dip in fresh water and draw out to the size
of a fine packthread.

As soon as the vessel was laid up in a secure place,
Tolstyk, Vassyutin, and Lasaroff, with several others,
went in four baidars to Kanaga. The first remained
upon that island; but the two others rowed in two baidars to Tsetchina, which is separated from Kanaga by a
strait about seven versts in breadth: the islanders received them amicably, and promised to pay tribute.
The several parties returned all safe to Kayachu, without
having procured any furs. Soon afterwards Tolstyk dis-
patched some hunters in four baidars to Tagalak, Atchu,
and Amlak, which lay to the East of Kayachu: none of
these parties met with any opposition from the natives:
they accordingly remained with great tranquillity upon
these several islands until the year 1764. Their success
in hunting was not however very great; for they caught
no more than 1880 full grown sea-otters, 778 middle-
aged, and 372 cubs.

Description of the Andrea-noffikie Islands.

The following is Lasaroff's description of the above-
mentioned six islands * which lie in a chain somewhat
to the North West of the Fox Islands, and must not be
blended with them. The first certain account was
brought by this vessel, the St. Andrean and Natalia,

* These are the six Islands described by Mr. Stæhlin in his description
of the New Archipelago. See Appendix I. N° V.

from

from whence they are called the Andreanoffſkie Oſtrova, or the Iſlands of St. Andrean.

Ayagh is about an hundred and fifty verſts in circum- Ayagh. ference: it contains ſeveral high and rocky mountains, the intervals of which are bare heath and moor ground: not one foreſt tree is to be found upon the whole iſland. The vegetables ſeem for the moſt part like thoſe which grow in Kamtchatka. Of berries there are found * crow or crake-berries and the larger ſort of bilberries, but in ſmall quantities. Of the roots of burnet and all kinds of ſnake weed, there is ſuch an abundance as to afford, in caſe of neceſſity, a plentiful proviſion for the inhabitants. The above-mentioned rivulet is the only one upon the iſland. The number of inhabitants cannot ſufficiently be aſcertained, becauſe the natives paſs continually from iſland to iſland in their baidars.

Kanaga ſtands Weſt from Ayagh, and is two hundred Kanaga. verſts in circumference. It contains an high volcano, where the natives find ſulphur in ſummer. At the foot of this mountain are hot ſprings, wherein they occaſion-ally boil their proviſion. There is no rivulet upon this iſland: and the low grounds are ſimilar to thoſe of Ayagh. The inhabitants are reckoned about two hun-dred ſouls.

* Empetrum, Vaccin. Uliginoſum, Sanguiſorba, & Biſtorta.

L 2   Tſetchina

Tſetchina.   Tſetchina lies Eaſtward about forty verſts from Kanaga, and is about eighty in circumference. It is full of rocky mountains, of which the Bielaia Sopka, or the White Peak, is the higheſt. In the valley there are alſo ſome warm ſprings, but no rivulet abounding in fiſh: the iſland contains only four families.

Tagalak.   Tagalak is forty verſts in circumference, ten Eaſt from Tſetchina: it contains a few rocks, but neither rivulets with fiſh, nor any vegetable production fit for nouriſhment. The coaſts are rocky, and dangerous to approach in baidars. This iſland is alſo inhabited by no more than four families.

Atchu.   Atchu lies in the ſame poſition forty verſts diſtant from Tagalak, and is about three hundred in circumference: near it is an harbour, where ſhips may ride ſecurely at anchor. It contains many rocky mountains; and ſeveral ſmall rivulets that fall into the ſea, and of which one running Eaſtwards abounds in fiſh. The roots which have juſt before been mentioned, and bulbs of white lilies, are found there in plenty. Its inhabitants amount to about ſixty ſouls.

Amlak.   Amlak is a mountainous iſland ſtanding to the Eaſt more than ſeven verſts from Atchu, and is alſo three hundred in circumference. It contains the ſame num

                                                                    ber

ber of inhabitants as Atchu, has a commodious haven, and produces roots in abundance. Of several small rivulets there is one only which flows towards the North, that contains any fish. Besides these a cluster of other islands were observed stretching farther to the East, which were not touched upon.

The inhabitants of these six islands are tributary to Russia. They live in holes dug in the earth, in which they make no fires even in winter. Their clothes are made like shirts, of the skins of the * guillimot and puffin, which they catch with springes. Over these in rainy weather they wear an upper garment, made of the bladders and other dried intestines of seals and sea-lions oiled and stitched together. They catch cod and turbot with bone-hooks, and eat them raw. As they never lay-in a store of provision, they suffer greatly from hunger in stormy weather, when they cannot go out to fish; at which time they are reduced to live upon small shellfish and sea-wrack, which they pick up upon the beach and eat raw. In May and June they kill sea-otters in the following manner: When the weather is calm, they row out to sea in several baidars: having found the animal, they strike him with harpoons, and follow him so closely, that he cannot easily escape. They take sea dogs in the same manner. In the severest weather they make no addition to their usual cloathing. In order to warm

Account of the Inhabitants.

* Colymbus Troile, Alca Arctica.

4

themselves

themfelves in winter, whenever it freezes very hard, they burn a heap of dry grafs, over which they ftand and catch the heat under their clothes. The clothes of the women and children are made of fea-otter fkins, in the fame form as thofe belonging to the men. Whenever they pafs the night at a diftance from home, they dig a hole in the earth, and lay themfelves down in it, covered only with their clothes and matts of platted grafs. Regardlefs of every thing but the prefent moment, deftitute of religion, and without the leaft appearance of decency, they feem but few degrees removed from brutes.

As foon as the feveral baidars fent out upon hunting parties were returned, and the veffel got ready for their departure, the Toigons of thefe iflands (excepting Kanaga) came in baidars to Tolftyk, accompanied with a confiderable number of the natives; their names were Tfarkulini, Tfhunila, Kayugotfk and Mayatok. They brought with them a voluntary tribute, making prefents of pieces of dried falmon, and unanimoufly expreffing their fatisfaction upon the good conduct of the Ruffians. Tolftyk gave them in return fome toys and other trifles, and defired them to recommend to the inhabitants of the other iflands the like friendly behaviour towards the Ruffian merchants who fhould come amongft them, if they had a mind to be treated in the fame manner.

June

June 14, 1764, they failed for Kamtchatka, and anchored on the 19th before Shemiya, one of the Aleütian Iflands. The 21ft they were forced from their anchor by tempeftuous winds, and driven upon a rocky fhore. This accident obliged them to fend the lading afhore, and to draw the fhip upon land in order to repair the damage, which was done not without great difficulty. On the 18th of Auguft they ftood out to fea and made towards Atchu, which they reached on the 20th. Having fprung a leak they again refitted the veffel; and, after taking on board the crew of a fhip which had been lately caft away, they failed for Kamtchatka. On the 4th of September they came in fight of that peninfula near Tzafchminfkoi Oftrog; and on the 18th, as they were endeavouring to run into the mouth of the Kamtchatka river, they were forced by a ftorm upon the coaft. The veffel was deftroyed, and the greateft part of the cargo loft.

The Veffel wrecked upon the Coaft of Kamtchatka.

C H A P.

C H A P.   VIII.

Voyage of the Zacharias and Elizabeth, fitted out by Kul-
koff, and commanded by Drufinin—They fail to Umnak
and Unalafhka, and winter upon the latter ifland—The
veffel deftroyed; and all the crew, except four, murdered
by the iflanders—The adventures of thefe four Ruffians,
and their wonderful efcape.

I SHALL here barely mention that a veffel was fitted
out in Auguft, 1760, at the expence of Terrenti
Tfebaëffkoi: but I fhall have occafion to be very circumftantial in my accounts concerning feveral others,
which failed during the following years: more copious
information concerning the Fox Iflands having been
procured from thefe voyages, although for the moft
part unfortunate, than from all the preceding ones.

In 1762 four veffels failed for the Fox Iflands: of
thefe only one returned fafe to Kamtchatka.

Voyage of
Drufinin in   The firft was the Zacharias and Elizabeth, fitted out
the Zacharias
and Elizabeth, by Kulkoff, a merchant of Vologda, and Company, under
1762.
          the command of Drufinin, and manned by thirty-four
Ruffians, and three Kamtchadals.

                                   September

September the 6th, they weighed anchor from Ochotſk, and arrived October the 11th in the haven of St. Peter and Paul, where they wintered. June the 24th, 1763, they again put to ſea, and having reached, after eleven days ſailing, the neareſt Aleütian Iſlands, they anchored before Attak. They ſtaid here about fourteen days, and took up ſeven Ruſſians who had been ſhipwrecked on this coaſt. Among theſe was Korelin, who returned to Kamtchatka, and brought back the following account of the voyage.

July the 17th, they ſailed from Attak towards the more diſtant iſlands. In the ſame month they landed upon an iſland, where the crew of the Andrean and Natalia was engaged in hunting; and, having laid in a proviſion of water, continued their voyage.

In the beginning of September they arrived at Um- nak, one of the Fox Iſlands, and caſt anchor about a verſt from the ſhore. They found there Glottoff's veſſel, whoſe voyage will be mentioned in a ſucceeding chapter*. Druſinin immediately diſpatched his firſt mate Maeſniſk and Korelin, with thirty-four of the crew, to land. They paſſed over to the Eaſtern extremity of the iſland, which was diſtant about ſeventy verſts from the veſſel; and returned ſafe on the 12th of September. During this ex-

Arrival at Umnak.

* Chap. X.

M

pedition,

pedition, they faw feveral remains of fox-traps which
had been fet by the Ruffians; and met with feveral
natives who fhewed fome tribute-quittances. The
fame day letters were brought by the iflanders from
Medvedeff and Korovin *, who were juft arrived at
Umnak and Unalafhka in two veffels fitted out by the
merchants Protaffoff and Trapefnikoff. Anfwers were
returned by the fame meffengers.

Winters at
Unalafhka.

On the 22d, Drufinin failed to the Northern point of
Unalafhka, which lies about fifteen verfts from Umnak:
the crew, having laid up the veffel in a fafe harbour,
and brought the lading afhore, made preparation to con-
ftruct an hut. Soon after their arrival, two Toigons
of the neareft village brought hoftages of their own accord; their example was immediately followed by feveral
of the more diftant villages. Here they received information of an hunting party fent from Trapefnikoff's
fhip. Upon which Maefnifk alfo difpatched three companies upon the fame errand, one confifting of eleven
men, among whom was Korelin, under the command of
Peter Tfekaleff; a fecond of the fame number, under
Michael Kudyakoff; and a third of nine men, under
Yephim Kafkitfyn. Of thefe three parties, Tfekaleff's
was the only one of which we have received any circumftantial account: for not a fingle perfon of the
other two parties, or of the crew remaining on board,
ever returned to Kamtchatka.

* See the following chapter.

Kafkitfyn

Kaſkitſyn remained near the haven, and the two other companies were diſpatched to the Northern point of the iſland. Kudyakoff ſtopped at a place called Kalaktak, which contained about forty inhabitants; Tſekaleff went on to Inalok, which lies about thirty verſts from Kalaktak. He found there a dwelling with about ſeventy inhabitants, whom he behaved to with kindneſs: he built an hut for himſelf and his companions, and kept a conſtant watch.

December the 4th, ſix of the party being diſpatched to look after the pit-falls, there remained only five Ruſſians: namely, Peter Tſekaleff, Stephen Korelin, Dmitri Bragin, Gregory Shaffyrin, and Ivan Kokovin: the iſlanders took this opportunity of giving the firſt proofs of their hoſtile intentions, which they had hitherto concealed. As Tſekaleff and Shaffyrin were upon a viſit to the iſlanders, the latter ſuddenly, and without any provocation, ſtruck Tſekaleff upon the head with a club, and afterwards ſtabbed him with knives. They next fell upon Shaffyrin, who defended himſelf with an hatchet; and, though deſperately wounded, forced his way back to his companions. Bragin and Korelin, who remained in the hut, had immediate recourſe to their fire-arms; but Kokovin, who was at a ſmall diſtance, was ſurrounded by the ſavages, and thrown down. They continued ſtabbing him with knives and darts, until Korelin came to his aſſiſtance; the latter, having

All the Crew, except four Ruſſians, deſtroyed by the Natives.

M 2 wounded

wounded two iſlanders, and driven away the others, brought Kokovin half-dead to the hut.

Soon afterwards the natives ſurrounded the hut, which the Ruſſians had taken the precaution to provide with ſhooting holes. The ſiege laſted four days without intermiſſion. The iſlanders were prevented indeed by the fire-arms from ſtorming the hut; but whenever the Ruſſians made their appearance, darts were immediately ſhot at them from all ſides; ſo that they could not venture to go out for water. At length, when Shaffyrin and Kokovin were a little recovered, they all ſallied out upon the iſlanders with their guns and lances; three perſons were killed upon the ſpot, and ſeveral wounded; upon which the others fled away and diſperſed. During the ſiege the ſavages were ſeen at a little diſtance bearing ſome arms and caps, and holding them up in triumph: theſe things belonged to the ſix Ruſſians, who had been ſent to the pit-falls, and had fallen a ſacrifice to the reſentment of the natives.

The latter no ſooner diſappeared, than the Ruſſians dragged the baidar into the ſea, and rowed without moleſtation out of the bay, which is about ten verſts broad. They next landed near a ſmall habitation: finding it empty, they drew the baidar aſhore, and went with their fire-arms and lances acroſs the mountains towards Kalaktak, where they had left Kudyakoff's party. As they

approached

approached that place towards evening, they fired from the heights; but no fignal being returned, they concluded, as was really the cafe, that this company had likewife been maffacred by the inhabitants. They themfelves narrowly efcaped the fame fate; for, immediately upon the report of the fire-arms, numerous bodies of the iflanders made their appearance, and clofely purfued the Ruffians: darknefs however coming on, the latter found means to efcape over the fandy fhore of a bay to a rock, where they were fheltered, and could defend themfelves. They here made fo good a ufe of their arms, that the iflanders thought proper to retire: the fugitives, as foon as their purfuers were withdrawn, feized the opportunity of proceeding towards the haven, where their veffel lay at anchor; they ran without interruption during the whole night, and at break of day, when they were about three verfts from the haven, they efpied a locker of the veffel lying on the fhore. Struck with aftonifhment at this alarming difcovery, they retreated with precipitation to the mountains, from whence they defcried feveral iflanders rowing in canoes, but no appearance of their own veffel. During that day they kept themfelves clofely concealed, and durft not venture again towards the haven before the evening. Upon their arrival they found the veffel broken to pieces, and the dead bodies of their companions lying mangled along the beach. Having collected all the provifion which had been untouched by the favages, they returned to the mountains.

The

The following day they fcooped out a cavity at the foot of a mountain fituated about three verfts from the haven, and covered it with a piece of a fail. In the evening they returned to the haven, and found there an image of a faint and a prayer book; all the tackle and lading were taken away, excepting the facks for provifion. Thefe facks were made of leather: the natives had ript them up, probably to fee if they contained any iron, and had left them, together with the provifion, behind as ufelefs. The Ruffians collected all that remained, and dragged as much as they were able to carry into the mountains to their retreat, where they lived in a very wretched ftate from the 9th of December to the 2d of February, 1764.

Mean while they employed themfelves in making a little baidar, which they covered with the leather of the facks. Having drawn it at night from the mountains to the fea, they rowed without waiting for break of day along the Northern coaft of Unalafhka, in order to reach Trapefnikoff's veffel, which, as they had reafon to think, lay at anchor fomewhere upon the coaft. They rowed at fome diftance from the fhore, and by that means paff- ed three habitations unperceived. The following day they obferved at fome diftance five iflanders in a baidar, who upon feeing them made to Makufhinfk, before

which

which place the fugitives were obliged to pafs. Darknefs coming on, the Ruffians landed on a rock, and paffed the night afhore. Early in the morning they difcovered the iflanders advancing towards them from the bay of Ma-kufhinfk. Upon this they placed themfelves in an ad-vantageous poft, and prepared for defence.

The favages rowed clofe to the beach: part landing, and part remaining in their baidars, they commenced the affault by a volley of darts; and notwithftanding the Ruffians did great execution with their fire arms, the fkirmifh continued the whole day. Towards evening the enemy retired, and the fugitives betook themfelves with their canoe to an adjoining cavern. The attack was again renewed during the night; but the Ruffians were fo ad-vantageoufly pofted, that they repulfed the affailants without much difficulty. In this encounter Bragen was flightly wounded. They remained in this place three days; but the fea rifing at a fpring-tide into the rock, forced them to fally out towards a neighbouring cavern, which they reached without lofs, notwithftand-ing the oppofition of the iflanders.

They were imprifoned in this cave five weeks, and kept watch by turns. During that time they feldom ven-tured twenty yards from the entrance; and were obliged to quench their thirft with fnow-water, and with the moifture dripping from the rock. They fuffered alfo

greatly

greatly from hunger, having no fuſtenance but ſmall ſhell-fiſh, which they occaſionally found means to col-lect upon the beach. Compelled at length by extreme want, they one night ventured to draw their baidar into the ſea, and were fortunate enough to get off unper-ceived.

Their Eſcape from Unalaſh-ka to Trapeſ-nikoff's Veſſel. They continued rowing at night, but in the day they hid themſelves on the ſhore; by this means they eſcaped unobſerved from the bay of Makuſhinſk, and reached Trapeſnikoff's veſſel the 30th of March, 1764. What happened to them afterwards in company with the crew of this veſſel will be mentioned in the ſucceeding chapter. Shaffyrin alone of all the four died of ſick-neſs during the voyage; but Korelin, Kokovin, and Bragin *, returned ſafe to Kamtchatka. The names of theſe brave men deſerve our admiration, for the courage and perſeverance with which they ſupported and over-came ſuch imminent dangers.

* Theſe Ruffians were well known to ſeveral perſons of credit, who have confirmed the authenticity of this relation. Among the reſt the celebrated naturaliſt Mr. Pallas, whoſe name is well known in the lite-rary world, ſaw Bragin at Irkutſk: from him he had a narrative of their adventures and eſcape; which, as he aſſured me, perfectly tallied with the above account, which is drawn from the journal of Korelin.

C H A P.

C H A P. IX.

Voyage of the veſſel called the Trinity, *under the command of* Korovin—*Sails to the* Fox Iſlands—*Winters at* Una-laſhka—*Puts to ſea the ſpring following—The veſſel is ſtranded in a bay of the iſland* Umnak, *and the crew attacked by the natives—Many of them killed—Others carried off by ſickneſs—They are reduced to great ſtreights —Relieved by* Glottoff, *twelve of the whole company only remaining—Deſcription of* Umnak *and* Unalaſhka.

THE ſecond veſſel which ſailed from Kamtchatka in the year 1762, was the Trinity, fitted out by the trading company of Nikiphor Trapeſnikoff, merchant of Irkutſk, under the command of Ivan Korovin, and manned with thirty-eight Ruſſians and ſix Kamtchadals. *Voyage of Korovin, 1762.*

September 15, they ſailed down the Kamtchatka river, and ſtood out to ſea the 29th, when they were driven at large for ten days by contrary winds. At laſt upon the 8th of October they came in ſight of Beering's and Copper Iſland, where they caſt anchor before the South ſide of the former. Here they were reſolved to winter on account of the late ſeaſon of the year. Accordingly they laid up the veſſel in a ſecure harbour, and brought *Departs from Kamtchatka.*

all the lading afhore.   They ftaid here until the firft of
Auguft, 1763: during that time they killed about 500
arctic foxes and 20 fea-otters; the latter animals reforted lefs frequently to this ifland, in confequence of
the difturbance given them by the Ruffian hunters.

Korovin, having collected a fufficient ftore of provifion, feveral fkins of fea-cows for the coverings of baidars, and fome iron which remained from the wreck of
Beering's fhip, prepared for his departure.   Upon his
arrival at Beering's Ifland the preceding autumn, he
found there a veffel fitted out by Jacob Protaffoff, merchant of Tiumen, under the command of Dennis Medvedeff *.   Korovin had entered into a formal contract
with Medvedeff for the divifion of the furs.   Here he
took on board ten of Medvedeff's crew, and gave him
feven in return.

Auguft 1, Korovin put to fea from Beering's Ifland with
thirty-feven men, and Medvedeff with forty-nine.   They
failed without coming in fight of the Aleütian Ifles: on
the 15th, Korovin made Unalafhka, where Glottoff lay
at anchor, and Medvedeff reached Umnak.   Korovin
received the news of the latter's fafe arrival, firft by
fome iflanders, and afterwards by letters; both veffels

---

* This is the fourth veffel which failed in 1762. As the whole crew
was maffacred by the favages, we have no account of the voyage.
Short mention of this maffacre is occafionally made in this and the following chapters.

lay

lay at no greater diftance from each other than about an hundred and fifty verfts, taking a ftreight line from point to point acrofs the firth.

Korovin caft anchor in a convenient bay at the diftance of fixty yards from the fhore. On the 16th he landed with fourteen men, and having found nothing but an empty fhed, he returned to the veffel. After having taken a reinforcement, he again went afhore in order to look for fome inhabitants. About feven verfts from the haven, he came to two habitations, and faw three hundred perfons affembled together. Among them were three Toigons, who recollected and accofted in a friendly manner one Barnafheff, a native of Tobolfk, who had been there before with Glottoff; they fhewed fome tribute-quittances, which they had lately received from the Coffac Sabin Ponomareff. Two of thefe Toigons gave each a boy of twelve years of age as an hoftage, whom they paffed for their children; and the third delivered his fon of about fifteen years of age, the fame who had been Glottoff's hoftage, and whom Korovin called Alexèy. With thefe hoftages he returned to the fhip, which he laid up in the mouth of a river, after having brought all the provifion and lading afhore. Soon afterwards the three Toigons came to fee the hoftages; and informed Korovin, that Medvedeff's veffel rode fecurely at anchor before Umnak.

N 2 September

September 15, when every thing was prepared for
wintering, Korovin and Barnafheff set out in two baidars,
each with nine men and one of the hoftages, who had
a flight knowledge of the Ruffian language. They
went along the Northern coaft of the ifland, towards
its Weftern extremity, in order to hunt, and to enquire
after a certain interpreter called Kafhmak, who had been
employed by Glottoff on a former occafion. Having
rowed about twenty verfts, they paffed by a village,
and landed at another which lay about five verfts further.   But as the number of inhabitants feemed to
amount to two hundred, they durft not venture to the
dwellings, but ftayed by the baidar.   Upon this the
Toigon of the place came to them, with his wife and
fon : he fhewed a tribute-quittance, and delivered his
fon, a boy of thirteen years of age and whom Korovin
called Stepanka, as an hoftage, for which he received a
prefent of corals.

They rowed now further to a third village, about
fifteen verfts from the former, where they found the
interpreter Kafhmak ; the latter accompanied them to
the two Toigons, who gave them a friendly reception,
and fhewed their tribute-quittances.   A few natives only
made their appearance; the others, as the Toigons pretended, were gone out to fifh.   The next morning each
Toigon gave a boy as an hoftage ; one of the boys Korovin called Gregory, and the other Alexey.   The Ruffians

fians were detained there two days by a violent ftorm; during which time a letter from Medvedeff was brought by an Aleutian, and an anfwer was returned by the fame perfon. The ftorm at length fomewhat abating, they rowed back to the next village, where they continued two nights without any apprehenfions from the favages. At length Korovin returned in fafety with the hoftages to the crew.

In the beginning of October they built a winter-hut, partly of wood and partly of feal-fkins, and made all the neceffary preparations for hunting. On the 14th, two companies, each confifting of eleven men, were fent out upon an hunting party to the Eaftern point of the ifland; they returned in four days with hoftages. About fixty verfts from the haven, they had met a party of twenty-five Ruffians, commanded by Drufinin. About the fame time fome Toigons brought a prefent of fturgeon and whale's blubber, and received in return fome beads and provifion.

Builds an Hut, and makes Preparations for Wintering.

Korovin and his company now thought themfelves fecure; for which reafon twenty-three men, under the command of the above-mentioned Barnafheff, were difpatched in two baidars upon an hunting party towards the Weftern point of the ifland. Eight mufkets were diftributed to each boat, a piftol and a lance to each

man,,

man, and alſo a ſufficient ſtore of ammunition and proviſion. The following day two accounts were ſent from
Barnaſheff; and letters were alſo received from the crew
of Protaſſoff's veſſel. From the 2d of November to the
8th of December, the Ruſſians, who remained with Korovin, killed forty-eight dark-coloured foxes, together
with an hundred and ſeventeen of the common ſort:
during this expedition one man was loſt. Some of the
natives came occaſionally in baidars, and exchanged ſea-
otters and fox-ſkins for corals. On the 8th of December letters were again brought from Barnaſheff and alſo
from the crew of Protaſſoff's ſhip. Anſwers were returned by the ſame meſſengers.

After the departure of theſe meſſengers, the mother
of Alexèy came with a meſſage from the Toigon her huſ-
band, importing, that a large number of iſlanders were
making towards the ſhip. Upon this Korovin ordered
the men to arms, and ſoon after ſeventy natives approached, and held up ſome ſea-otter ſkins. The Ruſſians cried
out that no more than ten at a time ſhould come over the
brook towards their hut: upon which the iſlanders left
their ſkins with Korovin, and returned without attempting any hoſtilities. Their apprehenſions were now ſomewhat quieted, but they were again raiſed by the arrival
of three Kamtchadals belonging to Kulkoff's ſhip, who
flew for protection to Korovin: they brought the account that the crew had been killed by the ſavages, and
the

the veffel deftroyed. It was now certain that the feventy iflanders above-mentioned had come with hoftile intentions. This information fpread fuch a fudden panic among the Ruffians, that it was even propofed to burn the veffel, and to endeavour to find their companions, who were gone upon hunting parties.

That day however paffed without any attack : but towards the evening of the 10th of December, the favages affembled in large bodies, and invefted the hut on all fides. Four days and nights they never ceafed annoying the Ruffians with their darts; two of the latter were killed, and the furvivors were nearly exhaufted by continual fatigue. Upon the fifth day the iflanders took poft in a neighbouring cavern, where they continued watching the Ruffians fo clofely during a whole month, that none of the latter durft venture fifty paces from their dwelling. Korovin, finding himfelf thus annoyed by the natives, ordered the hut to be deftroyed : he then retired to his veffel, which was brought for greater fecurity out of the mouth of the rivulet to the diftance of an hundred yards from the beach. There they lay at anchor from the 5th of March to the 26th of April, during which time they fuffered greatly from want of provifion, and ftill more from the fcurvy.

The Ruffians attacked by the Natives.

During

During this period they were attacked by a large body
of the natives, who advanced in forty baidars with the
hopes of furprifing the veffel. Korelin had been warned
of their approach by two of the inhabitants, one of whom
was a relation of the interpreter Kafhmak: accordingly
he was prepared for their reception. As foon as
the favages came near the veffel, they brandifhed
their darts and got ready for the attack. Korovin however had no fooner fired and killed one perfon, than they
were ftruck with a panic and rowed away. They were fo
incenfed at this failure of fuccefs, that they immediately
put to death the two good-natured natives, who had be-
trayed their defign to the Ruffians. Soon afterwards the
father of Alexèy came and demanded his fon, who was
reftored to him: and on the 30th of March Korovin and
his three companions arrived as it is mentioned in the
preceding chapter. By this reinforcement the number
of the crew amounted to eighteen perfons.

Korovin puts
to Sea. The
Veffel ftranded
upon Umnak.
April 26, Korovin put to fea from Unalafhka with the
crew and eleven hoftages. The veffel was driven until
the 28th by contrary winds, and then ftranded in a bay
of the ifland Umnak. The ammunition and fails, together with the fkins for the conftruction of baidars,
were brought afhore with great difficulty. During the
difembarkation one fick man was drowned, another died
as foon as he came to land, and eight hoftages ran away
                                                      amidft

amidft the general confufion.   There ftill remained the faithful interpreter Kafhmak and three hoftages.   The whole number of the Ruffians amounted to only fix-teen perfons ; and of thefe three were fick of the fcurvy. Under thefe circumftances they fecured themfelves be-tween their baidar and fome empty barrels, which they covered with feal-fkins, while the fails were fpread over them in form of a tent.   Two Ruffians kept watch ; and there being no appearance of any iflanders, the others retired to fleep.

Before break of day, about an hundred favages ad-vancing fecretly from the fea-fide, threw their darts at the diftance of twenty yards with fuch force, that many of them pierced through the baidar and the fkins; others fell from above through the fails.   By this dif-charge, the two perfons who kept watch, together with the three hoftages, were killed on the fpot; and all the Ruffians were wounded.   The latter indeed were fo effectually furprifed, as to be prevented from having recourfe to their fire-arms.   In this diftrefs Korovin fallied out, in company with four Ruffians, and at-tacked the enemy with lances : two of the favages were killed, and the others driven to flight.   Korovin and his party were fo feverely wounded, that they had fcarcely ftrength fufficient to return to their tent.

The Ruffians in Danger of being deftroy-ed by the Na-tives.

The latter repulfed.

O   During

During the night the ſtorm increaſed to ſuch a degree, that the veſſel was entirely daſhed to pieces. The
greateſt part of the wreck, which was caſt on ſhore
by the ſea, was carried away by the iſlanders. They
alſo broke to pieces the barrels of fat, emptied the ſacks
of proviſion, and deſtroyed moſt of the furs: having
thus ſatisfied their reſentment, they went away; and
did not again make their appearance until the 30th of
April. Upon their retiring, the Ruſſians collected the
wretched remains which had been left untouched by
the ſavages, or which the waves had caſt on ſhore ſince
their departure.

April 30, a body of an hundred and fifty natives
advanced from the Eaſtern point of the iſland towards
the tent; and, at the diſtance of an hundred yards,
ſhot at the Ruſſians with fire-arms, but luckily without
execution. They alſo ſet on fire the high graſs, and
the wind blew the flames towards the tent; but the
Ruſſians firing forced the enemy to flight, and gained
time to extinguiſh the flames.

This was the laſt attack which was made upon Korovin;
although ſickneſs and miſery detained him and his companions upon this ſpot until the 21ſt of July. They then
put to ſea in a baidar eight yards long, which they
had conſtructed in order to make to Protaſſoff's veſſel,
with

with whofe fate they were as yet unacquainted. Their number was now reduced to twelve perfons, among whom were fix Kamtchadals.

After having rowed ten days they landed upon the beach of the fame ifland Umnak; there they obferved the remains of a veffel which had been burnt, and faw fome clothes, fails, and ropes, torn to pieces. At a fmall diftance was an empty Ruffian dwelling, and near it a bath-room, in which they found, to their inexpreffible terror, twenty dead bodies in their clothes. Each of them had a thong of leather, or his own girdle, faftened about the neck, with which he had been dragged along. Korovin and his companions recollected them to have been fome of thofe who had failed in Protaffoff's veffel; and could diftinguifh among the reft the commander Medvedeff. They difcovered no further traces of the remaining crew; and as none ever appeared, we have no account of the circumftances with which this cataftrophe was attended.

The Ruffians difcover the dead Bodies of their Countrymen who had been murdered by the Natives.

After having buried his dead countrymen, Korovin and his companions began to build an hut: they were prevented however from finifhing it, by the unexpected arrival of Stephen Glottoff*, who came to them with a fmall party by land. Korovin and his companions accordingly joined Glottoff, and rowed the next day to his veffel.

Relieved from their Diftreffes by the Arrival of Glottoff.

* See the following chapter.

O 2

Soon

Soon afterwards Korovin was fent with a party of twenty men to coaft the ifland of Umnak, in order to difcover if any part of Medvedeff's crew had made their efcape from the general maffacre : but his enquiries were without fuccefs. In the courfe of this expedition, as he lay at anchor, in September, before a fmall ifland fituated between Umnak and Unalafhka, fome favages rowed towards the Ruffians in two large baidars ; and having fhot at them with fire-arms, though without effect, inftantly retired. The fame evening Korovin entered a bay of the ifland Umnak, with an intention of paffing the night on fhore : but as he came near the coaft, a large number of favages in an hundred baidars furrounded and faluted him with a volley of darts. Korovin fired, and foon difperfed them ; and immediately made to a large baidar, which he faw at fome diftance, in hopes of finding fome Ruffians. He was however miftaken ; the iflanders who were aboard landed at his approach, and, after fhooting at him from their fire-arms, retired to the mountains.

Korovin found there an empty baidar, which he knew to be the fame in which Barnafheff had failed, when he was fent upon an hunting party. Within were nothing but two hatchets and fome iron points for darts. Three women were feized at the fame time ; and two natives, who refufed to furrender themfelves, were put to death.

They

They then made to the dwelling, from which all the inhabitants had run away, and found therein pieces of Ruffian leather, blades of fmall knives, fhirts, and other things, which had belonged to the Ruffians. All the information which they could procure from the women whom they had taken prifoners, was, that the crew had been killed, and this booty taken away by the inhabitants, who had retired to the ifland Unalafhka. Korovin gave thefe women their liberty, and, being apprehenfive of frefh attacks, returned to the haven.

Towards winter Korovin, with a party of twenty-two men, was fent upon an hunting expedition to the Weftern point of Unalafhka: he was accompanied by an Aleütian interpreter, called Ivan Glottoff. Being informed by fome iflanders, that a Ruffian fhip, under the command of Ivan Solovioff*, was then lying before Unalafhka, he immediately rowed towards the haven where fhe was at anchor. On the way he had a fharp encounter with the natives, who endeavoured to prevent him from landing: of thefe, ten were killed upon the fpot; and the remainder fled away, leaving behind them fome women and children.

Korovin ftaid three days aboard Solovioff's veffel, and then returned to the place where he had been fo lately attacked. The inhabitants however, for this

* Chap. XI.

time,

time, made no oppofition to his landing; on the contrary, they received him with kindnefs, and permitted
him to hunt: they even delivered hoftages; and entered
into a friendly traffic, exchanging furs for beads. They
were alfo prevailed upon to reftore feveral mufkets
and other things, taken from the Ruffians who had
been maffacred.

A fhort time before his departure, the inhabitants
again fhewed their hoftile intentions; for three of them
came up to the Ruffian centinel, and fuddenly fell upon
him with their knives. The centinel however difen-
gaging himfelf, and retreating into the hut, they ran
away. The Toigons of the village protefted ignorance
of this treachery; and the offenders were foon afterwards difcovered and punifhed. Korovin, as he was
returning to Glottoff, was forced to engage with the
iflanders upon Unalafhka, and alfo upon Umnak, where
they endeavoured to prevent him from landing. Before the end of the year a ftorm drove the baidar upon
the beach of the latter ifland; and the tempeftuous
weather fetting in, they were detained there until the
6th of April, 1765. During this time they were reduced, from a fcarcity of provifion, to live chiefly upon
fea-wrack and fmall fhell-fifh. On the 22d they returned to Glottoff; and as they had been unfuccefsful
in hunting, their cargo of furs was very inconfiderable.
Three days after his arrival, Korovin quitted Glottoff,
and went over with five other Ruffians to Solovioff, with

4   whom

whom he returned the following year to Kamtchatka.
The six Kamtchadals of Korovin's party joined Glottoff.

According to Korovin's account, the islands Umnak Korovin's Description of Umnak and Unalashka.
and Unalashka are situated not much more Northwards
than the mouth of the Kamtchatka river ; and, according to the ship's reckoning, about the distance of 1700
versts Eastwards from the same place. The circumference of Umnak is about two hundred and fifty versts;
Unalashka is much larger. Both these islands are wholly
destitute of trees; drift-wood is brought ashore in large
quantities. There were five lakes upon the Northern
coast of Unalashka, and but one upon Umnak, of which
none were more than ten versts in circumference. These
lakes give rise to several small rivulets, which flow only
a few versts before they empty themselves into the sea:
the fish enter the rivulets in the middle of April,
they ascend the lakes in July, and continue there until
August. Sea-otters and other sea-animals resort but
seldom to these islands; but there is great abundance of
red and black foxes. North Eastwards from Unalashka
two islands appeared in sight, at the distance of five or
ten versts ; but Korovin did not touch at them.

The inhabitants of these islands row in their small Account of the Inhabitants.
baidars from one island to the other. They are so
numerous, and their manner of life so unsettled, that
their number cannot exactly be determined. Their
dwelling

dwelling caves are made in the following manner. They
firft dig an hole in the earth proportioned to the fize of
their intended habitation, of twenty, thirty, or forty
yards in length, and from fix to ten broad. They
then fet up poles of larch, firs, and afh driven on the
coaft by the fea. Acrofs the top of thefe poles they
lay planks, which they cover with grafs and earth.
They enter through holes in the top by means of ladders. Fifty, an hundred, and even an hundred and fifty
perfons dwell together in fuch a cave. They light little
or no fires within, for which reafon thefe dwellings are
much cleaner than thofe of the Kamtchadals. When
they want to warm themfelves in the winter, they make
a fire of dry herbs, of which they have collected a large
ftore in fummer, and ftand over it until they are fufficiently warmed. A few of thefe iflanders wear fur-
ftockings in winter; but the greateft part go bare-footed,
and all are without breeches. The fkins of cormorants,
puffins, and fea-divers, ferve for the mens cloathing; and
the women wear the fkins of fea-bears, feals, and fea-otters.
They fleep upon thick mats, which they twift out of a
foft kind of grafs that grows upon the fhore, and have
no other covering but their ufual clothes. Many of the
men have five or fix wives; and he that is the beft
hunter or fifher has the greateft number. The women
make their needles of the bones of birds wings, and ufe
finews for thread.

Their

Their weapons are bows and arrows, lances and darts, which they throw like the Greenlanders to the diftance of fixty yards by means of a little hand-board. Both the darts and arrows are feathered: the former are about an ell and an half long; the fhaft, which is well made confidering their want of inftruments, is often compofed of two pieces that join into each other: the point is of flint, fharpened by beating it between two ftones. Thefe darts as well as the lances were formerly tipped with bone, but at prefent the points are commonly made of the iron which they procure from the Ruffians, and out of which they ingenioufly form little hatchets and two-edged knives. They fhape the iron by rubbing it between two ftones, and whetting it frequently with fea-water. With thefe inftruments and ftone hatchets they build their baidars. They have a ftrange cuftom of cutting holes in the under-lip and through the griftle of the nofe. They place in the former two little bones, wrought in the form of teeth, which projeét fome inches from the face. In the nofe a piece of bone is placed crofsways. The deceafed are buried with their boat, weapons, and clothes *.

* The author repeats here feveral circumftances which have been mentioned before, and many of them will occur again : but my office as a tranflator would not fuffer me to omit them.

C H A P.

CHAP. X.

Voyage of Stephen Glottoff—*He reaches the* Fox Iflands—
Sails beyond Unalafhka *to* Kadyak—*Winters upon that
Ifland—Repeated attempts of the Natives to deftroy the
Crew—They are repulfed, reconciled, and prevailed upon
to trade with the* Ruffians—*Account of* Kadyak—*Its
inhabitants—animals—productions—*Glottoff *fails back
to* Umnak—*Winters there—Returns to* Kamtchatka—
Journal of his voyage.

THE following voyage, which extended farther, and
terminated more fortunately, than the laft mentioned expeditions, is one of the moft memorable yet made.

Voyage of
Glottoff in the
Andrean and
Natalia, 1762. Terenty Tfebaeffſkoi and company, merchants of
Lalſk, fitted out the Andrean and Natalia under the command of Stephen Glottoff, an experienced and ſkilful
ſeaman of Yarenſk. This veſſel ſailed from the bay of
the river Kamtchatka the 1ſt of October, 1762, manned
with thirty-eight Ruffians and eight Kamtchadals. In
eight days they reached Mednoi Oftroff, or Copper Ifland,
where having fought out a convenient harbour, they
Winters upon
Copper Ifland. unloaded and laid up the veſſel for the winter. Their
firft care was to fupply themfelves with provifions ; and
they

they killed afterwards a quantity of ice-foxes, and a confiderable number of fea-otters.

For the benefit of the crown and their own ufe in cafe of need, they refolved to take on board all the remaining tackle and iron work of Beering's fhip, which had been left behind on Commander's Ifland, and was buried in the beach. For this purpofe they difpatched, on the 27th of May, Jacob Malevinfkoy (who died foon after) with thirteen men in a baidar to that ifland, which was feventy verfts diftant. They brought back with them twenty-two pood of iron, ten of old cordage fit for caulker's ufe, fome lead and copper, and feveral thoufand beads,

Copper Ifland has its name from the native copper found on the coaft, particularly at the Weftern point on its South fide. Of this native copper Malevinfkoy brought with him two large pieces weighing together twelve pounds, which were picked up between a rock and the fea on a ftrand of about twelve yards in breadth. Amongft other floating bodies which the fea drives upon the fhores of this ifland, the true right camphor wood, and another fort of wood very white, foft, and fweet-fcented, are occafionally found.

Every preparation for continuing the voyage being Sails to the made, they failed from Copper Ifland the 26th of July, Fox Iflands. 1763, and fteered for the iflands Umnak and Aguna-

lafhka,

lafhka, where Glottoff had formerly obferved great numbers of black foxes.   On account of ftorms and contrary
winds, they were thirty days before they fetched Umnak.

Arrives at
Kadyak.
Here they arrived the 24th of Auguft, and without drop-
ping anchor or lofing any time, they refolved to fail further for the difcovery of new iflands: they paffed eight
contiguous to each other and feparated by ftraits, which,
according to their eftimation, were from twenty to an
hundred verfts broad.   Glottoff however did not land
till he reached the laft and moft Eaftward of thefe iflands,
called by the inhabitants Kadyak, from which the natives faid it was not far to the coaft of a wide extended
woody continent.   No land however was to be feen from
a little ifland called by the natives Aktunak, which is fituated about thirty verfts more to the Eaft than Kadyak.

September 8th, the veffel ran up a creek, lying South
Eaft of Aktunak, through which a rivulet empties itfelf
into the fea; this rivulet comes from a lake fix verfts
long, one broad, and about fifty fathoms deep.   During
the ebb of the tide the veffel was left aground; but the
return of the water fet her again afloat.   Near the fhore
were four large huts, fo crouded with people, that their
number could fcarcely be counted: however, foon after
Glottoff's arrival, all thefe inhabitants quitted their dwellings, and retired with precipitation.   The next day fome
iflanders in baidars approached the veffel, and accofted
                                                    the

the people on board : and as Ivan Glottoff, the Aleütian interpreter, did not well underftand the language of thefe iflanders, they foon afterwards returned with a boy whom they had formerly taken prifoner from Ifanak, one of the iflands which lie to the Weft of Kadyak. Him the Aleütian interpreter perfectly underftood : and by his means every neceffary explanation could be obtained from the iflanders.

In this manner they converfed with the favages, and endeavoured to perfuade them to become tributary ; they ufed alfo every argument in their power to prevail upon them to give up the boy for an interpreter ; but all their entreaties were for the prefent without effect. The favages rowed back to the cliff called Aktalin, which lies about three verfts to the South of Kadyak, where they feemed to have habitations.

On the 6th of September Kaplin was fent with thirteen men to the cliff, to treat peaceably with the iflanders. He found there ten huts, from which about an hundred of the natives came out. They behaved feemingly in a friendly manner, and anfwered the interpreter by the boy, that they had nobody proper for an hoftage ; but that they would deliver up the boy to the Ruffians agreeably to their defire. Kaplin received him very thankfully, and brought him on board, where he was properly taken care of : he afterwards accompanied Glottoff

to

to Kamtchatka, and was baptized by the name of Alex-
ander Popoff, being then about thirteen years of age.
For some days after this conference the islanders came off
in companies of five, ten, twenty, and thirty: they were
admitted on board in small numbers, and kindly received,
but with a proper degree of circumspection.

On the 8th of September the vessel was brought further up the creek without unloading her cargo ; and on
the 9th Glottoff with ten men proceeded to a village on
the shore about two hundred yards from the vessel,
where the natives had begun to reside : it consisted of
three summer-huts covered only with long grass ; they
were from eight to ten yards broad, twelve long, and
about four high. They saw there about an hundred men,
but neither women nor children.

Finding it impossible to persuade the savages to give
hostages, Glottoff resolved to let his people remain together, and to keep a strong guard.

The islanders visited them still in small bodies; it was
however more and more visible that their intentions were
The Natives hostile.   At last on the 1st of October, by day-break, a
attack the
Ruffians, but great number having assembled together in the remote
are defeated. parts of the island, came unexpectedly across the country. They approached very near without being discovered by the watch, and seeing nobody on deck but those

on

on duty, fhot fuddenly into the veffel with arrows. The watch found refuge behind the quarter boards, and gave the alarm without firing. Glottoff immediately ordered a volley to be fired over their heads with fmall arms; upon which they immediately retreated with great expedition. As foon as it was day there was no enemy to be feen: but they difcovered a number of ladders, feveral bundles of hay in which the favages had put fulphur, likewife a quantity of birch-tree bark, which had been left behind in their precipitate flight.

They now found it very neceffary to be on their guard againft the attempts of thefe perfidious incendiaries. Their fufpicions were ftill further increafed by the fubfequent conduct of the natives: for though the latter came to the veffel in fmall bodies, yet it was obferved that they examined every thing, and more particularly the watch, with the ftricteft attention; and they always returned without paying any regard to the friendly propofitions of the Ruffians.

On the 4th of October about two hundred iflanders made their appearance, carrying wooden fhields before them, and preparing with bows and arrows for an attack. Glottoff endeavoured at firft by perfuafion to prevail upon them to defift; but obferving that they ftill continued advancing, he refolved to venture a fally. This in-

4. trepidity

trepidity difconcerted the iflanders, and they immediately retreated without making the leaft refiftance.

The 26th of October they ventured a third attack, and advanced towards the veffel for that purpofe by day-break : the watch however gave the alarm in due time, and the whole crew were immediately under arms. The approach of day-light difcovered to their view different parties of the enemy advancing under the protection of wooden fcreens. Of thefe moving breaft-works they counted feven ; and behind each from thirty to forty men armed with bone lances. Befides thefe a croud of armed men advanced feparately to the attack, fome of them bearing whale jaw-bones, and others wooden fhields. Diffuafion proving ineffectual, and the arrows beginning to fall even aboard the fhip, Glottoff gave orders to fire.

The Natives are finally repulfed by the Ruffians. The fhot from the fmall arms however not being of force enough to pierce the fcreens, the iflanders advanced under their protection with fteadinefs and intrepidity. Glottoff neverthelefs determined to rifk a fally of his whole crew armed with mufkets and lances. The iflanders inftantly threw down their fcreens, and fled with precipitation until they gained their boats, into which they threw themfelves and rowed off. They had about feventeen large baidars and a number of fmall canoes. The fkreens which they left behind were made of three rows of ftakes placed per-pendicularly, and bound together with fea-weed and ofiers; they were twelve feet broad, and above half a yard thick.

The

The iflanders now appearing to be fufficiently intimi- The Ruffians winter at Kadyak.
dated, the Ruffians began to build a winter hut of floated
wood, and waited in a body the appearance of fpring
without further annoyance. Although they faw none of
the inhabitants before the 25th of December, yet Glottoff
kept his people together; fending out occafionally fmall
hunting and fifhing parties to the lake, which lay about
five verfts from the creek. During the whole winter
they caught in the lake feveral different fpecies of trout
and falmon, foles, and herrings of a fpan and a half
long, and even turbot and cod-fifh, which came up with
the flood into the lake.

At laft, on the 25th of December, two iflanders came
to the fhip, and converfed at a diftance by means of
interpreters. Although propofals of peace and trade
were held out to them in the moft friendly manner,
yet they went off without feeming to put much confidence in thefe offers: nor did any of them appear
again before the 4th of April, 1764. Want of fufficient exercife in the mean time brought on a violent
fcurvy among the crew, by which diforder nine perfons
were carried off.

On the 4th of April four of the natives made their appearance, and feemed to pay more attention to the propofals: one of them at laft advanced, and offered to barter
two fox-fkins for beads. They did not fet the leaft value

Q

The Natives
are reconciled
to the Ruf-
fians.
lue upon other goods of various kinds, such as shirts,
linen, and nankeen, but demanded glafs beads of different
colours, for which they exchanged their fkins with
pleafure. This friendly traffic, together with Glottoff's
entreaties, operated fo powerfully, that, after holding a
confultation with their countrymen, they returned with
a folemn declaration, that their brethren would in future
commit no hoftilities againft the Ruffians. From that
time until their departure a daily intercourfe was carried
on with the iflanders, who brought all forts of fox and
fea-otter fkins, and received in exchange a ftipulated
number of beads. Some of them were even perfuaded
to pay a tribute of fkins, for which receipts were given.

Amongft other wares the Ruffians procured two fmall
carpets, worked or platted in a curious manner, and on
one fide fet clofe with beaver-wool like velvet : they
could not however learn whether thefe carpets were
wrought by the iflanders. The latter brought alfo for
fale well-dreffed fea-otter fkins, the hair of which was
fhorn quite fhort with fharp ftones, in fuch a manner,
that the remainder, which was of a yellowifh brown
colour, gliftened and appeared like velvet. Their caps
had furprifing and fometimes very ornamental decora-
tions : fome of them had on the forepart combs adorned
with manes like an helmet; others, feemingly peculiar
to the females, were made of inteftines ftitched together with rein-deer hair and finews in a moft elegant
                                                            tafte,

tafte, and ornamented on the crown with long ftreamers of hair died of a beautiful red. Of all thefe curiofities Glottoff carried famples to Kamtchatka*.

The natives differ confiderably in drefs and language from the inhabitants of the other Fox Iflands: and feveral fpecies of animals were obferved upon Kadyak, which are not to be found upon the other iflands, viz. ermines, martens, beavers, river-otters, wolves, wild boars, _{Animals of Kadyak.} and bears: the laft-mentioned animal was not indeed actually feen by the Ruffians, but the prints of its feet were traced. Some of the inhabitants had clothes made of the fkins of rein-deer and jevras; the latter of which is a fort of fmall marmofet. Both thefe fkins were probably procured from the continent of America†. Black, brown, and red foxes, were feen in great numbers; and the coaft abounds with fea-dogs, fea-bears, fea-lions, and fea-otters. The birds are cranes, geefe, ducks, gulls, ptarmigans, crows, and magpies; but no uncommon fpecies was any where difcovered. The vegetable pro-

---

* Thefe and feveral other ornaments of a fimilar kind are preferved in the cabinet of curiofities at the Academy of Sciences of St. Peterfburg: a cabinet which well merits the attention of the curious traveller; for it contains a large collection of the dreffes of the Eaftern nations. Amongft the reft one compartment is entirely filled with the dreffes, arms, and implements, brought from the New-difcovered iflands.

† Although this conjecture is probable, yet, when the reader recollects that the ifland Alakfu is faid to contain rein-deer, he will perceive that the inhabitants of Kadyak might have been fupplied with the fkins of that animal from thence. See p. 68.

Q 2 ductions

Production. ductions are bilberries, cranberries, wortleberries, and wild lily-roots. Kadyak likewife yields willows and alders, which circumftance affords the ftrongeft proof that it lies at no great diftance from the continent of America. The extent of Kadyak cannot be exactly afcertained, as the Ruffians, through apprehenfion of the natives, did not venture to explore the country.

Account of the Inhabitants. The inhabitants, like thofe of the Aleütian and nearer iflands, make holes in the under-lips and through the griftle of the nofe, in which they infert the bones of birds and animals worked into the form of teeth. Their clothes are made of the fkins of birds, foxes, fea-otters, young rein-deer, and marmofets; they few them together with finews. They wear alfo fur-ftockings of rein-deer fkins, but no breeches. Their arms are bows, arrows, and lances, whofe points, as well as their fmall hatchets, are of fharp flint: fome few make knives and lance points of rein-deer bones. Their wooden fhields are called kuyaky, which amongft the Greenlanders fignifies a fmall canoe. Their manners are altogether rude. They have not the leaft difpofition to give a courteous reception to ftrangers: nor does there appear amongft themfelves any kind of deference or fubmiffion from one to another.

Their canoes are fome of them fo fmall as to contain only one or two perfons; others are large baidars fimilar

to

to the women's boats of the Greenlanders. Their food
confifts chiefly of raw and dried fifh, partly caught at
fea with bone hooks, and partly in rivulets, in bag-nets
made of finews platted together. They call themfelves Kanagift, a name that has no fmall refemblance to
Karalit; by which appellation, the Greenlanders and Efquimaux on the coaft of Labradore diftinguifh themfelves;
the difference between thefe two denominations is occafioned perhaps by a change of pronunciation, or by a
miftake of the Ruffian failors, who may have given it
this variation. Their numbers feem very confiderable
on that part of the ifland, where they had their fixed
habitations.

The ifland Kadyak * makes, with Aghunalafhka, Umnak, and the fmall iflands lying between them, a continued
Archipelago, extending N. E. and E. N. E. towards America: it lies by the fhip's reckoning in 230 degrees of
longitude; fo that it cannot be far diftant from that
part of the American coaft which Beering formerly
touched at.

The large ifland Alakfu, lying Northward from Kadyak where Pufhkaref† wintered, muft be ftill nearer the

* Kadyak is not laid down upon any chart of the New difcovered
iflands: for we have no chart of Glottoff's voyage; and no other Ruffian navigator touched at that ifland.

† See Chap. VI.

4

continent:

continent : and the account given by its inhabitants of a great promontory, called Atachtak, ſtretching from the continent N.E. of Alakſu, is not at all improbable.

Although the conduct of the iſlanders appeared more friendly, yet on account of their numbers Glottoff reſolved not to paſs another winter upon Kadyak, and accordingly prepared for his departure. He wanted hoops for repairing his water-caſks; and being told by the natives that there were trees on the iſland at no great diſtance from the bay, he diſpatched, on the 25th of April, Lukas Ftoruſkin with eleven men for the purpoſe of felling wood. Ftoruſkin returned the ſame day with the following intelligence: that after rowing along the South coaſt of the iſland forty or fifty verſts from the haven, he obſerved, about half a verſt from the ſhore, a conſiderable number of alders, ſimilar to thoſe found in Kamtchatka, growing in vallies between the rocks. The largeſt trunks were from two to four verſhocks in diameter. Of this wood he felled as much as he had occaſion for; and returned without having met with either iſlander or habitation.

Departure
from Kadyak,
May, 1764.
They brought the veſſel down the creek in May; and, after taking in all the peltry and ſtores, left Kadyak on the 24th. Contrary winds retarded their voyage, and drove them near the iſland Alakſu, which they paſſed; their water being nearly exhauſted, they afterwards

landed

landed upon another ifland, called Saktunak, in order to procure a frefh ftock.   At laft on the 3d of July, they arrived again at Umnak, and anchored in a bay which Glottoff had formerly vifited. He immediately went afhore in a baidar, and foon found out his former hut, which was in ruins : near it he obferved another Ruffian dwelling, that had been built in his abfence, in which lay a murdered Ruffian, but whofe face none of them knew.   Glottoff, refolving to procure further information, went acrofs the ifland the 5th of July, accompanied by fixteen of his crew.   He difcovered the remains of a burnt veffel, fome prayer books, images, &c.; all the iron work and cordage were carried off.   Near the fpot he found likewife a bathing room filled with murdered Ruffians in their clothes.   From fome marks, he concluded that this was the veffel fitted out by Protaffoff; nor was he miftaken in his conjectures.

Alarmed at the fate of his countrymen, Glottoff returned to the fhip, and held a confultation upon the meafures neceffary to be taken; and it was unanimoufly refolved that they fhould endeavour to procure more intelligence concerning the veffel.   In the mean time feven iflanders came rowing off in baidars, and pretended that they wanted to trade.   They fhewed fea-otter fkins at a diftance, but would not venture on board;

and

and by the interpreter defired Glottoff and two of his people to come on fhore and barter. Glottoff however, having fufficient caufe to diftruft the favages, refufed to comply with their demands: upon this they immediately landed, and fhot from the fhore with fire-arms, but without doing any execution. They were even bold enough to get into their canoes a fecond time, and to row near the veffel. In order if poffible to procure intelligence from them, every method of perfuading them to peace was tried by means of the interpreters; and at laft one of them approached the fhip and demanded victuals, which being thrown to him, he came on board. He then related the fate of the above-mentioned veffel, of which the iflanders had made themfelves mafters; and gave likewife fome intelligence concerning the remaining fmall body of fugitives under the command of Korovin. He alfo confeffed, that their defign was to entice Glottoff on fhore, and then to kill him; for which purpofe more than thirty iflanders were pofted in ambufh behind the neareft rocks. After cutting off the leader, they imagined it would be an eafy matter to feize upon the fhip. Upon this information Glottoff detained the iflander on board, and landing with a ftrong party attacked the favages; the latter fhot with arrows, as well as from the mufkets which they had feized, but without effect, and were foon forced to retire to their canoes.

July

July the 14th a violent ftorm arofe, in which Glot-toff's veffel parted her cable, and was forced on fhore without any other lofs than that of an anchor. The crew likewife, through want of frefh proviſions, began to grow fo fickly, that they were almoft in a defencelefs ſtate. Glottoff however, with ten men, fet out the 28th of July for that part of the ifland, where according to information they expected to find Korovin. They dif-covered only parts of the wreck, but none of the crew, fo that they now gave them up for loft. But on the 2d of Auguft, as Glottoff was on his way back, five iflanders approached him in canoes, and afked why the baidar had been out; to which a falfe anfwer being given, they told him, that on the other fide of the ifland he would find Korovin with his people, who were building an hut on the fide of the rivulet. Upon re-ceiving this intelligence, Glottoff and his companions went over land to the place pointed out by the iflanders, and found every thing agreeable to their information: in this Korovin had not the leaft fhare, not having been made privy to the tranfaction. The circumftances of his joining, and afterwards feparating from Glottoff, have already been mentioned *.

* See the preceding chapter.

Glottoff

Glottoff win-
tes upon
Umnak.
Glottoff now refolved to winter upon Umnak, and accordingly laid up his veffel for that purpofe.   On the 2d
of September Korovin, as is before related, was at his
own defire fent out with a hunting party in two baidars.
On his return, in May 1765, they had the firft intelligence
of the arrival of Solovioff's veffel, which lay before
Unalafhka, and of which an account fhall be given *.
None of the iflanders appeared near the harbour during
the winter, and there were none probably at that time
upon Umnak ; for Glottoff made excurfions on all fides,
and went once round the ifland.   He likewife looked
into the habitations of the iflanders, and found them
empty : he examined the country, and caufed a ftrict fearch
to be made after the remains of the plundered veffel.

According to his account Umnak is about 300 verfts in
circumference.   It contains feveral fmall rivulets, which
take their rife from lakes, and fall into the fea after a
very fhort courfe.   No trees were obferved upon the
ifland, and the vegetables were the fame as thofe of
Kamtchatka.

Chap. XI.

The

The following fummer fmall parties of the inhabitants were feen ; but they immediately fled upon the approach of the Ruffians. Some of them however were at laft perfuaded to a friendly intercourfe and to pay a tribute : by thefe means they got back part of the arms, anchors, and iron work, of the plundered veffel. They continued to barter with the natives during the fummer of 1765, exchanging beads for the fkins of foxes and fea otters.

The following winter hunting parties were fent out Departure from Umnak. in Umnak as well as to Unalafhka ; and in July 1766 Glottoff, without meeting with any more difficulties, began his voyage homewards. We fhall here conclude with giving a copy of the journal kept on board Glottoff's veffel, the Andrean and Natalia ; from which infe- rences with regard to the fituation of the iflands may be drawn.

Journal

Journal of Glottoff, on board the Andrean and Natalia.

1762.

Oct. 1. Sailed from Kamtchatka Bay.

2. Wind Southerly, steered between E. and S. E. three hours.

3. Wind S. E. worked at N. E. course, 16 hours.

4. From midnight sailed East with a fair wind, 18 hours.

5. At six o'clock A. M. discovered Beering's Island distant about 18 versts.

6. At 1 o'clock came to anchor on the South East point of Copper Island.

7. At 8 A. M. sailed to the South side of the Island, anchored there at 10 o'clock.

1763.

July 26. Sailed from Copper Island at 5 P. M.

27. Sailed with a fair S. S. W. wind, 17 hours.

28. Made little way.

29. Drove—wind E. N. E.

30. Ditto.

31. Ditto.

Aug. 1. Ditto.

2. At 11 A. M. wind N. E. steered E.

3. Wind W. S. W. sailed 8 knots an hour, 250 versts.

4. Wind South—sailed 150 versts.

5. Wind ditto—sailed 126 versts.

6. Wind

6. Wind ditto, 3 knots, 45 verſts.

7. Calm.

8. During the night gentle S. E. wind, ſteered N. E. at $2\frac{1}{2}$ knots.

9. Forenoon calm.　At 2 o'clock P. M. gentle N. E. wind, ſteered between E. N. E. and S. E. at the rate of three knots.

10. Morning, wind E. N. E. afterwards S. S. W. with which ſteered N. E.

11. At 5 o'clock the wind S. S. E. ſteered E. N. E. at the rate of three knots.

12. Wind S. ſteered E. at $2\frac{1}{2}$ knots, ſailed 50 verſts.

13. Wind S. S. E. ſteered E. at $4\frac{1}{2}$ knots, ſailed 90 verſts.

14. Wind W. N. W. at 2 knots, ſailed 30 verſts.

15. The wind freſhened, at 4 knots, ſailed 60 verſts.

16. Wind N. N. E. ſteered E. S. E. at 3 knots, ſailed 30 verſts.

17. Wind E. S. E. and S. E. light breezes and changeable.

18. Wind S. E. ſteered N. E. at $3\frac{1}{2}$ knots, ſailed in 12 hours 22 verſts.

19. Wind S. and light breezes, ſteered E. at 3 knots, ſailed in 8 hours 11 verſts.

20. Before day-break calm; three hours after ſun-riſe a breeze ſprung up at S. E. ſteered E. N. E. at 3 knots, and ſailed 20 verſts.

22. Calm

22. Calm.

23. Wind S. S. E. during the night, the ſhip ſailed at the rate of two knots; the wind afterwards came round to the S. S. W. and the ſhip ſailed at 5 to 6 knots theſe 24 hours 150 verſts.

24. Saw land at day-break, at 3 knots ſailed 45 verſts.

25. Wind W. S. W. ſailed along the coaſt theſe 24 hours 50 verſts.

26. Wind N. W. ſteered N. E. at $5\frac{1}{2}$ knots, 100 verſts.

27. Wind E. N. E. the ſhip drove towards land, on which diſcovered a high mountain.

28. Wind N. E. and ſtormy, the ſhip drove.

29. Wind N. W. ſteered E. N. E. at the rate of 3 knots.

30. Wind S. S. E. at 6 knots, ſteering again towards land.

31. A violent ſtorm, wind weſt.

Sept. 1. Wind Weſt, ſteered N. E. at the rate of 3 knots towards land.

2. Wind S. W. ſteered N. E. towards land at 5 knots.

3. Wind S. W. drove N. N. E. along the coaſt.

4. Wind W. N. W. ſteered N. E. at 4 knots, ſailed 100 verſts.

5. Wind N. W. ſteered E. N. E. at 3 knots, and towards evening came to anchor off the Iſland Kadyak.

1764.

1764.

May 24. Sailed from Kadyak.

25. Wind N. W. and made but little way W. S. W.

26. Wind W. ſhip drove towards S. E.

27. Wind W. S. W. ſhip drove E. S. E.   The ſame day the wind came round to the S. when ſteered again towards Kadyak.

28. Wind E. S. E. fell in with the iſland Alaſka or Alakſu.

29. Wind S. W. ſteered N. W.

30. Wind W. N. W. the ſhip drove under the foreſail.

31. Wind W. drove to the Southward.

June 1. Wind W. S. W. landed on the Iſland Saktunak, for a ſupply of water.

2. Wind S. E. ſteered S. W. along the iſland at 3 knots.

3. Wind N. E. ſteered W. S. W. at the rate of 3 to 4 knots, ſailing in theſe 24 hours 100 verſts.

4. Calm.

5. At 8 o'clock A. M. a ſmall breeze S. E.

6. Wind E. afterwards calm. Towards evening the Wind S. E. ſteered S. W. at 3 knots, and unexpectedly diſcovered land ahead, which kept clear of with difficulty.

From the 7th to the 10th at anchor off a ſmall cliff.

10. A hard gale at S. the ſhip drove foul of the anchor, ſtood out to ſea ſteering E.

11. An-

11. Anchored again at a small distance from land.

13. Wind S. S. W. stood out to sea and steered E. S. E.

14. Wind W. S. W. steered S. S. E. at the rate of 1 knot.

15. Calm.

16. Wind S. steered W. at 1 knot, the ship drove a little to the Northward.

17. Wind S. S. E. steered W. S. W. at 3 knots.

18. Calm.

19. Ditto.

20. Wind N. E. steered S. W. and sailed this day about 87 versts.

21. The wind blowing right ahead, came to anchor off an unknown island, where continued till the

25. When stood out to sea early in the morning.

26. Wind W. N. W. afterwards W. steered S. E.

27. Calm, in the night a small but favourable breeze.

28. Wind N. W. continued the course, at the rate of 2 to 3 knots *.

29. Wind N. E. steered W. at 3 to 4 knots, and saw land.

30. Wind N. E. steered S. W. at the rate of 7 knots.

* Lief man bey nordweſt wind auf den curs zu 2 bis 3 knoten.

July

July 1. With the same wind and course, at the rate of 5 knots, sailed 200 versts.

2. Fell in with the island Umnak, and came to an anchor under a small island until next day; when brought the ship into the harbour, and laid her up.

1766.

June 13. Brought the ship into the harbour, and continued at anchor there until the 3d of July.

July 3. Got under way.

4. Wind E.

5. A South West wind drove the ship about 50 versts N. E.

6. Wind S. failed about 60 versts W.

7. Wind W. S. W. the ship drove to the Northward.

8. Wind N. W. steered S. at the rate of one knot.

9. Wind N. W. steered the whole day W. S. W.

10. Wind S. S. W. failed about 40 versts W. N. W.

11. Wind S. W. continued the same course, failing only 5 versts.

12. Continued the same course, and failed 55 versts.

13. For the most part calm.

14. Wind W. N. W. and stormy, the ship drove under the foresail.

15. Wind S. failed on the proper course 100 versts.

16. Wind E. S. E. failed W. S. W. at the rate of 6 knots, 100 versts.

17. Wind N. N. W. failed S. W. at the rate of 2 knots, 30 versts.

S   18 Wind

18. Wind S. fteered W. at the rate of 5 knots, and failed 130 verfts.

19. Wind S. W. the fhip drove under the forefail.

20. Wind E. N. E. fteered W. N. W. at the rate of 3 knots.

21. Wind E. N. E. at the rate of 4 to 5 knots, failed 200 verfts.

22. Wind N. E. at $4\frac{1}{2}$ knots, 150 verfts.

23. Wind E. N. E. fteered W. at 3 knots, 100 verfts.

24. Wind E. fteered W. at the rate of 3 knots, 50 verfts.

25. Wind N. E. fteered W. at 5 knots 100 verfts.

26. The wind continued N. E. and frefhened, fteered W. at the rate of 7 knots, 200 verfts.

27. A fmall breeze N. N. W. with which however failed 150 verfts.

28. Wind being W. S. W. drove 24 hours under bare-poles.

29. Wind South, fteered W. at the rate of 2 knots, 48 verfts—this day faw land.

30. Wind S. S. E. failed, at the rate of 4 knots, 96 verfts, and approached the land, which found to be the ifland Karaga—From the 1ft to the 13th of Auguft, continued our voyage towards the mouth of Kamtchatka river, fometimes plying to windward, fometimes driving, and at laft arrived happily with a rich cargo.

C H A P. XI.

Solovioff's voyage—he reaches Unalafhka, and paffes two winters upon that ifland—relation of what paffed there —fruitlefs attempts of the natives to deftroy the crew— Return of Solovioff to Kamtchatka—journal of his voyage in returning—defcription of the iflands Umnak and Unalafhka—productions—inhabitants—their manners—cuftoms, &c. &c.

IN the year 1764, Jacob Ulednikoff, merchant of Irkutfk, and company, fitted out a fhip called the Holy Apoftles Peter and Paul, under the command of Ivan Solovioff: fhe failed from the mouth of Kamtchatka river the 25th of Auguft. The crew confifted of fifty-five men, amongft whom were fome of the owners, and thirteen Kamtchadals.

Voyage of Solovioff in the St. Peter and Paul, 1764.

They fteered at firft S. E. with the wind at N. W. but on its coming foutherly they afterwards fhaped their courfe E. N. E. The 27th one of the Ruffian failors died off Kamtchatka point; the 31ft they made Beering's Ifland, which they paffed leaving it on their left. The 1ft and 2d of September they were becalmed, and afterwards the wind fpringing up at W. S. W. they continued

their

their former courſe ; until the 5th they ſailed on with the wind at South ; but on the 5th and 6th, from changeable breezes and dead calms, made no progreſs ; from the 7th to the 13th, they ſailed E. S. E. with Southerly and Weſterly winds ; and from that time to the 15th Eaſt, with the wind at Weſt.

September 16, they made the iſland Umnak, where Solovioff had formerly been in Nikiphoroff's veſſel. As they ſailed along the Northern coaſt, three iſlanders came to them in baidars ; but, the crew having no interpreter, they would not come on board. As they found no good bay on that ſhore, they proceeded through a ſtrait of about a verſt broad, which ſeparates Umnak from Una-

Arrival at
Unalaſhka.laſhka. They lay-to during the night ; and early on the 17th dropped anchor at the diſtance of about two hundred yards from the ſhore, in a bay on the North ſide of the laſt mentioned iſland.

From thence the captain diſpatched Gregory Korenoff at the head of twenty men in a baidar, with orders to land, reconnoitre the country, find out the neareſt habitations, and report the diſpoſition of the people. Korenoff returned the ſame day, with an account that he had diſcovered one of the dwelling-caves of the ſavages, but abandoned and demoliſhed, in which he had found traces of Ruſſians, viz. a written legend, and a broken muſket-ſtock. In conſequence of this intelligence, they brought

the

the ſhip near the coaſt, and endeavoured to get into the mouth of a river called by the natives Tſikanok, and by the Ruſſians Oſernia, but were prevented by ſhallow water. They landed however their tackle and lading. No natives made their appearance until the 22d, when two of them came of their own accord, and welcomed the Ruſſians on their arrival. They told their names, and were recognized by Solovioff; he had known them on a former expedition, when Agiak, one of the two, had ſerved as an interpreter; the other, whoſe name was Kaſhmak, had voluntarily continued ſome time with the crew on the ſame occaſion.

Theſe two perſons recounted the particular circumſtances which attended the loſs of Kulkoff's, Protaſſoff's, and Trapefnikoff's veſſels; from the laſt of which Kaſhmak had, with great hazard of his life, eſcaped by flight. Agiak had ſerved as interpreter to Protaſſoff's company, and related that the iſlanders, after murdering the hunting detachments of the Ruſſians, came to the harbour, and entered the ſhip under the moſt friendly appearances. Finding the crew in perfect ſecurity, they ſuddenly attacked and ſlew them, together with their commander. He added, that he had hid himſelf under a bench until the murderers were gone: that ſince that time, he, as well as Kaſhmak, had lived as fugitives; and in the courſe of their wanderings had learned the following intelligence from the girls who were gathering berries in

the

the fields. The Toigons of Umnak, Akutan, and Tofhko, with their relations of Unalafhka, had formed a confederacy. They agreed not to difturb any Ruffians on their firft landing, but to let them go out on different hunting excurfions; being thus feparated and weakened, the intention of the Toigons was to attack and cut them off at the fame time, fo that no one party fhould have affiftance from any of the others. They acquainted him alfo with Glottoff's arrival at Umnak.

Thefe unfavourable reports filled Solovioff with anxiety; he accordingly doubled his watch, and ufed every precaution in his power againft attacks from the favages. But wanting wood to repair his veffel, and wifhing for more particular information concerning the fituation of the ifland, he difpatched the 29th a party of thirty men, with the above-mentioned interpreter, to its weftern extremity. In three or four hours they rowed to Ankonom, a point of land, where they faw a village, confifting of two large caves, and over againft it a little ifland at no great diftance. The moment the inhabitants faw them approaching, they got into their baidars, and put out to fea, leaving their dwellings empty. The Ruffians found therein feveral fkeletons, which, in the interpreter's opinion, were the remains of ten murdered failors of Trapefnikoff's company. With much perfuafion the interpreter prevailed on the iflanders to return to the place which they had juft quitted: they kept however at a

wary

wary diftance, and were armed for whatever might occur.

Solovioff attempting to cut off their retreat, in order to fecure if poffible fome hoftages, they took the alarm, and began themfelves the attack. Upon this the Ruffians fired upon and purfued them ; four were killed, and feven taken prifoners, among whom was the Toigon of the little ifland Sedak. Thefe prifoners, being bound and examined, confeffed that a number of Korovin's crew had been murdered in this place ; and the Toigon fent people to bring in a number of mufkets, fome kettles and tackle, which the natives had taken upon that occa-fion. They alfo brought intelligence that Korovin, with a party in two baidars, had taken fhelter at a place called Inalga. Upon this information, letters were immediately fent to Korovin ; upon the receipt of which he joined them the 2d of October.

At the time of Korovin's arrival, the favages made another attack on Solovioff's watch with knives ; which obliged the latter to fire, and fix of the affailants were left dead on the fpot. The captive Toigon excufed this attempt of his people by afcribing it to their fears, left Korovin out of revenge fhould put all the prifoners to death ; on which account this effort was made to refcue them. Solovioff, for the greater fecurity, fent the pri-foners by land to the haven, while Korovin and his

party

party went to the fame place by fea. The Toigon however was treated kindly, and even permitted to return
home on condition of leaving his fon as an hoftage. In
confequence of this kind behaviour the inhabitants of
three other villages, Agulak, Kutchlok, and Makufki, prefented hoftages of their own accord.

Solovioff lays up the Veffel, and winters upon Una-lafhka.

From the remaining timber of the old dwelling the
Ruffians built a new hut ; and on the fourteenth they
laid up the veffel. Koronoff was then fent upon a reconnoitring party to the Southern fide of the ifland, which
in that part was not more than five or fix verfts broad :
he proceeded on with his companions, fometimes rowing
in canoes, fometimes travelling by land and dragging
them after. He returned the twentieth, and reported
that he had found upon the coaft on the further fide of
the ifland an empty habitation. That he rowed from
thence Eaftward along the fhore, and behind the firft point
of land came to an ifland in the next bay; there he found
about forty iflanders of both fexes lodged under their
baidars, who by his friendly behaviour had been induced
to give him three hoftages. Thefe people afterwards
fettled in the above-mentioned empty hut, and came frequently to the harbour.

On the 28th of October, Solovioff himfelf went alfo
upon a reconnoitring party along the North coaft, towards
the North-Eaft end of the ifland. He rowed from the

firft

firſt promontory acroſs a bay ; and found on the oppoſite
point of land a dwelling place called Agulok, which lies
about four hours row from the harbour. He found there
thirteen men and about forty women and children, who
delivered up ſeveral gun-barrels and ſhip-ſtores, and likewiſe informed him of two of Korovin's crew who had
been murdered.

November 5, they proceeded farther; and after five or
ſix hours rowing, they ſaw on a point of land another
dwelling called Ikutchlok, beyond which the interpreter
ſhewed them the haven, where Korovin's ſhip had been
at anchor. This was called Makuſhinſky Bay ; and on
an iſland within it they found two Toigons, called Itchadak and Kagumaga, with about an hundred and eighty
people of both ſexes employed in hunting ſea-bears.
Theſe natives were not in the leaſt hoſtile, and Solovioff
endeavoured to eſtabliſh and confirm a friendly intercourſe
between them and his people. He remained with them
until the 10th, when the Toigons invited him to their
winter quarters, which lay about five hours ſail farther
Eaſt: there he found two dwelling caves, each of forty
yards ſquare, near a rivulet abounding with fiſh which
fell from a lake into a little bay. In the neighbourhood
of this village is a hot ſpring below the ſea mark, which
is only to be ſeen at ebb tide. From hence he departed
T the

the 25th, but was forced back by ftorms, and detained there until the 6th of December.

Kagumaga then accompanied him to another village called Totchikala; both the Toigon and the interpreter advifed him to be on his guard againft the natives, whom they reprefented as very favage, fworn enemies to the Ruffians, and the murderers of nine of Kulkoff's crew. Solovioff for thefe reafons paffed the night on the open coaft, and next morning fent the Toigon before to infpire the natives with more friendly fentiments. Some of them liftened to his reprefentations; but the greateft part fled upon Solovioff's approach, fo that he found the place confifting of four large dwelling caves almoft empty, in which he fecured himfelf with fuitable precaution. Here he found three hundred darts and ten bows with arrows, all which he deftroyed, only referving one bow and fe-venteen arrows as fpecimens of their arms. By the moft friendly arguments he urged the few natives who re-mained to lay afide their enmity, and to perfuade their leaders and relations to return to their habitations and live on terms of amity and friendfhip.

On the 10th about an hundred men and a ftill greater number of women returned. But the faireft fpeeches had no effect on thefe favages, who kept aloof and pre-pared for hoftilities, which they began on the 17th by an open attack. Nineteen of them were killed, amongft whom

Renewal of
Hoftilities.

whom was Inlogufak one of their leaders, and the moft inveterate fomenter of hoftilities againft the Ruffians. The other leader Aguladock being taken alive confeffed, that on receiving the firft news of Solovioff's arrival, they had refolved to attack the crew and burn the fhip. Notwithftanding this confeffion, no injury was offered to him : in confequence of this kind ufage, he was prevailed upon to give his fon as an hoftage, and to order his people to live on friendly terms with the Ruffians. During the month of January the natives delivered in three anchors, and a quantity of tackle, which had been faved from a veffel formerly wrecked on that coaft; and at the fame time they brought three boys and two young girls as hoftages and pledges of their future fidelity.

January 25, Solovioff fet out for the haven where his fhip lay : before his departure the Toigons of Makufhinfk paid of their own accord a double tribute.

February 1, Kagumaga of Makufhinfk, Agidalok of Totzikala, and Imaginak of Ugamitzi, Toigons of Unalafhka, with a great number of their relations, came to Solovioff; they acquainted him with the arrival of a Ruffian fhip at Unimak, the fixth ifland to the Eaft of Agunalafhka, adding that they knew none of the crew excepting a Kamtchadal named Kirilko, who had been there on a former occafion. They likewife informed him that the natives, after having cut off part of the

T 2

crew

crew who had been fent out in two baidars, had
found means to overpower the remainder and to deftroy
the veffel.   From the name of the Kamtchadal they concluded that this muft have been another veffel fitted out
by Nikiphor Trapefnikoff and company, of which no
farther intelligence was ever received.   Willing to procure farther intelligence, they endeavoured to perfuade
the Toigons to fend a party of their people to the above-
mentioned ifland; but the latter excufed themfelves, on
account of the great diftance and their dread of the
iflanders.

February 16, Solovioff fet out a fecond time for the
Weft end of the ifland, where they had formerly taken
prifoner, and afterwards fet at liberty, the Toigon of
Sedak.   From thence he proceeded to Ikolga, which
lies on the bay, and confifts of only one hut.   On the
26th he came to Takamitka, where there is likewife
only one hut on a point of land by the fide of a rivulet,
which falls from the mountains into the fea.   Here he
met with Korovin, in whofe company he cut the blubber
of a whale, which the waves had caft on fhore; after
this Korovin went acrofs the gulph to Umnak, and he
proceeded to Ikaltfhinfk, where on the 9th one of his
party was carried off by ficknefs.

March 15, he returned to the haven, having met with
no oppofition from the iflanders during this excurfion.

I   On

On his return he found one of the crew dead, and a dreadful fcurvy raging amongft the reft; of that diftemper five Ruffians died in March, eight and a Kamtchadal in April, and fix more in May. About this time the iflanders were obferved to pay frequent vifits to the hoftages; and upon enquiring privately into the reafon, fome of the latter difcovered, that the inhabitants of Makufhinfk had formed the defign of cutting off the crew, and of making themfelves mafters of the veffel. Solovioff had now great reafons to be apprehenfive, for the crew were afflicted with the fcurvy to fuch a violent degree, that out of the whole number only twelve perfons were capable of defending themfelves. Thefe circumftances did not efcape the obfervation of the natives; and they were accordingly infpired with frefh courage to renew their hoftilities.

On the 27th of May the Ruffians perceived the Toigon of Itchadak, who had formerly paid a voluntary tribute, near the fhore: he was accompanied by feveral iflanders in three baidars. Solovioff calling to him by the interpreter, he came on fhore, but kept at a diftance defiring a conference with fome of his relations. Solovioff gave orders to feize him; and they were lucky enough to take him prifoner, together with two of his companions. He immediately confeffed, that he had come with a view of enquiring of the hoftages how many Ruffians were ftill remaining: having procured the neceffary intelligence,

his

his intention was to furprife the watch at a convenient feafon, and afterwards to fet fire to the fhip. As they faw feveral iflanders row paft the harbour at the fame time, and the Toigon likewife informed them that they were affembling to execute the abovementioned defign; Solovioff refolved to be much upon his guard. They feparated, however, without attempting any hoftilities.

June 5, Glottoff arrived at the harbour on a vifit, and returned on the 8th to his fhip. The captive Toigon was now fet at liberty, after being ferioufly exhorted to defift from hoftilities. In the courfe of this month two more of the crew died; fo that the arrival of Korovin, who joined them about this time, with two of his own and two of Kulkoff's crew, was of courfe a very agreeable circumftance. The fick likewife began to recover by degrees.

July 22, Solovioff, with a party of his people, in two baidars, made another excurfion Northwards; he paffed by the places formerly mentioned as far as Igonok, which lies ten verfts beyond Totzikala. Igonok confifts of one dwelling cave on the fide of a rivulet, which falls from the mountains, and empties itfelf into the fea. The inhabitants amounted to about thirty men, who dwelt there with their wives and children. From thence Solovioff proceeded along the fhore into a bay; five verfts

further

further he found another rivulet, which has its fource among the hills, and flows through a plain.

Upon the fhore of the fame bay, oppofite to the mouth of this rivulet, lay two villages, one of which only was inhabited; it was called Ukunadok, and confifted of fix dwelling caves. About thirty-five of the inhabitants were at that time employed in catching falmon in the rivulet. Kulkoff's fhip had lain at anchor about two miles from thence; but there were no remains of her to be found. After coming out of the bay he went forwards to the fummer village Umgaina, diftant about feven or eight leagues, and fituated on the fide of a rivulet, which takes its rife in a lake abounding with falmon. Here he found the Toïgon Amaganak, with about ten of the natives, employed in fifhing. Fifteen verfts farther along the fhore they found another fummer village called Kalaktak, where there was likewife another rivulet, which came from the hills. The inhabitants were fixty men and an hundred and feventy women and children: they gave Solovioff a very friendly reception; and delivered up two hoftages, who were brought from the neighbouring ifland Akutan; with thefe he fet out on his return, and on the 6th of Auguft joined his crew.

On

On the 11th he went over to the ifland Umnak, accompanied by Korovin, to bring off fome fhips ftores
left there by the latter; and returned to the haven on
the 27th. On the 31ft Shaffyrin died, the fame perfon
whofe adventures have been already related*.

Sept. 19, Korenoff was fent northwards upon an
hunting party; he returned the 30th of January, 1766.
Although the Ruffians who remained at the haven met
with no moleftation from the natives during his abfence;
yet he and his companions were repeatedly attacked.
Having diftributed to the inhabitants of the feveral villages through which he paffed nets for the purpofe of
catching fea-otters, he went to the Eaft part of the ifland
as far as Kalaktak, with an intention of hunting. Upon
his arrival at that place, on the 31ft of October, the inhabitants fled with precipitation; and as all his efforts to
conciliate their affections were ineffectual, he found it requifite to be upon his guard. Nor was this precaution un-
neceffary; for on the following day they returned in a
confiderable body, armed with lances, made with the
iron of the plundered veffels. Korenoff, however, and
his companions, who were prepared to receive them,
killed twenty-fix, and took feveral prifoners; upon
which the others became more tractable.

* Chap. VIII.

Nov.

Nov. 19, Korenoff, upon his return to the haven, came to Makufhinfk, where he was kindly received by a Toigon named Kulumaga; but with regard to Itchadak, it was plain that his defigns were ftill hoftile. Inftead of giving an account of the nets which had been left with him, he withdrew privately: and on the 19th of January, accompanied by a numerous body of iflanders, made an attempt to furprife the Ruffians. Victory, however, again declared for Korenoff; and fifteen of the affailants, amongft whom was Itchadak himfelf, remained dead upon the fpot. Kulumaga affured them, in the ftrongeft manner, that the defign had been carried on without his knowledge; and protefted, that he had often prevented his friend from committing hoftilities againft the Ruffians.

Korenoff returned to the haven on the 30th of January; and on the 4th of February he went upon another hunting expedition toward the Weftern point of the ifland. During this excurfion he met with a party fent out by Glottoff, at a place called Takamitka; he then rowed over to Umnak, where he collected a fmall tribute, and returned on the 3d of March. During his abfence Kyginik, Kulumaga's fon, paid a vifit to the Ruffians, and requefted that he might be baptized, and be permitted to go aboard the veffel; his demand was immediately complied with.

U

May

May 13th, Korovin went, with fourteen men, to
Umnak, to bring off an anchor, which was buried in the
sand.   On his return preparations were made for their
departure.   Before the arrival of Korovin the hunters
had killed 150 black and brown foxes, and the same
number of old and young sea-otters; since his arrival
they had caught 350 black foxes, the same number of
common foxes, and 150 sea-otters of different sizes.

This cargo being put on board, the interpreter Kash-
mak set at liberty, with a certificate of, and presents for
his fidelity, and the hostages delivered up to the Toigons
and their relations, who had assembled at the haven,
Solovioff put to sea on the 1st of June, with an Easterly
wind.   Before his departure he received a letter from
Glottoff, informing him that he was likewise preparing
for his return.

Journal of the
Voyage home-
wards.

June 2. The wind being contrary, they got but a small
            way from land.

        5. Steered again towards the shore, came to an
            anchor, and sent a boat for a supply of water,
            which returned without having seen any
            body.

        6. Weighed and steered W. with a S. E. wind.

        7. Favourable wind at N.E. and in the afternoon
            at N.

                                        8. Wind

8. Wind at N. W. and ftormy, the ſhip drove under the forefail.

9 & 10. Sailed Northwards, with a Wefterly wind.

11. Calm till noon; afterwards breeze ſprung up at S. with which they fteered W. till next day at noon; when the wind coming round to the Weft, they changed their courfe, and fteered N. W.

12. Calm during the night.

13. A ſmall breeze of Northerly wind, with which they fteered W. in the afternoon it fell calm, and continued fo till the

16. At noon, when a breeze ſpringing up at Eaft, they fteered W. on which courfe they continued during the

18. with a S. S. E. wind.

From the 19 to the 22. The wind was changeable from the S. W. to N. W. with which they ftill made a ſhift to get to the Weftward.

23. The wind E. they fteered betwixt N. & W. which courfe they continued the

24th, 25th, 26th, with a Northerly wind.

27. A. M. the wind changed to S. W.

28, 29, 30. Wind at Weft.

July 1. The wind changed to E. with which they fteered between W. and S. W. with little variations, till the 3d.

U 2   4. They

4. They reached Kamtchatkoi Nofs, and on the

5th. Brought the ſhip, in good condition, into Kamtchatka river.

Solovioff's De-
ſcription of the
Fox Iſlands.
Solovioff's deſcription of theſe iſlands and the inhabitants, being more circumſtantial than the accounts
given by former navigators, deſerves to be inſerted at
full length.   According to his eſtimation, the iſland
Unalaſhka lies between 1500 and 2000 verſts due Eaſt
from the mouth of the Kamtchatka river : the other
iſlands to the Eaſtward ſtretch towards N. E.   He reckons the length of Akutan at eighty verſts ; Umnak at
an hundred and fifty, and Unalaſhka at two hundred. No
large trees were ſeen upon any of the iſlands which he
touched at. They produce underwood, ſmall ſhrubs, and
plants, for the moſt part ſimilar to the common ſpecies
found in Kamtchatka.   The winter is much milder than
in the Eaſtern parts of Siberia, and continues only from
November to the end of March.   The ſnow ſeldom lies
upon the ground for any time.

Rein-deer, bears, wolves, ice-foxes, are not to be
found on theſe iſlands ; but they abound in black, grey,
brown, and red foxes ; for which reaſon they have got
the name of Lyſſie Oſtrova, or Fox Iſlands.   Theſe foxes
are ſtronger than thoſe of Yakutſk, and their hair is
much coarſer. During the day they lie in caves and
                                                        clifts

clifts of rocks; towards evening they come to the fhore in fearch of food; they have long ago extirpated the brood of mice, and other fmall animals. They are not in the fmalleft degree afraid of the inhabitants, but diftinguifh the Ruffians by the fcent; having experienced the effects of their fire-arms. The number of fea-animals, fuch as fea-lions, fea-bears, and fea-otters, which refort to thefe fhores, are very confiderable. Upon fome of the iflands warm fprings and native fulphur are to be found.

The Fox-iflands are in general very populous; Unalafhka, which is the largeft ifland, is fuppofed to contain Manners and Cuftoms of the Inhabitants. feveral thoufand inhabitants. Thefe favages live together in feparate communities, compofed of fifty, and fometimes of two or even three hundred perfons; they dwell in large caves from forty to eighty yards long, from fix to eight broad, and from four to five high. The roof of thefe caves is a kind of wooden grate, which is firft fpread over with a layer of grafs, and then covered with earth. Several openings are made in the top, through which the inhabitants go up and down by ladders: the fmalleft dwellings have two or three entrances of this fort, and the largeft five or fix. Each cave is divided into a certain number of partitions, which are appropriated to the feveral families; and thefe partitions are marked by means of ftakes driven into the earth. The men and women fit

on

on the ground ; and the children lie down, having their legs bound together under them, in order to make them learn to fit upon their hams.

Although no fire is ever made in thefe caves, they are generally fo warm, that both fexes fit naked. Thefe people obey the calls of nature openly, and without efteeming it indecent. They wafh themfelves firft with their own urine, and afterwards with water. In winter they go always bare-footed : and when they want to warm themfelves, efpecially before they go to fleep, they fet fire to dry grafs and walk over it. Their habitations being almoft dark, they ufe particularly in winter a fort of large lamps, made by hollowing out a ftone, into which they put a rufh-wick and burn train oil. A ftone fo hollowed is called Tfaaduck. The natives * are whites with black hair ; they have flat faces, and are of a good ftature. The men fhave with a fharp ftone or knife the circumference and top of the head, and let the hair which remains hang from the crown †. The women cut their hair in a ftreight line over the forehead ; behind they let it grow to a confiderable length,

* Von geficht find fie platt undweifs durchgaengig mit fchwarzen haaren.

† The original in this paffage is fomewhat obfcure. Die maenner fcheeren mit einem Scharfen Stein oder meffer den Umkreifs des haarkopfs und die platte, und laffen die haare um die krone des kopfs rundum ueberhangen.

and tie it in a bunch. Some of the men wear their beards; others fhave or pull them out by the roots.

They mark various figures on their faces, the backs of their hands, and lower parts of their arms, by pricking them firft with a needle, and then rubbing the parts with a fort of black clay. They make three incifions in the under-lip; they place in the middle one a flat bone, or a fmall coloured ftone; and in each of the fide-ones they fix a long pointed piece of bone, which bends and reaches almoft to the ears. They likewife make a hole through the griftle of the nofe, into which they put a fmall piece of bone in fuch a manner as to keep the noftrils extended. They alfo pierce holes in their ears, and wear in them what little ornaments they can procure.

Their drefs confifts of a cap and a fur-coat, which reaches down to the knee. Some of them wear common caps of a party coloured bird-fkin, upon which they leave part of the wings and tail. On the fore-part of their hunting and fifhing caps they place a fmall board like a fcreen, adorned with the jaw-bones of fea-bears, and ornamented with glafs beads, which they receive in barter from the Ruffians. At their feftivals and dancing parties they ufe a much more fhowy fort of caps. Their fur-coats are made like fhirts, being clofe behind and before, and are put on over the head. The

drefs

drefs of the men is made of bird fkins, that of the women of fea-otters and fea-bears. Thefe fkins are died with a fort of red earth, and neatly fewed with finews, and ornamented with various ftripes of fea-otter fkins and leathern fringes. They have alfo upper garments made of the inteftines of the largeft fea-calves and fea-lions.

Their veffels confift of two forts: the larger are lea-thern boats or baidars, which have oars on both fides, and are capable of holding thirty or forty people. The fmaller veffels are rowed with a double paddle, and re-femble the canoes of the Greenlanders, containing only one or two perfons: they never weigh above thirty pounds, being nothing but a thin fkeleton of a boat covered with leather. In thefe however they pafs from one ifland to another, and even venture out to fea to a confiderable diftance. In calm weather they go out in them to catch turbot and cod with bone-hooks and lines made of finews or fea-weed. They ftrike fifh in the rivulets with darts. Whales and other fea-animals thrown afhore by the waves are carefully looked after, and no part of them is loft. The quantity of provi-fions which they procure by hunting and fifhing being far too fmall for their wants, the greateft part of their food confifts of fea-wrack and fhell-fifh, which they find on the fhore.

No

No ftranger is allowed to hunt or fifh near a village, or to carry off any thing fit for food. When they are on a journey, and their provifions are exhaufted, they beg from village to village, or call upon their friends and relations for affiftance.

They feed upon the flefh of all forts of fea-animals, and generally eat it raw. But if at any time they choofe to drefs their victuals, they make ufe of an hollow ftone; having placed the fifh or flefh therein, they cover it with another, and clofe the interftices with lime or clay. They then lay it horizontally upon two ftones, and light a fire under it. The provifion intended for keeping is dried without falt in the open air. They gather berries of various forts, and lily roots of the fame fpecies with thofe which grow wild at Kamtchatka. They are unacquainted with the manner of dreffing the cow-parfnip, as practifed in that Peninfula; and do not underftand the art of diftilling brandy or any other ftrong liquor from it. They are at prefent very fond of fnuff, which the Ruffians have introduced among them.

No traces were found of any worfhip, neither did they feem to have any forcerers * among them. If a

* In the laft chapter it is faid that there are forcerers among them.

whale happens to be caſt on ſhore, the inhabitants aſ-
ſemble with great marks of joy, and perform a number
of extraordinary ceremonies. They dance and beat
drums * of different ſizes: they then cut up the fiſh,
of which the greateſt and beſt part is conſumed on
the ſpot. On ſuch occaſions they wear ſhowy caps;
and ſome of them dance naked in wooden maſks, which
reach down to their ſhoulders, and repreſent various ſorts
of ſea-animals. Their dances conſiſt of ſhort ſteps forwards, accompanied with many ſtrange geſtures.

Marriage ceremonies are unknown among them;
and each man takes as many wives as he can maintain,
but the number ſeldom exceeds four. Theſe women
are occaſionally allowed to cohabit with other men;
they and their children are alſo not unfrequently bar-
tered in exchange for commodities. When an iſlander
dies, the body is bound with thongs, and afterwards ex-
poſed to the air in a ſort of wooden cradle hung upon

* The expreſſion in the original is " Schlagen auf groſſen platten
" handpauken von verſchiedenen Klang," which, being literally tran-
ſlated, ſignifies " They beat upon large flat hand-kettle drums of dif-
" ferent ſounds."

By the accounts which I procured at Peterſburg, concerning the
form of theſe drums, they ſeem to reſemble in ſhape thoſe made uſe of
by the ſorcerers of Kamtchatka, and are of different ſizes. I had an
opportunity of ſeeing one of the latter in the Cabinet of Curioſities. In
is of an oval form, about two feet long and one broad: it is covered
only at one end like the tambour de baſque, and is worn upon the arm
like a ſhield.

a croſs-a crofs-bar, fupported by forks. Upon thefe occafions they cry, and make bitter lamentations.

Their Toigons or Princes are thofe who have nume-rous families, and are fkilful and fuccefsful in hunting and fifhing.

Their weapons confift of bows, arrows, and darts: they throw the latter very dexteroufly, and to a great diftance, from a hand-board. For defence they ufe wooden fhields, called kuyakin. Thefe iflanders are, notwithftanding their favagenefs, very docile; and the boys, whom the Ruffians keep as hoftages, foon ac-quire a knowledge of their language.

C H A P. XII.

Voyage of Otcheredin—*He winters upon* Umnak—*Arrival of* Levasheff *upon* Unalashka—*Return of* Otcheredin *to* Ochotsk.

Voyage of
Otcheredin in
the St. Paul,
1765.

IN the year 1765 three merchants, namely, Orechoff of Yula, Lapin of Solikamsk, and Shiloff of Ustyug, fitted out a new vessel called the St. Paul, under the command of Aphanassei Otcheredin. She was built in the harbour of Ochotsk: his crew consisted of sixty-two Russians and Kamtchadals; and she carried on board two inhabitants of the Fox Islands, named John and Timothy Surgeff, who had been brought to Kamtchatka and baptised.

September 10, they sailed from Ochotsk, and arrived the 22d in the bay of Bolcheresk where they wintered. August 1, 1776, they continued their voyage, and having passed the second of the Kuril Isles, steered on the 6th into the open sea; on the 24th they reached the nearest of the Fox Islands, which the interpreters called * Atchak. A storm arising, they cast anchor in a bay, but saw no inhabitants upon the shore. On the 26th

* Called in a former journal Atchu, p. 63.

they

they failed again, difcovered on the 27th Sagaugamak, along which they fteered North Eaft, and on the 31ft came within feven miles of the ifland Umnak; where, on account of the latenefs of the feafon and the want of provifion and water, they determined to winter. Accordingly on the 1ft of September, by the advice of the interpreters, they brought the veffel into a convenient bay near a point of land lying N. W. where they faftened it to the fhore with cables.

Arrival at Umnak.

Upon their landing they difcovered feveral pieces of a wreck; and two iflanders, who dwelled on the banks of a rivulet which empties itfelf into the bay, informed them, that thefe were the remains of a Ruffian veffel, whofe commander's name was Denys. From this intelligence they concluded that this was Protaffoff's veffel, fitted out at Ochotfk. The inhabitants of Umnak, Unalafhka, and of the Five Mountains, had affembled and murdered the crew, when feparated into different hunting parties. The fame iflanders alfo mentioned the fate of Kulkoff's and Trapefnikoff's fhips upon the ifland Unalafhka. Although this information occafioned general apprehenfions, yet they had no other refource than to draw the veffel afhore, and to take every poffible precaution againft a furprize. Accordingly they kept a conftant watch, made prefents to the Toigons and the principal inhabitants, and demanded fome children as hoftages. For fome time the iflanders behaved very peaceably, until the Ruffians endeavoured to perfuade them to become

tributary :

4

tributary : upon which they gave such repeated signs of
their hostile intentions, that the crew lived under continual alarms.   In the beginning of September information was brought them of the arrival of a vessel, fitted
out by Ivan Popoff, merchant of Lalsk, at Unalashka.

About the end of the said month the Toigon of the
Five Mountains came to Otcheredin, and was so well sa-
tisfied with his reception, that he brought hostages, and
not only assured them of his own friendship, but promised to use his influence with the other Toigons, and
to persuade them to the same peaceable behaviour.   But
the other Toigons not only paid no regard to his persua-
sions, but even barbarously killed one of his children.
From these and other circumstances the crew passed the
winter under continual apprehensions, and durst not venture far from the harbour upon hunting parties.   Hence
ensued a scarcity of provisions; and hunger, joined to
the violent attacks of the scurvy, made great havock
amongst them, insomuch that six of them died, and several of the survivors were reduced to so weak a condition,
that they were scarce able to move.

The health of the crew being re-established in the
spring, twenty-three men were sent on the 25th of
June in two boats to the Five Mountains, in order to
persuade the inhabitants to pay tribute.   On the 26th
they landed on the island Ulaga, where they were attacked

tacked with great fpirit by a large body of the inhabitants; and though three of the Ruffians were wounded,
yet the favages were repulfed with confiderable lofs: they
were fo terrified by their defeat, that they fled before the
Ruffians during their continuance on that ifland. The
latter were detained there by tempeftuous weather until
the 9th of July; during which time they found two
rufty firelocks belonging to Protaffoff's crew. On the
10th they returned to the harbour; and it was immediately refolved to difpatch fome companies upon hunting expeditions.

Accordingly on the 1ft of Auguft Matthew Polofkoff,
a native of Ilinfk, was fent with twenty-eight men in
two boats to Unalafhka with the following orders;
that if the weather and other circumftances were favourable, they were to make to Akutan and Akun, the
two neareft iflands to the Eaft, but to proceed no further.
In confequence of this, Polofkoff reached Akutan about
the end of the month; and being kindly received by
the inhabitants, he left fix of his party to hunt; with
the remainder he went to Akun, which lies about two
verfts from Akutan. From thence he difpatched five
men to the neighbouring iflands, where he was informed
by the interpreters there were great quantities of foxes.

Polofkoff and his companions continued the whole
autumn upon Akun without being annoyed; but on the

12th of December the inhabitants of the different iflands affembled in great numbers, and attacked them by land and fea.   They informed Polofkoff, by means of the interpreters, that the Ruffians whom he had fent to the neighbouring iflands were killed; that the two veffels at Umnak and Unalafhka were plundered, and the crew put to death; and that they were now come to make him and his party fhare the fame fate.   The Ruffian fire arms however kept them in due refpect; and towards evening they difperfed.   The fame night the interpreter deferted, probably at the inftigation of his countrymen, who neverthelefs killed him, as it was faid, that winter.

January 16, the favages ventured to make a fecond attack.   Having furprifed the guard by night, they tore off the roof of the Ruffian dwelling, and fhot down into the hut, making at the fame time great outcries: by this unexpected affault four Ruffians were killed, and three wounded; but the furvivors no fooner had recourfe to their fire-arms, than the enemy was driven to flight.   Meanwhile another body of the natives attempted to feize the two veffels, but without fuccefs; they however cut off the party of fix men left by Polofkoff at Akutan, together with the five hunters difpatched to the contiguous iflands, and two of Popoff's crew who were at the Wefternmoft part of Unalafhka.

Polofkoff

Polofkoff continued upon Akun in great danger until the 20th of February; when, the wounded being recovered, he failed over with a fair wind to Popoff's veffel at Unalafhka; and on the 10th of May returned to Otcheredin.

In April, Popoff's veffel being got ready for the voyage, all the hoftages, whofe number amounted to forty, were delivered to Otcheredin. July the 30th a veffel belonging to the fame Popoff arrived from Beering's Ifland, and caft anchor in the fame bay where Otcheredin's lay; and both crews entered into an agreement to fhare in common the profits of hunting. Strengthened by this alliance, Otcheredin prevailed upon a number of the inhabitants to pay tribute. Auguft the 22d Otcheredin's mate was fent with fix boats and fifty-eight men to hunt upon Unalafhka and Akutan; and there remained thirty men with the veffels in the harbour, who kept conftant watch.

Soon afterwards Otcheredin and the other commander received a letter from Levafheff Captain Lieutenant of the Imperial fleet, who accompanied Captain Krenitzin in the fecret expedition to thofe iflands. The letter was dated September 11, 1768: it informed them he was arrived at Unalafhka in the St. Paul, and lay at anchor in the fame bay in which Kulkoff's veffel had

Otcheredin receives an Account of Levafheff's Arrival at Unalafhka.

Y   been

been loft.   He likewife required a circumftantial account of their voyages.   By another order of the 24th
he fent for four of the principal hoftages, and demanded
the tribute of fkins which had been exacted from the
iflanders. But as the weather was generally tempeftuous
at this feafon of the year, they deferred fending them
till the fpring.   May the 31ft Levafheff fet fail for
Kamtchatka; and in 1771 returned fafely from his expedition at St. Peterfburg.

The two veffels remained at Umnak until the year
1770, during which time the crews met with no oppofition from the iflanders.   They continued their hunting parties, in which they had fuch good fortune, that
the fhare of Otcheredin's veffel (whofe voyage is here
chiefly related) confifted in 530 large fea-otter fkins,
40 young ones and 30 cubs, the fkins of 656 fine black
foxes, 100 of an inferior fort, and about 1250 red fox
fkins.

With this large cargo of furs Otcheredin fet fail on the
22d of May, 1770, from Umnak, leaving Popoff's crew
behind.   A fhort time before their departure, the other
interpreter Ivan Surgeff, at the inftigation of his relations,
deferted.

Return of
Otcheredin to   After having touched at the neareft of the Aleütian
Ochotfk.
Iflands, Otcheredin and his crew arrived on the 24th of
                                                         July

July at Ochotſk. They brought two iſlanders with them, whom they baptized. The one was named Alexèy Solovieff; the other Boris Otcheredin. Theſe iſlanders unfortunately died on their way to Peterſburg; the firſt between Yakutſk and Irkutſk; and the latter at Irkutſk, where he arrived on the 1ſt of February, 1771.

HAP.

C H A P. XIII.

Conclusion—General position and situation of the Aleütian *and* Fox *Islands—their distance from each other—Further description of the dress, manners, and customs of the inhabitants—their feasts and ceremonies, &c.*

Position of
Beering's and
Copper Islands.

ACCORDING to the latest informations brought by Otcheredin's and Popoff's vessels, the North West point of Commandorskoi Ostroff, or Beering's Island, lies due East from the mouth of the Kamtchatka river, at the distance of 250 versts. It is from 70 to 80 versts long, and stretches from North West to South East, in the same direction as Copper Island. The latter is situated about 60 or 70 versts from the South East point of Beering's Island, and is about 50 versts in length.

Of the Aleü-
tian Isles.

About 300 versts East by South of Copper Island lie the Aleütian Isles, of which Attak is the nearest : it is rather larger than Beering's Island, of the same shape, and stretches from West to South East. From thence about 20 versts Eastwards is situated Semitshi, extending from West to East, and near its Eastern point another small island. To the South of the strait, which separates the two latter islands, and at the distance of

40 verfts from both of them, lies Shemiya in a fimilar pofition, and not above 25 verfts in length. All thefe iflands ftretch between 54 and 55 degrees of North latitude.

The Fox Iflands are fituated E. N. E. from the Aleü- Of the Fox Iflands. tians: the neareft of thefe, Atchak, is about 800 verfts diftant; it lies in about 56 degrees North latitude, and extends from W. S. W. towards E. N. E. It greatly refembles Copper Ifland, and is provided with a commodious harbour on the North. From thence all the other iflands of this chain ftretch in a direction towards N. E. by Eaft.

The next to Atchak is Amlak, about 15 verfts diftant; it is nearly of the fame fize; and has an harbour on its South fide. Next follows Sagaugamak, at about the fame diftance, but fomewhat fmaller; from that it is 50 verfts to Amuchta, a fmall rocky ifland; and the fame diftance from the latter to Yunakfan, another fmall ifland. About 20 verfts from Yunakfan there is a clufter of five fmall iflands, or rather mountains, Kigalgift, Kagamila, Tfigulak, Ulaga, and Tana-Unok, and which are therefore called by the Ruffians Pät Sopki, or the Five Mountains. Of thefe Tana-Unok lies moft to the N. E. towards which the Weftern point of Umnak advances within the diftance of 20 verfts.

Umnak

Umnak ftretches from S.W. to N.E.; it is 150 verfts in length, and has a very confiderable bay on the Weft end of the Northern coaft, in which thcre is a fmall ifland or rock, called Adugak; and on the South fide is Shemalga, another rock. The Weftern point of Aghunalafhka, or Unalafhka, is feparated from the Eaft end of Umnak by a ftrait near 20 verfts in breadth. The pofition of thefe two iflands is fimilar; but Aghunalafhka is much the largeft, and is above 200 verfts long. It is divided towards the N.E. into three promontories, one of which runs out in a Wefterly direction, forming one fide of a large bay on the North coaft of the ifland: the fecond ftretches out N.E. ends in three points, and is connected with the ifland by a fmall neck of land. The third or moft Southerly one is feparated from the laft mentioned promontory by a deep bay. Near Unalafhka towards the Eaft lies another fmall ifland, called Skirkin.

About 20 verfts from the North Eaft promontory of Aghunalafhka lie four iflands: the firft, Akutan, is about half as big as Umnak; a verft further is the fmall ifland Akun; a little beyond is Akunok; and laftly Kigalga, which is the fmalleft of thefe four, and ftretches with Akun and Akunok almoft from N. to S. Kigalga is fituated about the 61ft degree of latitude. About

100

100 verſts from thence lies an iſland called Unimak*, upon which Captain Krenitzin wintered; and beyond it the inhabitants ſaid there was a large tract of country called Alaſhka, of which they did not know the boundaries.

The Fox Iſlands are in general very rocky, without containing any remarkable high mountains: they are deſtitute of wood, but abound in rivulets and lakes, which are moſtly without fiſh. The winter is much milder than in Siberia; the ſnow ſeldom falls before the beginning of January, and continues on the ground till the end of March.

There is a volcano in Amuchta; in Kagamila ſulphur flows from a mountain; in Taga-Unok there are warm ſprings hot enough to boil proviſions; and flames of ſulphur are occaſionally ſeen at night upon the mountains of Unalaſhka and Akutan.

The Fox Iſlands are tolerably populous in proportion to their ſize. The inhabitants are entirely free, and pay tribute to no one: they are of a middle ſtature; and live, both in ſummer and winter, in holes dug in the earth. No ſigns of religion were found amongſt them.

Account of the Inhabitants of the Fox Iſlands.

* Krenitzin wintered in the ſtraits of Alaxa, which ſeparate Unimak from Alaxa. See Appendix I. N° I. p. 254.

Several

Several perfons indeed pafs for forcerers, pretending to
know things paft and to come, and are accordingly
held in high efteem, but without receiving any emo-
lument. Filial duty and refpect towards the aged are
not held in eftimation by thefe iflanders. They are
not however deficient in fidelity to each other; they
are of lively and chearful tempers, though rather impe-
tuous, and naturally prone to anger. In general, they
do not obferve any rules of decency, but follow all the
calls of nature publicly, and without the leaft referve.
They wafh themfelves with their own urine.

Their Food.   Their principal food confifts in fifh and other
fea-animals, fmall fhell-fifh and fea-plants: their
greateft delicacies are wild lilies and other roots, together with different kinds of berries. When they have
laid in a ftore of provifions, they eat at any time of the
day without diftinction; but in cafe of neceffity they
are capable of fafting feveral days together. They feldom heat their dwellings; but when they are defirous
of warming themfelves, they light a bundle of hay, and
ftand over it; or elfe they fet fire to train oil, which
they pour into a hollow ftone.

They feed their children when very young with the
coarfeft flefh, and for the moft part raw. If an infant
cries, the mother immediately carries it to the fea-fide,
and be it fummer or winter holds it naked in the

water

water until it is quiet. This custom is so far from doing the children any harm, that it hardens them against the cold, and they accordingly go bare-footed through the winter without the least inconvenience. They are also trained to bathe frequently in the sea; and it is an opinion generally received among the islanders, that by that means they are rendered bold, and become fortunate in fishing.

The men wear shirts made of the skins of cormo- Dress. rants, sea-divers, and gulls; and, in order to keep out the rain, they have upper garments of the bladders and other intestines of sea-lions, sea-calves, and whales, blown up and dried. They cut their hair in a circular form close to their ears; and shave also a round place upon the top. The women, on the contrary, let the hair descend over the forehead as low as the eye-brows, and tie the remaining part in a knot upon the top of the head. They pierce the ears, and hang therein bits of coral which they get from the Russians. Both sexes make holes in the gristle of the nose, and in the under-lips, in which they thrust pieces of bone, and are very fond of such kind of ornaments. They mark also and colour their faces with different figures. They barter among one another sea-otters, sea-bears, clothes made of bird-skins and of dried intestines, skins of sea-lions and sea-calves for the coverings of baidars,

Z

wooden

wooden mafks, darts, thread made of finews and reindeer hair, which they get from the country of Alafka.

Their houfhold utenfils are fquare pitchers and large troughs, which they make out of the wood driven afhore by the fea. Their weapons are bows and arrows pointed with flints, and javelins of two yards in length, which they throw from a fmall board. Inftead of hatchets they ufe crooked knives of flint or bone. Some iron knives, hatchets, and lances, were obferved amongft them, which they had probably got by plundering the Ruffians.

Arms.

According to the reports of the oldeft inhabitants of Umnak and Unalafhka, they have never been engaged in any war either amongft themfelves or with their neighbours, except once with the people of Alafhka, the occafion of which was as follows : The Toigon of Um-nak's fon had a maimed hand; and fome inhabitants of Alafhka, who came upon a vifit to that ifland, faftened to his arm a drum, out of mockery, and invited him to dance. The parents and relations of the boy were offended at this infult : hence a quarrel enfued; and from that time the two people have lived in continual enmity, attacking and plundering each other by turns. According to the reports of the iflanders, there are mountains upon Alafhka, and woods of great extent at fome diftance from the coaft. The natives wear clothes made of

the

the ſkins of reindeer, wolves, and foxes, and are not tributary to any of their neighbours. The inhabitants of the Fox-iſlands ſeem to have no knowledge of any country beyond Alaſhka.

Feaſts are very common among theſe iſlanders; and more particularly when the inhabitants of one iſland are viſited by thoſe of the others. The men of the village meet their gueſts beating drums, and preceded by the women, who ſing and dance. At the concluſion of the dance the hoſts invite them to partake of the feaſt; after which ceremony the former return firſt to their dwellings, place mats in order, and ſerve up their beſt proviſion. The gueſts next enter, take their places, and after they are ſatisfied the diverſions begin.

Firſt, the children dance and caper, at the ſame time making a noiſe with their ſmall drums, while the owners of the hut of both ſexes ſing. Next, the men dance almoſt naked, tripping after one another, and beating drums of a larger ſize: when theſe are weary, they are relieved by the women, who dance in their clothes, the men continuing in the mean time to ſing and beat their drums. At laſt the fire is put out, which had been kindled for the ceremony. The manner of obtaining fire is by rubbing two pieces of dry wood, or moſt commonly by ſtriking two flints together, and letting the ſparks fall

upon

upon fome fea-otter's hair mixed with fulphur. If any forcerer is prefent, it is then his turn to play his tricks in the dark; if not, the guefts immediately retire to their huts, which are made on that occafion of their canoes and mats. The natives, who have feveral wives, do not withhold them from their guefts; but where the owner of the hut has himfelf but one wife, he then makes the offer of a female fervant.

Their hunting feafon is principally from the end of October to the beginning of December, during which time they kill large quantities of young fea-bears for their clothing. They pafs all December in feaftings and diverfions fimilar to that above mentioned: with this difference, however, that the men dance in wooden mafks, reprefenting various fea-animals, and painted red, green, or black, with coarfe coloured earths found upon thefe iflands.

During thefe feftivals they vifit each other from village to village, and from ifland to ifland. The feafts concluded, mafks and drums are broken to pieces, or depofited in caverns among the rocks, and never afterwards made ufe of. In fpring they go out to kill old feabears, fea-lions, and whales. During fummer, and even in winter when it is calm, they row out to fea, and catch cod and other fifh. Their hooks are of bone; and for

lines

lines they make use of a string made of a long tenacious sea-weed, which is sometimes found in those seas near one hundred and sixty yards in length.

Whenever they are wounded in any encounter, or bruised by any accident, they apply a sort of yellow root to the wound, and fast for some time. When their head achs, they open a vein in that part with a stone lancet. When they want to glue the points of their arrows to the shaft, they strike their nose till it bleeds, and use the blood as glue.

Murder is not punished amongst them, for they have no judge. With respect to their ceremonies of burying the dead, they are as follow: The bodies of poor people are wrapped up in their own clothes, or in mats; then laid in a grave, and covered over with earth. The bodies of the rich are put, together with their clothes and arms, in a small boat made of the wood driven ashore by the sea: this boat is hung upon poles placed crofs-ways; and the body is thus left to rot in the open air.

The customs and manners of the inhabitants of the Aleütian Isles are nearly similar to those of the inhabitants of the Fox Islands. The former indeed are ren-

dered

dered tributary, and entirely ſubject to Ruſſia; and moſt of them have a ſlight acquaintance with the Ruſſian language, which they have learned from the crews of the different veſſels who have landed there.

PART

PART II.

CONTAINING

THE CONQUEST OF SIBERIA,

AND

THE HISTORY

OF THE

TRANSACTIONS AND COMMERCE

BETWEEN RUSSIA AND CHINA.

CHAP. I.

First irruption of the Russians *into* Siberia—*second inroad*
—Yermac, *driven by the* Tzar *of* Muscovy *from the*
Volga, *retires to* Orel, *a* Russian *settlement—Enters*
Siberia, *with an army of* Cossacs—*his progress and*
exploits—Defeats Kutchum Chan — *conquers his do-*
minions—cedes them to the Tzar—*receives a rein-*
forcement of Russian *troops—is surprized by* Kutchum
Chan—*his defeat and death—veneration paid to his*
memory—Russian *troops evacuate* Siberia—*re-enter*
and conquer the whole country—their progress stopped by
the Chinese.

SIBERIA was scarcely known to the Russians before
the middle of the sixteenth century *: for although
an expedition was made, under the reign of Ivan Vassilievitch I. into the North-Western Parts of that country,
as far as the river Oby, by which several Tartar tribes
were rendered tributary, and some of their chiefs brought
prisoners to Moscow ; yet this incursion bore a greater
resemblance to the desultory inroads of barbarians, than
to any permanent establishment of empire by a civilized
nation. Indeed the effects of that expedition soon va-

First Irrupti
of the Russians
into Siberia,
under the
Reign of Ivan
Vassilievitch I.

---

* S. R. G. VI. p. 119—211. Fif. Sib. Gef. Tom. I.'

A a   nished;

nifhed; nor does any trace of the leaft fubfequent communication with Siberia appear in the Ruffian hiftory
before the reign of Ivan Vaffilievitch II. At that period
Siberia again became an object of attention, by means
of one Anika Strogonoff, a Ruffian merchant, who had
eftablifhed fome falt-works at Solvytfhegodfkaia, a town
in the government of Archangel.

Anika Strogo-
noff trades
with the Peo-
ple of Siberia. This perfon carried on a trade of barter with the inhabitants of the North-Weftern parts of Siberia, who
brought every year to the abovementioned town large
quantities of the choiceft furs. Upon their return to
their country, Strogonoff was accuftomed to fend with
them fome Ruffian merchants, who croffed the mountains, and traded with the natives. By thefe means a confiderable number of very valuable furs were procured at
an eafy rate, in exchange for toys and other commodities
of trifling value.

This traffic was continued for feveral years, without
any interruption; during which Strogonoff rapidly
amaffed a very confiderable fortune *. At length the
Tzar Ivan Vaffilievitch II. forefeeing the advantages
which would accrue to his fubjects, from eftablifhing a
more general and regular commerce with thefe people,

* S. R. G. VI. p. 220—223. Fif. Sib. Gef. p. 182.

determined

determined to enlarge the communication already opened with Siberia. Accordingly he sent a body of troops into that country. They followed the same route which had been discovered by the Russians in the former expedition, and which was lately frequented by the merchants of Solvytshegodskaia. It lay along the banks of the Petschora, and from thence crossed the Yugorian mountains, which form the North-Eastern boundary of Europe. These troops, however, do not seem to have passed the Irtish, or to have penetrated further than the Western branch of the river Oby. Some Tartar tribes were indeed laid under contribution; and a chief, whose name was Yediger, consented to pay an annual tribute of a thousand sables. But this expedition was not productive of any lasting effects; for soon afterwards Yediger was defeated, and taken prisoner by Kutchum Chan; the latter was a lineal descendant of the celebrated Zinghis Chan; and had newly established his empire in those parts.

Second Irruption of the Russians into Siberia in the Reign of Ivan VassilievitchII.

This second inroad was probably made about the middle of the sixteenth century; for the Tzar Ivan Vassilievitch assumed the title of Lord of all the Siberian lands so early as 1558, before the conquests made by Yermac in that kingdom *. But probably the name of Siberia was at that time only confined to the district

* S. R. G. VI. p. 217.

A a 2

then

then rendered tributary ; and as the Ruffians extended their conquefts, this appellation was afterwards applied to the whole tract of country which now bears that name.

For fome time after the above-mentioned expedition, the Tzar does not appear to have made any attempts towards recovering his loft authority in thofe diftant regions. But his attention was again turned to that quarter by a concurrence of incidents; which, though begun without his immediate interpofition, terminated in a vaft acceffion of territory.

Strogonoff
forms Settlements upon
the Kama and
Tchuffovaia.
Strogonoff, in recompence for having firft opened a trade with the inhabitants of Siberia, obtained from the Tzar large grants of land. Accordingly he founded colonies upon the banks of the rivers Kama and Tchuffovaia; and thefe fettlements gave rife to the entire fubjection of Siberia by the refuge which they not long afterwards afforded to Yermac Timofeeff.

This perfon was nothing more than a fugitive Coffac of the Don, and chief of a troop of banditti who infefted the fhores of the Cafpian fea. But as he was the inftrument by which fuch a vaft extent of dominion was added to the Ruffian Empire, it will not be uninterefting to develop the principal circumftances, which brought this

Coffac

Coffac from the fhores of the Cafpian to the banks of the Kama; and to trace the progrefs which he afterwards made in the diftant regions of Siberia.

By the victories which the Tzar Ivan Vaffilievitch had gained over the Tartars of Cafan and Aftracan, that monarch extended his dominions as far as the Cafpian Sea; and thereby eftablifhed a commerce with the Perfians and Bucharians. But as the merchants who traded to thofe parts were continually pillaged by the Coffacs of the Don; and as the roads which lay by the fide of that river, and of the Volga, were infefted with thofe banditti; the Tzar fent a confiderable force againft them. Accordingly, they were attacked and routed; part were flain, part made prifoners, and the reft efcaped by flight: among the latter was a corps of fix thoufand Coffacs, under the command of the above-mentioned Yermac Timofeeff *.

Yermac is driven from the Shores of the Cafpian Sea. A. D. 1577.

This celebrated adventurer, being driven from his ufual haunts, retired, with his followers, into the interior part of the province of Cafan. From thence he directed his courfe along the banks of the Kama, until he came to Orel †. That place was one of the Ruffian fettlements recently planted, and was governed by Maxim grandfon

He retires to Orel, one of the Ruffian Settlements.

* S. R. G. VI. p. 232. Fif. Sib. Gef. I. p. 185.
† S. R. G. VI. p. 233.

of

of Anika Strogonoff. Yermac, inftead of ftorming the place, and pillaging the inhabitants, acted with a degree of moderation unufual in a chief of banditti. Being hofpitably received by Strogonoff, and fupplied with every thing that was neceffary for the fubfiftence of his troops, he fixed his winter quarters at that fettlement. His reftlefs genius however did not fuffer him to continue for any length of time in a ftate of inactivity; and from the intelligence he procured concerning the fituation of

Determines to invade Siberia. the neighbouring Tartars of Siberia, he turned his arms toward that quarter.

State of Siberia. Siberia was at that time partly divided among a number of feparate princes; and partly inhabited by the various tribes of independent Tartars. Of the former Kutchum Chan was the moft powerful Sovereign. His dominions confifted of that tract of country which now forms the South-Weftern part of the province of Tobolfk; and ftretched from the banks of the Irtifh and Oby to thofe of the Tobol and Tura. His principal refidence was at Sibir *, a fmall fortrefs upon the river Irtifh, not

far

* Several authors have fuppofed the name of Siberia to derive its origin from this fortrefs, foon after it was firft taken by the Ruffians under Yermac. But this opinion is advanced without fufficient foundation; for the name of Sibir was unknown to the Tartars, that fort being by them called Ifker. Befides, the Southern part of the province of Tobolfk, to which the name of Siberia was originally applied, was thus

deno-

far from the prefent town of Tobolfk; and of which
fome ruins are ftill to be feen. Although his power
was very confiderable, yet there were fome circumftances which feemed to enfure fuccefs to an enterpriz-
ing invader. He had newly acquired a large part of
his territories by conqueft; and had, in a great meafure,
alienated the affections of his idolatrous fubjects by the
intolerant zeal, with which he introduced and diffeminated
the Mahometan religion *.

Strogonoff did not fail of difplaying to Yermac this
inviting pofture of affairs, as well with a view of removing him from his prefent ftation, as becaufe he himfelf
was perfonally exafperated againft Kutchum Chan: for
the latter had fecretly inftigated a large body of Tartars
to invade the Ruffian fettlements upon the river Tchuffovaia; and had afterwards commenced open hoftilities
againft them with a body of forces under the command
of his coufin Mehemet Kul. And although both thefe
attempts had failed of fuccefs, yet the troops engaged in
them had left traces of havock and devaftation too lafting
to be eafily effaced †.

denominated by the Ruffians before the invafion of Yermac. This
denomination probably firft came from the Permians and Sirjanians,
who brought the firft accounts of Siberia to the Ruffians.
S. R. G. VI. p. 180.

* S. R. G. VI. p. 180.
† Fif. Sib. Gef. I. p. 187.

All

Marches to-
wards Siberia.

All thefe various confiderations were not loft upon Yermac: having therefore employed the winter in preparations for his intended expedition, he began his march in the fummer of the following year, 1578, along the banks of the Tchuffovaia. The want of proper guides, and a neglect of other neceffary precautions, greatly retarded his march; and he was overtaken by the winter before he had made any confiderable progrefs. And at the appearance of fpring he found his ftock of

Returns to
Orel.

provifions fo nearly exhaufted, that he was reduced to the neceffity of returning to Orel.

But this failure of fuccefs by no means extinguifhed his ardour for the profecution of the enterprize; it only ferved to make him ftill more folicitous in guarding againft the poffibility of a future mifcarriage. By threats he extorted from Strogonoff every affiftance which the nature of the expedition feemed to require. Befides a fufficient quantity of provifions, all his followers, who were before unprovided with fire-arms, were fupplied with mufkets and ammunition; and, in order to give the appearance of a regular army to his troops, colours were diftributed to each company, which were ornamented with the images of faints, after the manner of the Ruffians.

Having

Having thus made all previous arrangements, he thought himself in a condition to force his way into Siberia. Accordingly, in the month of June, 1579, he set out upon this second expedition. His followers His second Expedition. amounted to five thousand men; adventurers inured to hardships, and regardless of danger: they placed implicit confidence in their leader, and feemed to be all animated with the fame spirit. He continued his route partly by land, and partly by water: the navigation however of the rivers was fo tedious, and the roads fo rugged and difficult, that eighteen months elapfed before he reached Tchingi, a fmall town upon Arrives upon the Banks of the Tura. the banks of the Tura *.

Here he muftered his troops, and found his army confiderably reduced: part had been exhaufted by fatigue, part carried off by ficknefs, and part cut off in fkirmifhes with the Tartars. The whole remaining number amounted to about fifteen hundred effective men; and yet with this handful of troops Yermac did not hefitate a moment in advancing againft Kutchum Chan. That prince was already upon his guard; and refolved to defend his crown to the laft extremity. Having collected his forces, he difpatched feveral flying parties againft Yermac, himfelf remaining behind with

* S. R. G. VI. p. 243—248—262.

B b the

the flower of his troops: but all thefe detachments were driven back with confiderable lofs; and worfted in many fucceffive fkirmifhes. Yermac continued his march without intermiffion, bearing down all refiftance until he reached the center of his adverfary's dominions.

Thefe fucceffes however were dearly bought; for his army was now reduced to five hundred men. Kutchum Chan was encamped* at no great diftance upon the banks of the Irtifh, with a very fuperior force, and determined to give him battle. Yermac, who was not to be daunted by the inequality of numbers, prepared for the engagement with a confidence which never forfook him; his troops were equally impatient for action, and knew no medium between conqueft and death. The event of the combat correfponded with this magnanimity. After an obftinate and well-fought battle, victory declared in favour of Yermac: the Tartars were entirely routed, and the carnage was fo general, that Kutchum Chan himfelf efcaped with difficulty.

Defeats Kutchum Chan. 1581.

This defeat proved decifive: Kutchum Chan was deferted by his fubjects; and Yermac, who knew how to improve as well as gain a victory, marched without

* The place where the Tartar army lay encamped was called Tfchuvatch: it is a neck of land wafhed by the Irtifh, near the fpot where the Tobol falls into that river. Fif. Sib. Gef. I. p. 203.

delay

delay to Sibir, the refidence of the Tartar princes. He was well aware, that the only method to fecure his conqueft was to get poffeffion of that important fortrefs. He expected therefore to have found in that place a confiderable garrifon, determined to facrifice their lives in its defence. But the news of the late defeat had diffufed univerfal confternation; and a body of troops whom he fent before him, to reduce the fortrefs, found it quite deferted: he himfelf foon after made his triumphant entry, and feated himfelf upon the throne without the leaft oppofition. Here he fixed his refidence, and received the allegiance of the neighbouring people, who poured in from all quarters upon the news of this unexpected revolution. The Tartars were fo ftruck with his gallant intrepidity and brilliant exploits, that they fubmitted to his authority without hefitation, and acquiefced in the payment of the ufual tribute.

Thus this enterprifing Coffac was fuddenly exalted from the ftation of a chief of banditti to the rank of a fovereign prince. It does not appear from hiftory whether his firft defign was to conquer Siberia, or folely to amafs a confiderable booty. The latter indeed feems the more probable conjecture. The rapid tide of fuccefs with which he was carried on, and the entire defeat of Kutchum Chan, afterwards expanded his views, and opened a larger fcene to his

B b 2   ambition.

Seats himfelf upon the Throne.

ambition. But whatever were his original projects,
he seems worthy, so far as intrepidity and prudence
form a basis of merit, of the final success which
flowed in upon him. For he was neither elated with
unexpected prosperity, nor dazzled with the sudden
glare of royalty: on the contrary, the dignity of his
deportment was as consistent and unaffected, as if he
had been born a sovereign.

And now Yermac and his followers seemed to enjoy
those rewards which they had dearly purchased by a
course of unremitted fatigue, and by victories which
almost exceeded belief. Not only the tribes in the
neighbourhood of Sibir wore the appearance of the most
unreserved submission; but even princes continued
flocking in from distant parts, to acknowledge themselves tributary, and to claim his protection. However,
Precarious Situation of Yermac. this calm was of short duration. Insurrections were
concerted by Kutchum Chan; who, though driven from
his dominions, yet still retained no small degree of
influence over his former subjects.

Yermac saw and felt the precariousness of his present grandeur; the inconsiderable number of his followers,
who had survived the conquest of Sibir, had been still
further diminished by an ambuscade of the enemy;
and as he could not depend on the affection of his
new subjects, he found himself under the necessity either
of

of calling in foreign affiftance, or of relinquifhing his dominion. Under thefe circumftances he had recourfe to the Tzar of Mufcovy; and made a tender of his new acquifitions to that monarch, upon condition of receiving immediate and effectual fupport. The judicious manner in which he conducted this meafure fhews him no lefs able in the arts of negotiation than of war.

One of his moft confidential followers was difpatched to Mofcow at the head of fifty Coffacs. He had orders to reprefent to the court the progrefs which the Ruffian troops, under the command of Yermac, had made in Siberia: he was artfully to add, that an extenfive Cedes his Conquefts to empire was conquered in the name of the Tzar; that the Tzar of Mufcovy. the natives were reduced to fwear allegiance to that monarch, and confented to pay an annual tribute. This reprefentation was accompanied with a prefent of the choiceft and moft valuable furs *. The embaffador was received at Mofcow with the ftrongeft marks of fatis-faction: a public thankfgiving was celebrated in the ca-thedral; the Tzar acknowledged and extolled the good 1582. fervices of Yermac; he granted him a pardon for all former offences; and, as a teftimony of his favour, dif-tributed prefents for him and his followers. Amongft thofe that were fent to Yermac was a fur robe, which the Tzar himfelf had worn, and which was the greateft

* S. R. G. VI. p. 304.

mark

mark of diſtinction that could be conferred upon a ſubject. To theſe was added a ſum of money, and a promiſe of ſpeedy and effectual aſſiſtance.

Meanwhile Yermac, notwithſtanding the inferior number of his troops, did not remain inactive within the fortreſs of Sibir. He defeated all attempts of Kutchum Chan to recover his crown; and took his principal general priſoner: he made occaſional inroads into the adjacent provinces, and extended his conqueſts up to the ſource of the river Taffda on one ſide, and on the other as far as the diſtrict which lies upon the river Oby above its junction with the Irtiſh.

Receives a Reinforcement of Ruſſian Troops.

At length the promiſed ſuccours arrived at Sibir. They conſiſted of five hundred Ruſſians, under the command of prince Bolkoſky, who was appointed wayvode or governor of Siberia. Strengthened by this reinforcement, Yermac continued his excurſions on all ſides with his uſual activity; and gained ſeveral bloody victories over different princes, who were imprudent enough to aſſert their independence.

In one of theſe expeditions he laid ſiege to Kullara, a ſmall fortreſs upon the banks of the Irtiſh, which ſtill belonged to Kutchum Chan: but he found it ſo bravely defended by that monarch, that all his efforts to carry it by ſtorm proved ineffectual. Upon his return to Sibir

he

he was followed at some diftance by that prince, who hung unperceived upon his rear; and was prepared to feize any fortunate moment of attack which might occur; nor was it long before a favourable opportunity prefented itfelf. The Ruffians to the number of about three hundred lay negligently pofted in a fmall ifland, formed by two branches of the Irtifh. The night was obfcure and rainy; and the troops, who were fatigued with a long march, repofed themfelves without fufpicion of danger. Kutchum Chan, apprifed of their fituation, filently advanced at midnight with a felect body of troops; and, having forded the river, came with fuch rapidity upon the Ruffians, as to preclude the ufe of their arms. In the darknefs and confufion of the night, the latter were cut to pieces almoft without oppofition; and fell a refiftlefs prey to thofe adverfaries, whom they had been accuftomed to conquer and defpife. The maffacre was fo univerfal, that only one man is recorded to have efcaped, and to have brought the news of this cataftrophe to his countrymen at Sibir.

Surprifed by Kutchum Chan.

Yermac himfelf perifhed in the rout, though he did not fall by the fword of the enemy. In all the hurry of furprife, he was not fo much infected with the general panic, as to forget his ufual intrepidity, which feemed to be encreafed rather than abated by the danger of his prefent fituation. After many defperate acts of heroifm,

Death of Yermac.

he

he cut his way through the troops who furrounded him, and made to the banks of the Irtifh*. Being clofely purfued by a detachment of the enemy, he endeavoured to throw himfelf into a boat which lay near the fhore; but ftepping fhort, he fell into the water, and, being incumbered with the weight of his armour, funk inftantly to the bottom†.

His body was not long afterwards taken out of the Irtifh, and expofed, by order of Kutchum Chan, to all the infults which revenge ever fuggefted to barbarians in the frenzy of fuccefs. But thefe firft tranfports of refentment had no fooner fubfided, than the Tartars teftified the moft pointed indignation at the ungenerous

* Many difficulties have arifen concerning the branch of the Irtifh in which Yermac was drowned; but it is now fufficiently afcertained that it was a canal, which fome time before this cataftrophe had been cut by order of that Coffac: Not far from the fpot where the Vagai falls into the Irtifh, the latter river forms a bend of fix verfts; by cutting a canal in a ftreight line from the two extreme points of this fweep, he fhortened the length of the navigation. S. R. G. p. 365, 366.

† Cyprian was appointed the firft archbifhop of Siberia in 1621. Upon his arrival at Tobolfk, he enquired for feveral of the antient followers of Yermac who were ftill alive; and from them he made himfelf acquainted with the principal circumftances attending the expedition of that Coffac, and the conqueft of Siberia. Thofe circumftances he committed to writing; and thefe papers may be confidered as the archives of the Siberian hiftory; from which the feveral hiftorians of that country have drawn their relations. Sava Yefimoff, who was himfelf one of Yermac's followers, is one of the moft accurate hiftorians of thofe times. He carries down his hiftory to the year 1636. Fif. Sib. Gef. I. p. 430.

ferocity

ferocity of their leader. The prowefs of Yermac, his confummate valour and magnanimity, virtues which barbarians know how to prize, rofe upon their recollection. They made a fudden tranfition from one extreme to the other: they reproached their leader for ordering, and themfelves for being the inftruments of indignity to fuch venerable remains. At length their heated imaginations proceeded even to confecrate his memory: they interred his body with all the rites of Pagan fuperftition; and offered up facrifices to his manes.

Many miraculous ftories were foon fpread abroad, and met with implicit belief. The touch of his body was fuppofed to have proved an inftantaneous cure for all diforders; and even his clothes and arms were faid to be endowed with the fame efficacy. A flame of fire was reprefented as fometimes hovering about his tomb, and fometimes as ftretching in one luminous body from the fame fpot towards the heavens. A prefiding influence over the affairs of the chace and of war was attributed to his departed fpirit; and numbers reforted to his tomb to invoke his tutelary aid in concerns fo interefting to uncivilized nations. Thefe idle fables, though they evince the fuperftitious credulity of the Tartars, convey at the fame time the ftrongeft teftimony of their veneration for the memory of Yermac; and this veneration

Veneration paid to his Memory.

C c　　　greatly

greatly contributed to the subsequent progress of the Russians in those regions *.

With Yermac expired for a time the Russian empire in Siberia. The news of his defeat and death no sooner reached the garrison of Sibir, than an hundred and fifty troops, the sad remains of that formidable army which had gained such a series of almost incredible victories, retired from the fortress, and evacuated Siberia. Notwithstanding this disaster, the court of Moscow did not abandon its design upon that country; which a variety of favourable circumstances still concurred to render a flattering object of Russian ambition. Yermac's sagacity had discovered new and commodious routes for the march of troops across those inhospitable regions : the rapidity with which he had overrun the territories of Kutchum Chan, taught the Russians to consider the Tartars as an easy prey. Many of the tribes who had been rendered tributary by Yermac, had testified a cheer-

The Russians quit Siberia.

* Even so late as the middle of the next century, this veneration for the memory of Yermac had not subsided. Allai, a powerful prince of the Calmucs, is said to have been cured of a dangerous disorder, by mixing some earth taken from Yermac's tomb in water, and drinking the infusion. That prince is also reported to have carried with him a small portion of the same earth, whenever he engaged in any important enterprize. This earth he superstitiously considered as a kind of charm; and was persuaded that he always secured a prosperous issue to his affairs by this precaution. S. R. G. VI. p. 391.

ful

ful acquiefcence under the fovereignty of the Tzar; and were inclined to renew their allegiance upon the firft opportunity: others looked upon all refiftance as unavailing, and had learned, from dear-bought experience, to tremble at the very name of a Ruffian. The natural ftrength of the country, which proved not to be irrefiftible even when united, was confiderably weakened by its inteftine commotions. Upon the retreat of the garrifon of Sibir, that fortrefs, together with the adjacent diftrict, was feized by Seyidyak, fon of the former fovereign, whom Kutchum Chan had dethroned and put to death: other princes availed themfelves of the general confufion to affert independency; and Kutchum Chan was able to regain only a fmall portion of thofe dominions, of which he had been ftripped by Yermac.

Influenced by thefe motives, the court of Mofcow fent a body of three hundred troops into Siberia, who penetrated to the banks of the Tura as far as Tfchingi almoft without oppofition. There they built the fort of Tumen, and re-eftablifhed their authority over the neighbouring diftrict. Being foon afterwards reinforced by an additional number of troops, they were enabled to extend their operations, and to erect the fortreffes of Tobolfk, Sirgut, and Tara. The erection of thefe and other fortreffes was foon attended with a

The Ruffians re-enter Siberia.

Re-conquer their ancient Territories.

C c 2   fpeedy

ſpeedy recovery of the whole territory, which Yermac
had reduced under the Ruſſian yoke.

This ſucceſs was only the fore-runner of ſtill greater
acquiſitions.   The Ruſſians puſhed their conqueſt far
and wide: wherever they appeared, the Tartars were
either reduced or exterminated; new towns were built;
and colonies were planted on all ſides.   Before a century

All Siberia
conquered and
colonized.

had well elapſed, all that vaſt tract of country now called
Siberia, which ſtretches from the confines of Europe to
the Eaſtern Ocean, and from the Frozen Sea to the preſent frontiers of China, was annexed to the Ruſſian
dominions.

Progreſs of
the Ruſſians
checked by
the Chineſe.

A ſtill larger extent of territory had probably been
won;   and all the various tribes of independent Tartary
which lie between the South-Eaſtern extremity of the
Ruſſian empire, and the Chineſe Wall, would have fol
lowed the fate of the Siberian hordes; if the power of
China had not ſuddenly interpoſed.

C H A P.

C H A P. II.

Commencement of hostilities between the Russians *and*
Chinese—Disputes concerning the limits of the two
empires—Treaty of Nershinsk—*Embassies from the court*
of Russia *to* Pekin—*Treaty of* Kiachta—*Establishment*
of the commerce between the two nations.

TOWARDS the middle of the seventeenth century
the Russians were rapidly extending themselves
Eastward through that important territory, which lies
on each side of the river * Amoor. They soon reduced
several independent Tungusian hordes; and built a chain
of small fortresses along the banks of the above-mentioned river, of which the principal were Albasin, and
Kamarskoi Ostrog. Not long afterwards, the Chinese
under † Camhi conceived a similar design of subduing
the

Rise of Animo-
sities between
the Russians
and Chinese.

---

* Amoor is the name given by the Russians to this river; it is called
Sakalin-Ula by the Manshurs, and was formerly denominated Karamu-
ran, or the Black River, by the Mongols.   S. R. G. II. p. 293.

† Camhi was the second emperor of the Manshur race, who made
themselves masters of China in 1624.
The Manshurs were originally an obscure tribe of the Tungusian Tartars, whose territories lay South of the Amoor, and bordered upon the
kingdom of Corea, and the province of Leaotong. They began to emerge
from

the fame hordes.   Accordingly the two great powers of
Ruffia and China, thus pointing their views to the fame
object, unavoidably claſhed; and, after feveral jealouſies
and intrigues, broke out into open hoſtilities about the
year 1680.   The Chineſe laid ſiege to Kamarſkoi Oſtrog,
and, though repulfed in this attempt, found means to cut
off feveral ftraggling parties of Ruffians.   Theſe animo-
fities induced the Tzar Alexèy Michaelovitch to ſend an
embaffy to Pekin ; but this meaſure did not produce the

Albaſin de-
ſtroyed by the
Chineſe.

deſired effect.   The Chineſe attacked Albaſin with a confiderable force :   having compelled the Ruffian garriſon
to capitulate, they demoliſhed that and all the Ruffian
forts upon the Amoor; and returned, with a large number of priſoners, to their own country.

Albaſin rebuilt
by the Ruffi-
ans, is beſieged
by the Chi-
neſe.

Not long after their departure, a body of ſixteen hundred Ruffians advanced along the Amoor; and conſtructed
a new fort, under the old name of Albaſin.   The Chineſe were no ſooner appriſed of their return, than they

from obſcurity at the beginning of the feventeenth century.   About that
time their chief Aiſchin-Giord reduced feveral neighbouring hordes;
and, having incorporated them with his own tribe, under the general
name of Manſhur, he became formidable even to the Chineſe. Shuntſchi,
grandſon of this chief, by an extraordinary concurrence of circumſtances,
was raiſed while an infant to the throne of China, of which his ſucceffors
ſtill continue in poffeffion.   Shuntſchi died in 1662, and was fucceeded
by Camhi, who is well known from the accounts of the jeſuit miſſion-
aries.
     For an account of the revolution of China, fee Duhalde Deſcr. de la
Chine, Bell's Journey to Pekin, and Fif. Sib. Gef. tom. I. p. 463.

marched

marched inftantly towards that river, and fat down before Albafin with an army of feven thoufand men, and
a large train of artillery. They battered the new fortrefs for feveral weeks, without being able to make a
breach, and without attempting to take it by ftorm. The
befieged, though not much annoyed by the unfkilful
operations of the enemy, were exhaufted with the complicated miferies of ficknefs and famine; and notwithftanding they continued to make a gallant refiftance,
they muft foon have funk under their diftreffes, if the
Chinefe had not voluntarily retired, in confequence of a
treaty being fet afoot between the two courts of Mofcow
and Pekin. For this purpofe the Ruffian embaffador
Golovin had left Mofcow fo early as the year 1685, accompanied by a large body of troops, in order to fecure
his perfon, and enforce refpect to his embaffy. The
difficulty of procuring fubfiftence for any confiderable
number of men in thofe defolate regions, joined to the
ruggednefs of the roads, and the length of the march,
prevented his arrival at Selenginfk until the year 1687.
From thence meffengers were immediately difpatched
with overtures of peace to the Chinefe government at
Pekin.

After feveral days, occafioned partly by policy, and
partly by the pofture of affairs in the Tartar country
through which the Chinefe were to pafs, embaffadors

4 left

left Pekin in the beginning of June 1689. Golovin
had propofed receiving them at Albafin; but while he
was proceeding to that fortrefs, the Chinefe embaffadors
prefented themfelves at the gates of Nerfhinfk, efcorted
by fuch a numerous army, and fuch a formidable train
of artillery, that Golovin was conftrained, from motives
of fear, to conclude the negotiation almoft upon their
own terms.

The conferences were held under tents, in an open
plain, near the town of Nerfhinfk; where the treaty
was figned and fealed by the plenipotentaries of the two
courts. When it was propofed to ratify it by oath, the
Chinefe embaffadors offered to fwear upon a crucifix;
but Golovin preferred their taking an oath in the name
of their own gods.

Treaty of
Nerfhinfk.

This treaty firft checked the progrefs of the Ruffian
arms in thofe parts; and laid the foundations of an important and regular commerce between the two nations.

By the firft and fecond articles, the South-Eaftern
boundaries of the Ruffian empire were formed by a
ridge of mountains, ftretching North of the Amoor
from the fea of Ochotfk to the fource of the fmall river
Gor-

Gorbitza*, then by that river to its influx into the
Amoor, and laftly by the Argoon, from its junction with
the Shilka up to its fource.

By the fifth article reciprocal liberty of trade was
granted to all the fubjects of the two empires, who fhould
be provided with tranfports from their refpective courts †.

This treaty was figned on the 27th of Auguft, in the
year 1689, under the reign of Ivan and Peter Alexie-
witch, by which the Ruffians loft, exclufively of a large
territory, the navigation of the river Amoor. The importance of this lofs was not at that time underftood;
and has only been felt fince the difcovery of Kamtchatka,
and of the iflands between Afia and America. The pro-
ducts of thefe new-difcovered countries might, by means
of the Amoor, have been conveyed by water into the
diftrict of Nerfhinfk, from whence there is an eafy

---

* There are two Gorbitzas; the firft falls into the Amoor, near the
conflux of the Argoon and Shilka; the fecond falls into the Shilka. The
former was meant by the Ruffians; but the Chinefe fixed upon the latter
for the boundary, and have carried their point. Accordingly the prefent
limits are fomewhat different from thofe mentioned in the text. They
are carried from the point, where the Shilka and Argoon unite to form
the Amoor, Weftward along the Shilka, until they reach the mouth of
the Weftern Gorbitza; from thence they are continued to the fource of
the laft-mentioned river, and along the chain of mountains as before. By
this alteration the Ruffian limits are fomewhat abridged.

† S. R. G. II. p. 435.

D d

transfport

tranſport by land to Kiachta: whereas the ſame merchandiſe, after being landed at Ochotſk, is now carried
over a large tract of country, partly upon rivers of difficult navigation, and partly along rugged and almoſt im-
paſſable roads.

Rife of the
Commerce
with China.

 In return, the Ruſſians obtained what they long and
repeatedly aimed at, a regular and permanent trade with
the Chineſe. The firſt intercourſe between Ruſſia and
China commenced in the beginning of the ſeventeenth
century *. At that period a ſmall quantity of Chineſe
merchandiſe was procured, by the merchants of Tomſk
and other adjacent towns, from the Calmucs. The rapid
and profitable ſale of theſe commodities encouraged
certain wayvodes of Siberia to attempt a direct and open
communication with China. For this purpoſe ſeveral
deputations were ſent at different times to Pekin from
Tobolſk, Tomſk, and other Ruſſian ſettlements: theſe
deputations, although they failed of obtaining the grant
of a regular commerce, were neverthleſs attended with
ſome important conſequences. The general good reception, which the agents met with, tempted the Ruſſian merchants to ſend occaſional traders to Pekin. By
theſe means a faint connection with that metropolis was
kept alive: the Chineſe learned the advantages of the

* S. R. G. VIII. p. 504, & ſeq.

Ruſſian

Ruffian trade, and were gradually prepared for its fubfequent eftablifhment. This commerce, carried on by
intervals, was entirely fufpended by the hoftilities upon
the river Amoor: but no fooner was the treaty of Nerfhinfk concluded, than the Ruffians engaged with extraordinary alacrity in this favourite branch of traffic. The
advantages of this trade were foon found to be fo confiderable, that Peter I. conceived an idea of ftill farther
enlarging it. Accordingly, in 1692, he fent Ifbrand
Ives, a Dutchman in his fervice, to Pekin, who requefted
and obtained, that the liberty of trading to China, which Caravans allowed to trade
by the late treaty was granted to individuals, fhould to Pekin.
be extended to caravans.

In confequence of this arrangement, fucceffive caravans went from Ruffia to Pekin, where a caravanfary
was allotted for their reception; and all their expences
during their continuance in that metropolis defrayed by
the Emperor of China. The right of fenuing thefe caravans, and the profits refulting from them, belonged to
the crown of Ruffia. In the mean time, private merchants continued as before to carry on a feparate trade
with the Chinefe, not only at Pekin, but alfo at the head
quarters of the Mongols. The camp of thefe roving
Tartars was generally to be found near the conflux of the
Orchon and Tola, between the Southern frontiers of
Siberia and the Mongol defert. A kind of annual fair

was

was held at this fpot by the Ruffian and Chinefe merchants: where they brought their refpective goods for
fale; and continued until they were difpofed of. This
rendezvous foon became a fcene of riots and confufion;
and repeated complaints were tranfported to the Chinefe
Emperor of the drunkennefs and mifconduct of the Ruffians. Thefe complaints made a ftill greater impreffion
from a coincidence of fimilar exceffes, for which the Ruffians at Pekin had become notorious.

Exafperated by the frequent reprefentations of his
fubjects, Camhi threatened to expell the Ruffians from
his dominions, and to prohibit them from carrying on
any commerce, as well in China as in the country of the
Mongols.

Embaffy of If-
mailoff to Pe-
kin.

Thefe untoward circumftances occafioned another
embaffy to Pekin in the year 1719. Leff Vaffilievitch
Ifmailoff, a captain of the Ruffian guards, who was fent
embaffador upon this occafion, fucceeded in the negotiation, and adjufted every difficulty to the fatisfaction
of both parties. At his departure he was permitted
to leave behind Laurence Lange, who had accompanied
him to Pekin, in the character of agent for the caravans;
for the purpofe of fuperintending the conduct of the Ruffians. His refidence however in that metropolis was but
fhort; for he was foon afterwards compelled, by the
Chinefe,

Chinefe, to return. His difmiffion was owing, partly, to a fudden caprice of that fufpicious people, and partly to a mifunderftanding, which had recently broke out between the two courts, in relation to fome Mongol tribes who bordered upon Siberia. A fmall number of thefe Mongols had put themfelves under the protection of Ruffia, and were immediately demanded by the Chinefe; but the Ruffians refufed compliance, under pretence that no article in the treaty of Nerfhinfk could, with any appearance of probability, be conftrued as extending to the Mongols. The Chinefe were incenfed at this refufal; and their refentment was ftill farther inflamed by the diforderly conduct of the Ruffian traders, who, freed from all controul by the departure of their agent, had indulged, without reftraint, their ufual propenfity to excefs. This concurrence of unlucky incidents extorted, in 1722, an order from Camhi for the total expulfion of the Ruffians from the Chinefe and Mongol territories. Thefe orders were rigoroufly executed; and all intercourfe between the two nations immediately ceafed.

Ruffians expelled from Pekin.

Affairs continued in this ftate until the year 1727, when the count Sava Vladiflavitch Ragufinfki, a Dalmatian in the fervice of Ruffia, was difpatched to Pekin. His orders were at all events to compofe the differences between the two courts relating to the Mongol tribes; to

Embaffy of Ragufinfki.

settle

settle the Southern frontiers of the Ruffian empire in that quarter; and to obtain the permiffion of renewing the trade with China. Accordingly that embaffador prefented a new plan for a treaty of limits and commerce to Yundfchin, fon and fucceffor of Camhi; by which the frontiers of the two empires were finally traced as they exift at prefent, and the commerce eftablished upon a permanent bafis, calculated to prevent as far as poffible all future fources of mifunderftanding. This plan being approved by the emperor, Chinefe commiffioners were immediately appointed to negotiate with the Ruffian embaffador upon the banks of the Bura, a fmall river which flows, South of the confines of Siberia, into the Orchon near its junction with the Selenga.

Treaty of
Kiachta.

At this conference, the old limits, fettled by the treaty of Nerfhinfk, were continued from the fource of the Argoon Weftwards as far as the mountain Sabyntaban, which is fituated at a fmall diftance from the fpot where the conflux of the two rivers Uleken and Kemtzak form the Yenifèi : this boundary feparates the Ruffian dominions from the territory of the Mongols, who are under the protection of China.

It was likewife ftipulated, that for the future all negotiations fhould be tranfacted between the tribunal of
foreign

foreign affairs at Pekin, and the board of foreign affairs at St. Peterſburg; or in matters of inferior moment between the two commanders of the frontiers*.

The moſt important articles relating to commerce, were as follow:

A caravan was allowed to go to Pekin every three years, on condition of its not confiſting of more than two hundred perſons; during their reſidence in that metropolis, their expences were no longer to be defrayed by the emperor of China. Notice was to be ſent to the Chineſe court immediately upon their arrival at the frontiers; where an officer was to meet and accompany them to Pekin.

Account of the Treaty relative to Commerce.

The privilege before enjoyed by individuals of carrying on a promiſcuous traffic in the Chineſe and Mongol territories was taken away; and no merchandize belonging to private perſons was permitted to be brought for ſale beyond the frontiers. For the purpoſe of preſerving, confiſtently with this regulation, the privilege of commerce to individuals, two places of reſort were

* This article was inſerted, becauſe the Chineſe emperor, from a ridiculous idea of ſuperiority, had contemptuouſly refuſed to hold any correſpondence with the court of Ruſſia.

appointed

appointed on the confines of Siberia: one called Kiachta, from a rivulet of that name near which it ftands;
and the other Zuruchaitu: at thefe places a free trade
was reciprocally indulged to the fubjects of the two
nations.

A permiffion was at the fame time obtained for
building a Ruffian church within the precincts of their
caravanfary; and for the celebration of divine fervice,
four priefts were allowed to refide at Pekin *. The
fame favour was alfo extended to fome Ruffian fcholars †,

* The firft Ruffian church at Pekin was built for the accommodation
of the Ruffians taken prifoners at Albafin. Thefe perfons were carried
to Pekin, and the place appointed for their habitation in that city was
called the Ruffian Street, a name it ftill retains. They were fo well received by the Chinefe, that, upon the conclufion of the treaty of Net-
fhinfk, they refufed to return to their native country. And as they
intermarried with the Chinefe women, their defcendants are quite natu-
ralized; and have for the moft part adopted not only the language, but
even the religion of the Chinefe. Hence, the above-mentioned church,
though it ftill exifts, is no longer applied to the purpofe of divine worfhip: its prieft was transferred to the church, which was built within
the walls of the caravanfary.

† The good effects of this inftitution have already been perceived.
A Ruffian, whofe name is Leontieff, after having refided ten years at Pekin, is returned to Peterfburg. He has given feveral tranflations and extracts of fome interefting Chinefe publications, viz. Part of the Hiftory of
China; the Code of the Chinefe Laws; Account of the Towns and Re-
venues, &c. of the Chinefe empire, extracted from a Treatife of Geography, lately printed at Pekin. A fhort account of this Extract is given
in the Journal of St. Petersburg for April, 1779.

                                                              for

for the purpofe of learning the Chinefe tongue : in order to qualify themfelves for interpreters between the
two nations.

This treaty, called the treaty of Kiachta, was, on the
fourteenth of June, 1728, concluded and ratified by the
count Ragufinfki and three Chinefe plenipotentaries upon
the fpot where Kiachta was afterwards built; it is the
bafis upon which all the fubfequent tranfactions between
Ruffia and China have been founded*.

One innovation in the mode of carrying on the trade
to China, which has been introduced fince the acceffion
of the prefent emprefs Catherine II. deferves to be mentioned in this place.   Since the year 1755 no caravans
have been fent to Pekin.   Their firft difcontinuance was Caravans dif-
continued.
occafioned by a mifunderftanding between the two courts
of Peterfburg and Pekin in 1759.   Their difufe after
the reconciliation had taken place arofe from the following circumftances.   The exportation and importation
of many principal commodities, particularly the moft
valuable furs, were formerly prohibited to individuals,
and folely appropriated to caravans belonging to the
crown.   By thefe reftrictions the Ruffian trade to China
was greatly fhackled and circumfcribed.   The prefent

* S. R. G. VIII. p. 513.

E e   emprefs

empreſs (who, amidſt many excellent regulations which characteriſe her reign, has ſhewn herſelf invariably attentive to the improvement of the Ruſſian commerce)

Monopoly of the Fur Trade aboliſhed. aboliſhed, in 1762, the monopoly of the fur trade; and renounced in favour of her ſubjects the excluſive privilege which the crown enjoyed of ſending caravans to Pekin*. By theſe conceſſions the profits of the trade have been conſiderably encreaſed: the great expence, hazard, and delay, of tranſporting the merchandiſe occaſionally from the frontiers of Siberia to Pekin, has been retrenched; and Kiachta is now rendered the center of the Ruſſian and Chineſe commerce.

* S. R. G. VIII. p. 520.

C H A P.

VIEW of the Chinese Frontier Town **MAI**

London; Published according to A...

N with the **BROOK KIACHTA**, *taken from the West.*)

1780 by J. Cadel in the Strand.

CHAP. III.

Account of the Ruffian *and* Chinefe *fettlements upon the* *confines of* Siberia——*defcription of the* Ruffian *frontier* *town* Kiachta——*of the* Chinefe *frontier town* Maimatf- chin——*its buildings, pagodas, &c.*

BY the laft mentioned treaty it was ftipulated, that the commerce between Ruffia and China fhould be tranfacted at the frontiers. Accordingly two fpots were marked out for that purpofe upon the confines of Siberia, where they border upon the Mongol defert; one near ^{Ruffian and Chinefe Settlement upon the Brook Kiachta.} the brook Kiachta, and the other at Zuruchaitu. The defcription of the former of thefe places fhall be the fub- ject of the prefent chapter.

This fettlement confifts of a Ruffian and Chinefe town, both fituated in a romantic valley, furrounded by high, rocky, and for the moft part well-wooded, moun- tains. This valley is interfected by the brook Kiachta, which rifes in Siberia, and, after wafhing both the Ruffian and Chinefe town, falls into the Bura, at a fmall diftance from the frontiers.

The Ruffian fettlement is called Kiachta from the ^{Situation of the Ruffian Fron tier Town Kiachta.} abovementioned brook: it lies in 124 degrees 18 mi-

E e 2   nutes

nutes longitude from the ifle of Fero, and 35 degrees N. latitude, at the diftance of 5514 verfts from Mofcow, and 1532 from Pekin.

The Fortrefs.

It confifts of a fortrefs and a fmall fuburb. The fortrefs, which is built upon a gentle rife, is a fquare enclofed with palifadoes, and ftrengthened with wooden baftions at the feveral angles. There are three gates, at which guards are conftantly ftationed: one of the gates faces the North, a fecond the South towards the Chinefe frontiers, and a third the Eaft clofe to the brook Kiachta. The principal public buildings in the fortrefs are a wooden church, the governor's houfe, the cuftom-houfe, the magazine for provifions, and the guard-houfe. It contains alfo a range of fhops and warehoufes, barracks for the garrifon, and feveral houfes belonging to the crown; the latter are generally inhabited by the principal merchants. Thefe buildings are moftly of wood.

Suburb.

The fuburb, which is furrounded with a wooden wall covered at the top with chevaux de frize, contains no more than an hundred and twenty houfes very irregularly built; it has the fame number of gates as the fortrefs, which are alfo guarded. Without this fuburb, upon the high road leading to Selenginfk, ftand a few houfes, and the magazine for rhubarb.

4

This

This fettlement is but indifferently provided with water both in quality and quantity ; for although the brook Kiachta is dammed up as it flows by the fortrefs, yet it is fo fhallow in fummer, that, unlefs after heavy rains, it is fcarcely fufficient to fupply the inhabitants. Its ftream is turbid and unwholefome, and the fprings which rife in the neighbourhood are either foul or brackifh : from thefe circumftances, the principal inhabitants are obliged to fend for water from a fpring in the Chinefe diftrict. The foil of the adjacent country is moftly fand or rock, and extremely barren. If the frontiers of Ruffia were extended about nine verfts more South to the rivulet of Bura; the inhabitants of Kiachta would enjoy good water, a fruitful foil, and plenty of fifh, all which advantages are at prefent confined to the Chinefe.

The garrifon of Kiachta confifts of a company of regular foldiers, and a certain number of Coffacs; the former are occafionally changed, but the latter are fixed inhabitants of the place. It is the province of the commander to infpect the frontiers, and, in conjunction with the prefident of the Chinefe merchants, to fettle all affairs of an inferior nature ; but in matters of importance recourfe muft be had to the chancery of Selenginfk, and to the governor of Irkutfk. The Ruffian merchants,

merchants, and the agents of the Ruffian trading company, are the principal inhabitants of Kiachta.

The limits Weftwards from this fettlement to the river Selenga, and Eaftwards as far as Tchikoi, are bounded with chevaux de frize, placed there to prevent a contraband trade in cattle, for the exportation of which a confiderable duty is paid to the crown. All the outpofts along the frontiers Weftwards as far as the government of Tobolfk, and Eaftwards to the mountains of fnow, are under the command of the governor of Kiachta.

The moft elevated of the mountains that furround the valley of Kiachta, and which is called by the Mongols Burgultei, commands the Ruffian as well as the Chinefe town; for this reafon, the Chinefe, at the conclufion of the laft frontier treaty, demanded the ceffion of this mountain, under the pretext that fome of their deified anceftors were buried upon its fummit. The Ruffians gave way to their requeft, and fuffered the boundary to be brought back to the North fide of the mountain.

Maimatfchin, the Chinefe Frontier-Town.

The Chinefe town is called, by the Chinefe and Mongols, Maimatfchin, which fignifies fortrefs of commerce. The Ruffians term it the Chinefe Village (Kitaifkaia Sloboda)

Sloboda) and alſo Naimatſchin, which is a corruption of Maimatſchin. It is ſituated about an hundred and forty yards South of the fortreſs of Kiachta, and nearly parallel to it. Midway between this place and the Ruſſian fortreſs, two poſts about ten feet high are planted in order to mark the frontiers of the two empires: one is inſcribed with Ruſſian, the other with Manſhur characters *.

Maimatſchin has no other fortification than a wooden wall, and a ſmall ditch of about three feet broad; the latter was dug in the year 1756, during the war between the Chineſe and the Calmucs. The town is of an oblong form: its length is about ſeven hundred yards, and its breadth four hundred. On each of the four ſides a large gate faces the principal ſtreets; over each of theſe gates there is a wooden guard-houſe for the Chineſe garriſon, which conſiſts of Mongols in tattered clothes, and armed with clubs. Without the gate, which looks to the Ruſſian frontiers, and about the diſtance of eight yards from the entrance, the Chineſe have raiſed a wooden ſcreen, ſo conſtructed as to intercept all view of the ſtreets from without.

* Upon the mountain to the Weſt of Kiachta, the limit is again marked; on the Ruſſian ſide by an heap of ſtones and earth, ornamented on the top with a croſs; and on the Chineſe by a pile of ſtones in the ſhape of a pyramid. Pallas Reiſe, P. III. p. 110.

This

This town contains two hundred houfes and about twelve hundred inhabitants. It has two principal ftreets of about eight yards broad, croffing each other in the middle at right angles, with two by-ftreets running from North to South. They are not paved, but are laid with gravel, and kept remarkably clean.

Houfes.

The houfes are fpacious, uniformly built of wood, of only one ftory, not more than fourteen feet high, plaiftered and white-wafhed; they are conftructed round a court yard of about feventy feet fquare, which is ftrewed with gravel, and has an appearance of neatnefs. Each houfe confifts of a fitting room, fome warehoufes, and a kitchen. In the houfes of the wealthier fort the roof is made of plank; but in meaner habitations of lath covered over with turf. Towards the ftreets moft of the houfes have arcades of wood projecting forwards from the roof like a penthoufe, and fupported by ftrong pillars. The windows are large after the European manner, but on account of the dearnefs of glafs and Ruffian talc are generally of paper, excepting a few panes of glafs in the fitting room.

The fitting room is feldom turned towards the ftreets; it is a kind of fhop, where the feveral patterns of merchandize are placed in receffes, fitted up with fhelves, and

and fecured with paper-doors for the purpofe of keeping
out the duft. The windows are generally ornamented
with little paintings, and the walls are hung with
Chinefe paper. Half the floor is of hard beaten
clay; the other half is covered with boards, and rifes
about two feet. Here the family fit in the day-time
and fleep at night. By the fide of this raifed part,
and nearly upon the fame level, there is a fquare brick
ftove, with a ftreight perpendicular cylindrical excava-
tion, which is heated with fmall pieces of wood. From
the bottom of this ftove a tube defcends, and is carried
zigzag under the boarded floor above-mentioned, and
from thence to a chimney which opens into the ftreet.
By this contrivance, although the ftove is always open
and the flame vifible, yet the room is never troubled
in the leaft degree with fmoke. There is fcarcely any
furniture in the room, excepting one large dining-table
in the lower part, and two fmall lackered ones upon
the raifed floor: one of thefe tables is always provided
with a chaffing-difh, which ferves to light their pipes
when the ftove is not heated.

In this room there are feveral fmall niches covered
with filken curtains, before which are placed lamps
that are lighted upon feftivals; thefe niches contain painted paper idols, a ftone or metal veffel, wherein
the afhes of incenfe are collected, feveral fmall orna-

F f   ments

ments and artificial flowers: the Chinese readily allow strangers to draw aside the curtains, and look at the idols.

The Bucharian * merchants inhabit the South West quarter of Maimatschin. Their houses are not so large nor commodious as those of the Chinese, although the greatest part of them carry on a very considerable commerce.

The Governor of Maimatschin.

The Surgutschei, or governor of Maimatschin, has the care of the police, as well as the direction of all affairs relating to commerce: he is generally a person of rank, oftentimes a Mandarin, who has misbehaved himself in another station, and is sent here as a kind of punishment. He is distinguished from the rest by the crystal button of his cap, and by a peacock's † fea-

* " The chief merchandizes which the Bucharians bring to Ruffia, " are cotton, stuffs, and half-silks, spun and raw cotton, lamb-skins, " precious stones, gold-dust, unprepared nitre, fal-ammoniac, &c." See Ruffia, or a complete Historical Account of all the nations that compose that Empire, V. II. p. 141, a very curious and interesting work lately published by Mr. Tooke.

† In China the princes of the blood wear three peacock's feathers; nobles of the highest distinction, two; and the lower class of the nobility, one. It is also a mark of high rank to keep a carriage with four wheels. The governor of Maimatschin rode in one with only two wheels. All the Chinese wear buttons of different colours in their caps, which also denote the rank. Pallas Reise, P. III. p. 126.

ther hanging behind. The Chinese give him the title of Amban, which signifies commander in chief; and no one appears before him without bending the knee, in which posture the person who brings a petition must remain until he receives the governor's answer. His salary is not large; but the presents which he receives from the merchants amount annually to a considerable sum.

The most remarkable public buildings in Maimatf-chin, are the governor's house, the theatre, and two pagodas.

The governor's house is larger than the others, and better furnished; it is distinguished by a chamber where the court of justice is held, and by two high poles before the entrance ornamented with flags. *House of the Governor.*

The theatre is situated close to the wall of the town near the great pagoda: it is a kind of small shed, neatly painted, open in front, and merely spacious enough to contain the stage; the audience stand in the street. Near it are two high poles, upon which large flags with Chinese inscriptions are hoisted on festivals. On such occasions the servants belonging to the merchants act short burlesque farces in honour of their idols. *Theatre.*

The

The small
Pagoda.

The Idol
Tien.

The fmalleft of the two Pagodas is a wooden building, ftanding upon pillars, in the centre of the town, at the place where the two principal ftreets crofs. It is a Chinefe tower of two ftories, adorned on the outfide with fmall columns, paintings, and little iron bells, &c. The firft ftory is fquare, the fecond octangular. In the lower ftory is a picture reprefenting the God Tien, which fignifies, according to the explanation of the moft intelligent Chinefe, the moft high God, who rules over the thirty-two heavens. The Manfhurs, it is faid, call this idol Abcho; and the Mongols, Tingheru heaven, or the Cod of heaven. He is reprefented fitting with his head uncovered, and encircled with a ray * of glory fimilar to that which furrounds the head of our Saviour in the Roman catholic paintings; his hair is long and flowing; he holds in his right hand a drawn fword, and his left is extended as in the act of giving a benediction. On one fide of this figure two youths, on the other a maiden and a grey-headed old man, are delineated.

* When Mr. Pallas obtained permiffion of the governor to fee this temple, the latter affured him that the Jefuits of Pekin and their converts adored this idol. From whence he ingenioufly conjectures, either that the refemblance between this idol, and the reprefentation of our Saviour by the Roman Catholicks, was the occafion of this affertion; or that the Jefuits, in order to excite the devotion of the converts, have, out of policy, given to the picture of our Saviour a refemblance to the Tien of the Chinefe. Pallas Reife, P. III. p. 119.

The

The upper ſtory contains the picture of another idol in a black and white checquered cap, with the ſame figures of three young perſons and a little old man. There are no altars in this temple, and no other ornaments except-ing theſe pictures and their frames. It is opened only on feſtivals, and ſtrangers cannot ſee it without permiſſion.

The great Pagoda *, ſituated before the governor's houſe, and near the principal gate looking to the South, is larger and more magnificent than the former. Strangers are allowed to ſee it at all times, without the leaſt difficulty, provided they are accompanied by one of the prieſts, who are always to be found in the area of the temple. This area is ſurrounded with chevaux de frize: the entrance is from the South through two gates with a ſmall building between them. In the inſide of this building are two receſſes with rails before them, be-hind which the images of two horſes as big as life are coarſely moulded out of clay; they are ſaddled and bridled, and attended by two human figures dreſſed like grooms: the horſe to the right is of a cheſnut colour, the other is dun with a black mane and tail, the former is in the

The great Pa-goda and its Idols.

* The great Pagoda is omitted in the engraving of Maimatſchin prefixed to this chapter; this omiſſion was owing to the artiſt's being obliged to leave Kiachta before he had time to finiſh the drawing. In every other reſpect, the view, as I was informed by a gentleman who has been on the ſpot, is complete, and repreſented with the greateſt exactneſs.

attitude

attitude of fpringing, the latter of walking.   Near each horfe a banner of yellow filk, painted with filver dragons, is difplayed.

In the middle of this area are two wooden turrets fur-rounded with galleries; a large bell of caft iron, which is ftruck occafionally with a large wooden mallet, hangs in the Eaftern turret; the other contains two kettle-drums of an enormous fize, fimilar to thofe made ufe of in the religious ceremonies of the Calmucs.   On each fide of this area are ranges of buildings inhabited by the priefts of the temple.

This area communicates by means of an handfome gateway with the inner court, which is bordered on each fide by fmall compartments open in front, with rails be-fore them; in the infide of thefe compartments the legendary ftories of the idols are exhibited in a feries of hiftorical paintings.   At the farther extremity of this court ftands a large building, conftructed in the fame ftyle of architecture as the temple.   The infide is fixty feet long and thirty broad: it is ftored with antient weapons, and inftruments of war of a prodigious fize; fuch as fpears, fcythes, and long pikes with broad blades, fhields, coats of arms, and military enfigns re-prefenting hands *, dragons heads, and other carved

---

* Thefe hands refemble the manipulary ftandards of the Romans.

figures.

figures. All thefe warlike inftruments are richly gilded, and ranged in order upon fcaffolds along the wall. Oppofite the entrance a large yellow ftandard, embroidered with foliage and filver dragons, is erected; under it, upon a kind of altar, there is a feries of little oblong tables, bearing Chinefe infcriptions.

An open gallery, adorned on both fides with flowerpots, leads from the back-door of the armoury to the colonade of the temple. In this colonade two flate tablets are placed, in wooden frames, about fix feet high and two broad, with long infcriptions relating to the building of the temple. Before one of thefe plates a fmall idol of an hideous form ftands upon the ground, enclofed in a wooden cafe.

The temple itfelf is an elegant Chinefe building, richly decorated on the outfide with columns, lackered and gilded carved-work, fmall bells, and other ornaments peculiar to the Chinefe architecture. Within there is a rich profufion of gilding, which correfponds with the gaudinefs of the exterior. The walls are covered thick with paintings, exhibiting the moft celebrated exploits of the principal idol.

This temple contains five idols of a coloffal ftature, fitting crofs-legged upon pedeftals in three receffes, which fill the whole Northern fide.

The

Gheffur Chan, the principal idol.

The principal idol is feated alone, in the middle receſs, between two columns ornamented with gilded dragons. Large ſtreamers of ſilk, hanging from the roof of the temple, veil in ſome meaſure the upper part of the image. His name is Ghedfur, or Gheffur Chan*; the Chineſe call him Loo-ye, or the firſt and moſt antient; and the Manſhurs, Guanlöe, or the ſuperior god. He is of a gigantic ſize, ſurpaſſing more than fourfold the human ſtature, with a face gliſtening like burniſhed gold, black hair and beard. He wears a crown upon his head, and is richly dreſſed in the Chineſe faſhion: his garments are not moulded out of clay, as thoſe of the other idols; but are made of the fineſt ſilk. He holds in his hands a kind of tablet, which he ſeems to read with deep attention. Two ſmall female figures, reſembling girls of about fourteen years of age, ſtand on

---

* The Mongols and Calmucs call him by this name of Gheffur Chan; and although they do not reckon him among their divinities, yet they conſider him as a great hero, the Bacchus and Hercules of Eaſtern Tartary, who was born at the ſource of the Koango, and who vanquiſhed many monſters. They have in their language a very long hiſtory of his heroical deeds. His title, in the Mongol tongue, is as follows: Arban Zeeghi Effin Gheffur Bogdo Chan: the king of the ten points of the compaſs, or the monarch Gheffur Chan.

I have in my poſſeſſion a copy of this manuſcript, containing the Hiſtory of Gheffur Chan; it is in the original Mongol language, and was a preſent to me from Mr. Pallas: I ſhould be very happy to communicate it to any perſon verſed in the Eaſtern languages.

each

each fide of the idol, upon the fame pedeftal; one of which grafps a roll of paper. At the right-hand of the idol lie feven golden arrows, and at his left a bow.

Before the idol is a fpacious enclofure, furrounded with rails, within which ftands an altar with four coloffal figures, intended probably to reprefent the principal mandarins of the deified Gheffur. Two of thefe figures are dreffed like judges, and hold before them fmall tablets, fimilar to that in the hands of the principal idol. The two other figures are accoutred in complete armour: one wears a turban; and carries, upon the left fhoulder, a large fword fheathed, with the hilt upwards. The other has an hideous copper-coloured face, a large belly, and grafps in his right-hand a lance with a broad blade.

Although all the remaining idols in the temple are of an enormous fize, yet they are greatly furpaffed in magnitude by Gheffur Chan.

The firft idol in the recefs to the right is called Maoo-ang, or the Otfchibanni of the Mongols. He has three ghaftly copper-coloured faces, and fix arms; two of his arms brandifh two fabres crofs-ways over the head; a third bears a looking-glafs, and a fourth a kind of fquare, which refembles a piece of ivory. The two remaining

Maooang.

G g

arms

arms are employed in drawing a bow, with an arrow laid upon it, ready to be difcharged. This idol has a mirror upon his breaft, and an eye in his navel : near it are placed two fmall figures; one holds an arrow, and the other a little animal.

Tfaudfing.

The next idol in the fame recefs is called by the Chinefe Tfaudfing, or the gold and filver god; and by the Mongols Tfagan-Dfambala. He wears a black cap, and is dreffed, after the Chinefe fafhion, in fumptuous robes of ftate; he bears in his hand a fmall jewel cafket. Near him alfo ftand two little figures, one of which holds a truncated branch.

Chufho.

In the recefs to the left is the god Chufho, called by the Manfhurs Chua-fchan, and by the Mongols Galdi, or the Fire God. He is reprefented with a frightful fiery reddifh face; clad in complete armour he wields a fword half-drawn out of the fcabbard, and feems as in the act of ftarting up from his feat. He is attended by two little halberdeers, one of whom is crying; and the other bears a fowl upon his hand, which refembles a feapheafant.

Niu-o.

The other idol in the fame recefs is the god of oxen, Niu-o. He appears to be fitting in a compofed pofture, is habited like a Mandarin, and diftinguifhed by a

4

crown

crown upon his head. He has, in common with the other idols, a mirror upon his breaft. The Chinefe imagine him to be the fame with the Yamandaga of the Mongols; and it is faid his Manfhurifh name is Chain Killova; his Mongol name, which relates to the hiftory of Gheffur, is Bars-Batir, the Hero of Tygers.

Before thefe feveral idols there are tables, or altars, on which cakes, paftry, dried fruit, and flefh, are placed on feftivals and prayer-days: on particular occafions even whole carcaffes of fheep are offered up. Tapers and lamps are kept burning day and night before the idols. Among the utenfils of the temple, the moft remarkable is a veffel fhaped like a quiver, and filled with flat pieces of cleft reed, on which fhort Chinefe devices are infcribed. Thefe devices are taken out by the Chinefe on new-year's day; and are confidered as oracles, which foretell the good or ill luck of the perfon, by whom they are drawn, during the following year. There lies alfo upon a table an hollow wooden black lackered helmet, which all perfons of devotion ftrike with a wooden hammer, whenever they enter the temple. This helmet is regarded with fuch peculiar awe, that no ftrangers are permitted to handle it, although they are allowed to touch even the idols themfelves.

The firft day of the new and full moon is appointed for the celebration of worfhip. Upon each of thofe days no Chinefe ever fails to make his appearance once in the temple; he enters without taking off his cap*, joins his hands before his face, bows five times to each idol, touches with his forehead the pedeftal on which the idol fits, and then retires. Their principal feftivals are held in the firft month of their year, which anfwers to February. It is called by them, as well as by the Mongols, the white month; and is confidered as a lucky time for the tranfaction of bufinefs; at that time they difplay flags before the temples, and place meat upon the tables of the idols, which the priefts take away in the evening, and eat in the fmall apartments of the interior court. On thefe folemnities plays are performed in the theatre, in honour of the idols: the pieces are generally of the fatyrical kind, and pointed againft unjuft magiftrates and judges.

Superftition of the Chinefe. But although the Chinefe have fuch few ceremonies in their fyftem of religious worfhip, yet they are remarkably infected with fuperftition. Mr. Pallas gives the following defcription of their behaviour at Maimatfchin during an eclipfe of the moon. At the clofe of the evening in which the eclipfe appeared, all the inhabitants feemed to vie with each other indefatigably in

* Among the Chinefe, as well as other Eaftern nations, it is reckoned a mark of difrefpect to uncover the head before a fuperior.

raifing

raifing an inceffant uproar, fome by hideous fhrieks, others by knocking wood, and beating cauldrons; the din was heightened by ftriking the bell and beating the kettle-drums of the great Pagoda. The Chinefe fuppofe, that during an eclipfe the wicked fpirit of the air, called by the Mongols Arachulla, is attacking the moon; and that he is frightened away by thefe hideous fhrieks and noifes. Another inftance of fuperftition fell under the obfervation of Mr. Pallas, while he was at Maimatfchin. A fire broke out in that town with fuch violence that feveral houfes were in flames. None of the inhabitants, however, attempted to extinguifh it; they ftood indeed in idle confternation round the fire; and fome of them fprinkled occafionally water among the flames, in order to footh the fire god, who, as they imagined, had chofen their houfes for a facrifice. Indeed if the Ruffians had not exerted themfelves in quenching the fire, the whole place would probably have been reduced to afhes *.

* This account of Kiachta and Maimatfchin is taken from Mr. Pallas's defcription of Kiachta, in the journal of his travels through Siberia, P. III. p. 109—126. Every circumftance relating to the religious worfhip of the Eaftern nations is in itfelf fo interefting, that I thought it would not be unacceptable to my readers to give a tranflation of the above paffages refpecting the Chinefe Pagodas and Idols; although in a work treating of the new difcoveries, and the commerce which is connected with them. In the abovementioned journal the ingenious author continues to defcribe from his own obfervations the manners, cuftoms, drefs, diet, and feveral other particulars relative to the Chinefe; which, although exceedingly curious and interefting, are too foreign to the immediate purpofe of thefe fheets to have been inferted in the prefent work.

No

No writer has placed the religion and history of the Tartar-nations in a more explicit point of view than Mr. Pallas; every page in his interesting journal affords striking proofs of this assertion. He has lately thrown new lights upon this obscure subject, in a recent publication concerning the Tartars, who inhabit parts of Siberia, and the territory which lies between that country and the Chinese-wall. Of this excellent work the first volume appeared in 1776, and contains the genealogy, history, laws, manners, and customs, of this extraordinary people, as they are divided into Calmucs, Mongols, and Burats. The second volume is expected with impatience, and will ascertain, with minuteness and accuracy, the tenets and religious ceremonies which distinguish the votaries of Shamanism from the followers of Dalai-Lama, the two great sects into which these tribes are distinguished. Pallas Samlung historischer Nachrichten ueber die Mongolischen Volkerschafter.

C H A P.

C H A P. IV.

Commerce between the Chinefe and Ruffians—lift of the principal exports and imports—duties—average amount of the Ruffian trade.

THE merchants of Maïmatfchin come from the Northern provinces of China, chiefly from Pekin, Nankin, Sandchue, and other principal towns. They are not fettled at this place with their wives and families: for it is a remarkable circumftance, that there is not one woman in Maïmatfchin. This reftriction arifes from the policy of the Chinefe government, which totally prohibits the women from having the flighteft intercourfe with foreigners. No Chinefe merchant engages in the trade to Siberia who has not a partner. Thefe perfons mutually relieve each other. One remains for a ftated time, ufually a year, at Kiachta; and when his partner arrives with a frefh cargo of Chinefe merchandize, he then returns home with the Ruffian commodities *.

Merchants of Maïmatfchin.

Moft of the Chinefe merchants underftand the Mongol tongue, in which language commercial affairs are

---

* Pallas Reife, P. III. p. 125.

generally

generally tranfacted. Some few indeed fpeak broken Ruffian, but their pronunciation is fo foft and delicate, that it is difficult to comprehend them. They are not able to pronounce the R, but inftead of it make ufe of an L; and when two confonants come together, which frequently occurs in the Ruffian tongue, they divide them by the interpofition of a vowel*. This failure in articulating the Ruffian language feems peculiar to the Chinefe, and is not obfervable in the Calmucs, Mongols ; and other neighbouring nations †.

The commerce between the Ruffians and Chinefe is entirely a trade of barter, that is, an exchange of one merchandize for another. The Ruffians are prohibited to export their own coin, nor indeed could the Chinefe

---

* Bayer, in his Mufeum Sinicum, gives feveral curious inftances of the Chinefe mode of articulating thofe founds, which they have not in their own language. For inftance they change BDRXZ into PTLSS.

Thus for Maria they fay Ma-li-ya ;

for crux,	cu-lū-fu ;
for baptizo,	pa-pe-ti-fo ;
for cardinalis,	kia-ul-fi-na-li-fu ;
for fpiritus,	fu-pi-li-tu-fu ;
for Adam,	va-tam ;
for Eva,	nge-va ;
for Chriftus,	ki-li-fu-tu-fu ;

Hoc, eft, corpus, meum——ho-ke, nge-fu-tu, co-ul-pu-fu, me-vum.

Bayer, Muf. Sin. Tom. I. p. 15.

† Pallas Reife, P. III. p. 134.

receive

receive it, even fhould that prohibition be taken off;
for no fpecie is current amongft them except bullion *.
And the Ruffians find it more advantageous to take
merchandize in exchange, than to receive bullion at
the Chinefe ftandard. The common method of tranf-
acting bufinefs is as follows. The Chinefe merchant
comes firft to Kiachta, and examines the merchandize he
has occafion for in the warehoufe of the Ruffian trader;

* The Chinefe have no gold or filver coin. Thefe metals are always
paid in bullion; and for the purpofe of afcertaining the weight, every
Chinefe merchant is conftantly provided with a pair of fcales. As gold
is very fcarce in China, filver is the great medium of commerce. When
feveral authors affirm that the Ruffians draw large quantities of filver
from China, they miftake an accidental occurrence for a general and
ftanding fact. During the war between the Chinefe and Calmucs, the
former had occafion to purchafe at Kiachta provifion, horfes, and camels,
for which they paid filver. This traffic brought fuch a profufion of that
metal into Siberia, that its price was greatly reduced below its real value.
A pound of filver was at that period occafionally fold at the frontiers for 8
or 9 roubles, which at prefent is worth 15 or 16. But fince the conclufion
of thefe wars by the total reduction of the Calmucs under the Chinefe
yoke, Ruffia receives a very fmall quantity of filver from the Chinefe.
S. R. G. III. p. 593 & feq.

The filver imported to Kiachta is chiefly brought by the Bucharian
merchants, who fell cattle to the Chinefe in exchange for that metal,
which they afterwards difpofe of to the Ruffians for European manufactures. Gold-duft is alfo occafionally obtained from the fame merchants; the quantity however of thofe metals procured at Kiachta is fo
inconfiderable, as fcarcely to deferve mention. The whole fum of gold
and filver imported to Kiachta, in 1777, amounted to only 18,215 roubles.
See p. 242.

H h

he

he then goes to the houfe of the latter, and adjufts the price over a difh of tea. Both parties next return to the magazine, and the goods in queftion are there carefully fealed in the prefence of the Chinefe merchant. When this ceremony is over, they both repair to Maimatfchin; the Ruffian choofes the commodities he wants, not forgetting to guard againft fraud by a ftrict infpection. He then takes the precaution to leave behind a perfon of confidence, who remains in the warehoufe until the Ruffian goods are delivered, when he returns to Kiachta with the Chinefe merchandize *.

Ruffian Exports.   The principal commodities which Ruffia exports to China are as follow:

FURS and PELTRY.

It would be uninterefting to enumerate all the furs and fkins † brought for fale to Kiachta, which form the moft important article of exportation on the fide of the Ruffians. The moft valuable of thefe firs are the fkins of fea-otters, beavers, foxes, wolves, bears, Bucharian lambs, Aftracan fheep, martens, fables, ermines, grey-fquirrels.

* Pallas Reife, P. III. p. 135.

† The lift of all the furs and fkins brought to Kiachta, with their feveral prices, is to be found in Pallas Reife, Part III. p. 136 to p. 142.

The

The greateſt part of theſe furs and ſkins are brought from Siberia and the New-diſcovered Iſlands : this ſupply however is not alone fully adequate to the demand of the market at Kiachta. Foreign furs are therefore imported to St. Peterſburg, and from thence ſent to the frontiers. England alone furniſhes a large quantity of beaver and other ſkins, which ſhe procures from Hudſon's Bay and Canada*.

CLOTH.

Cloth forms the ſecond article of exportation which Ruſſia exports to China.

* Liſt of furs ſent from England to Petersburg in the following years :

	Beaver-ſkins.	Otter-ſkins.
1775,	46460	7143
1776,	27700	12086
1777,	27316	10703

The fineſt Hudſon's beavers have been ſold upon an average at Petersburg, from   70— 90 roubles per 10 ſkins.

Inferior ditto and beſt Canada beavers from 50— 75

Young or cub-beavers from   20— 35

Beſt otter-ſkins from   90—100

Inferior ones from   60— 80

The qualities of theſe ſkins being very different occaſion great variations in the prices.

At Kiachta, the beſt Hudſon's Bay beaver is ſold from   —   —   7 to 20 roubles per ſkin.

Otter's ditto   —   —   6—35

Black foxes ſkins from Canada are alſo ſometimes ſent from England to Petersburg.

At Kiachta they fetch from 1 to 100 roubles per skin.

H h 2   The

The coarse sort is manufactured in Ruffia; the finer sort is foreign, chiefly English, Pruffian, and French.

An arshire of foreign cloth fetches, according to its fineness, from   2 to 4 roubles.

Camlets.

Calimancoes.

Druggets.

White flannels, both Ruffian and foreign.

The remaining articles are,

Rich stuffs.

Velvets.

Coarfe linen, chiefly manufactured in Ruffia.

Ruffia leather.

Tanned hides.

Glafs ware and looking glaffes.

Hardware, namely knives, fciffars, locks, &c.

Tin.

Ruffian talk.

Cattle, chiefly camels, horfes, and horned cattle.

The Chinefe alfo pay very dear for hounds, greyhounds, barbets, and dogs for hunting wild boars.

Provifions *.

---

* In the year 1772, the Chinefe purchafed meat at Kiachta, at the following prices:

A pound of beef 3¾ copecs.

lamb 2¼

Horfe-flesh for the Tartars ¼. Pallas Reife P. III.

Meal.

Meal. — The Chinese no longer import such large quantities of meal as formerly, since they have employed the Mongols to cultivate the lands lying near the river Orchon *, &c. &c.

List of the most valuable commodities procured from China.

RAW AND MANUFACTURED SILK.   Imports.

The exportation of raw silk is prohibited in China under pain of death : large quantities however are smuggled every year into Kiachta, but not sufficient to answer the demands of the Russian merchants.

A pood of the best sort is estimated at 150 roubles ;
          of the worst sort at   75
The manufactured silks are of various sorts, fashions, and prices, viz. sattins, taffaties, damasks, and gauzes, scanes of silk died of all colours, ribbands, &c. &c.

RAW AND MANUFACTURED COTTON.

Raw cotton is imported in very large quantities ; a great part of this commodity is employed in packing up the china ware, and by these means is conveyed into

* S. R. G. III. p. 495—571. Pallas Reise, P. III. p. 136—144.

the

the inland part of Ruffia without any additional expence of carriage.

A pood fells for — from 4 roubles, 80 cop. to 12.

Of the manufactured cotton, that which the Ruffians call Kitaika, and the Englifh Nankeen, has the moft rapid fale. It is the moft durable, and, in proportion to its goodnefs, the cheapeft of all the Chinefe ftuffs; it is ftained red, brown, green, and black.

T E A S.

The teas which are brought into Ruffia are much fuperior in flavour and quality to thofe which are fent to Europe from Canton. The original goodnefs of the teas is probably the fame in both cafes.: but it is conjectured, that the tranfport by fea confiderably impairs the aromatic flavour of the plant. This commodity, now become fo favourite an object of European luxury, is efteemed by the Ruffian merchants the moft profitable article of importation.

At Kiachta a pound of the beft tea * is
estimated at   —   —   2 roubles.

Common ditto at   1

Inferior at   —   —   40 copecs.

* At Petersburg a pound of the beft green tea fetches 3 roubles.

P O R C E-

PORCELAIN OF ALL SORTS.

For some years paft the Chinefe have brought to Kiachta, parcels of porcelain, painted with European figures, with copies of feveral favourite prints and images of the Grecian and Roman deities.

Furniture, particularly Japan cabinets and cafes, lackered and varnifhed tables and chairs, boxes inlaid with mother-of-pearl, &c. &c.

Fans, toys, and other fmall wares.

Artificial flowers.

Tiger and panther fkins.

Rubies *, but neither in large quantities nor of great value.

White lead, vermilion, and other colours.

Canes.

Tobacco.

Rice.

Sugar Candy,

Preferved ginger, and other fweetmeats.

Rhubarb †.

Mufk, &c. &c.

---

* Rubies are generally procured by fmuggling; and by the fame means, pearls are occafionally difpofed of to the Chinefe, at a very dear rate. Pearls are much fought for by the Chinefe; and might be made a very profitable article.

† See Appendix II.

It

It is very difficult to procure the genuine Thibet mufk, becaufe the Chinefe purchafe a bad fort, which comes from Siberia, with which they adulterate that which is brought from Thibet *.

Advantages of this Trade to Ruffia.

Ruffia derives great advantages from the Chinefe trade. By this traffic, its natural productions, and particularly its furs and fkins, are difpofed of in a very profitable manner. Many of thefe furs, procured from the moft eafterly parts of Siberia, are of fuch little value that they would not anfwer the expence of carriage into Ruffia; while the richer furs, which are fold to the Chinefe at a very high price, would, on account of their dearnefs, feldom meet with purchafers in the Ruffian dominions. In exchange for thefe commodities the Ruffians receive from China feveral valuable articles of commerce, which they would otherwife be obliged to buy at a much dearer rate from the European powers, to the great difadvantage of the balance of their trade.

I have before obferved, that formerly the exportation and importation of the moft valuable goods were prohibited to individuals; at prefent only the following articles are prohibited. Among the exports, fire-arms and artillery; gun-powder and ball; gold and filver, coined

* S. R. G. III. p. 572—592. Pallas Reife, P. III. p. 144—153.

and

and uncoined, ftallions and mares; fkins of deer, rein-deer, elks, and horfes; beaver's hair, potafh, rofin, thread, and * tinfel-lace: among the imports, falt, brandy, poifons, copper-money, and rhubarb.

The duties paid by the Ruffian merchants are very confiderable; great part of the merchandife is taxed at   25 per cent.

Furs, cattle, and provifions, pay a duty of 23.

Ruffian manufactures   18.

One per cent. is alfo deducted from the price of all goods for the expence of deepening the river Selenga; and 7 per cent for the fupport of the cuftom-houfe.

Some articles, both of export and import, pay no duty. The exported are, writing, royal, and poft paper, Ruffian cloth of all forts and colours, excepting peafants cloth. The imported are, fattins, raw and ftained cottons, porce-lain, earthen-ware, glafs corals, beads, fans, all mu-fical inftruments, furniture, lackered and enamelled or-naments, needles, white-lead, rice, preferved ginger, and other fweet-meats †.

---

* Tinfel lace is fmuggled to the Chinefe, with confiderable profit; for they pay nearly as much for it as if it was folid filver.

S. R. G. III. p. 588.

† Pallas Reife, P. lII. p. 154.

The importance of this trade will appear from the following table.

Table of exportation and importation at Kiachta, in the year 1777.

	Roubles.	Cop.
Cuftom-houfe duties,	481,460.	59½.
Importation of Chinefe goods, to the value of	1,466,497.	3¾.
Of gold and filver	18,215.	
Total of Importation	1,484,712.	3¾.
Exportation of Ruffian commodities	1,383,621.	35.

From this table it appears, that the total fum of export and import amounts to 2,868,333.

In this calculation however the contraband trade is not included, which is very large; and as the year 1777 was not fo favourable to this traffic as the preceding years*, we may venture to eftimate the grofs amount

* In the year 1770, 1771, 1772, the cuftom-houfe duties at Kiachta (according to Mr. Pallas, P. III. p. 154.) produced 550,000 roubles.

By

amount of the average trade to China at near 4,000,000 Roubles.

By taking therefore the medium between that sum and 481,460, the amount of the duties in 1777, the average sum of the duties will be 515,730; and, as the duties in 1777 make nearly a sixth of the whole sum of exportation and importation, by multiplying 515,730 by 6, we have the grofs amount of the average exports and imports at 3,094,380. But as feveral goods pay no duty, and as the contraband trade according to the loweft valuation is eftimated at the fifth part of the exports and imports, the grofs amount of the average trade to China may be fairly computed at near 4,000,000, the fum ftated above.

CHAP.

C H A P.   V.

Defcription of Zuruchaitu—and its trade—Tranfport of the merchandife through Siberia.

AS almoft the whole traffic between Ruffia and China is confined to Kiachta, the general account of that has been given in the preceding chapter. The defcription therefore of Zuruchaitu, the other place fixed upon by the treaty of Kiachta for the purpofe of carrying on the fame trade, will neceffarily be comprifed in a narrow compafs.

Defcription of Zuruchaitu.

Zuruchaitu is fituated in 137° longitude, and 49° 20' N. latitude, upon the Weftern branch of the river Argoon, at a fmall diftance from its fource. It is provided with a fmall garrifon, and a few wretched barracks furrounded with chevaux de frife. No merchants are fettled at this place; they come every fummer from Nerfhinfk, and other Ruffian towns, in order to meet two parties of Mongol troops: thefe troops are fent from the Chinefe towns Naun and Merghen, and arrive at the frontiers about July. They encamp near Zuruchaitu upon the other fide of the river Argoon, and barter with the

Siberian

Siberian merchants a few Chinefe commodities, which they bring with them.

Formerly the commerce carried on at Zuruchaitu was more confiderable; but at prefent it is fo trifling, that it hardly deferves to be mentioned. Thefe Mongols furnifh the diftrict of Nerfhinfk with bad tea and to- Commerce. bacco, bad filks, and fome tolerable cottons. They receive in return ordinary furs, cloth, cattle, and Ruffian leather. This trade lafts about a month or fix weeks, and the annual duties of the cuftoms amount upon an average to no more than 500 roubles. About the middle of Auguft the Mongols retire; part proceed immediately to China, and the others defcend the ftream of the Amoor as far as its mouth, in order to obferve if there has been no ufurpation upon the limits. At the fame time the Ruffian merchants return to Nerfhinfk, and, were it not for the fmall garrifon, Zuruchaitu would remain uninhabited *.

The Ruffian commodities are tranfported by land Tranfport of the Ruffian and Chinefe Commodities through Si- beria. from Peterfburg and Mofcow to Tobolfk. From thence the merchants fometimes embark upon the Irtifh down to its junction with the Oby; then they either tow up their boats, or fail up the laft mentioned river as far as

* S. R. G. III. p. 465. Pallas Reife, P. III. p. 428.

Narym,

Narym, where they enter the Ket, which they afcend to Makoffſkoi Oſtrog. At that place the merchandize is carried about ninety verſts by land to the Yeniſèi. The merchants then afcend that river, the Tunguſka, and Angara, to Irkutſk, crofs the lake Baikal, and go up the river Selenga almoſt to Kiachta.

It is a work of fuch difficulty to afcend the ſtreams of fo many rapid rivers, that this navigation Eaſtwards can hardly be finiſhed in one fummer *; for which reafon the merchants commonly prefer the way by land. Their general rendezvous is the fair of Irbit near To- bolſk ; from thence they go in ſledges during winter to Kiachta, where they arrive about February, the feafon in which the chief commerce is carried on with the Chinefe. They buy in their route all the furs they find in the fmall towns, where they are brought from the adjacent countries. When the merchants return in fpring with the Chinefe goods, which are of greater bulk and weight than the Ruffian commodities, they proceed by water : they then defcend the ſtreams of moſt of the rivers, namely, the Selenga, Angara, Tunguſka, Ket, and Oby to its junction with the Irtiſh ; they afcend that river to Tobolſk, and continue by land to Mofcow and Peterſburg.

* Some of thefe rivers are only navigable in fpring when the fnow water is melting ; in winter the rivers are in general frozen.

Before

Before the paſſage from Ochotſk to Bolchereſk was diſcovered in 1716, the only communication between Kamtchatka and Siberia was by land; and the road lay by Anadirſk to Yakutſk. The furs * of Kamtchatka and of the Eaſtern Iſles are now conveyed from that peninſula by water to Ochotſk; from thence to Yakutſk by land on horſe-back, or by rein-deer: the roads are ſo very bad, lying either through a rugged mountainous country, or through marſhy fo-reſts, that the journey laſts at leaſt ſix weeks. Yakutſk is ſituated upon the Lena, and is the principal town, where the choiceſt furs are brought in their way to Kiachta, as well from Kamtchatka as from the Northern parts of Siberia, which lie upon the rivers Lena, Yana, and Indigirka. At Yakutſk the goods are embarked upon the Lena, towed up the ſtream of that river as far as Vercholenſk, or ſtill farther to Katſheg; from thence they are tranſported over a ſhort tract of land to the rivulet Buguldeika, down that ſtream to the lake Baikal, acroſs that lake to the mouth of the Selenga, and up that river to the neighbourhood of Kiachta.

* The furs, which are generally landed upon the Eaſtern coaſt of Kamtchatka, are either ſent by ſea to Bolchereſk, or are tranſported acroſs the peninſula in ſledges drawn by dogs. The latter conveyance is only uſed in winter: it is the common mode of travelling in that coun-try. In ſummer there is no conveyance, as the Peninſula contains nei-ther oxen, horſes, or rein-deer. S. R. G. III. p. 478.

In

In order to give the reader fome notion of that vaft tract of country, over which the merchandize is frequently tranfported by land-carriage, a lift of the diftances is here fubjoined.

From Peterfburg to Mofcow		734 verfts.
Mofcow to Tobolfk	—	2385
Tobolfk to Irkutfk	—	2918
Irkutfk to Kiachta	—	471
		6508

From Irbit to Tobolfk	—	420

From Irkutfk to Nerfhinfk		1129
Nerfhinfk to Zuruchaitu		370

From Ochotfk to Yakutfk	—	927
Yakutfk to Irkutfk	—	2433

From Selenginfk to Zuruchaitu		850
Zuruchaitu to Pekin	—	1588
Kiachta to Pekin	—	1532

The Chinefe tranfport their goods to Kiachta chiefly upon camels. It is four or five days journey from Pekin to the wall of China, and forty-fix from thence acrofs the Mongol defert to Kiachta*.

* Pallas Reife, P. III. p. 134.

3   PART

PART III.

APPENDIX I. & II.

CONTAINING

SUPPLEMENTARY ACCOUNTS

OF THE

RUSSIAN DISCOVERIES, &c. &c.

K k

APPENDIX I.

Extract from the journal of a voyage made by Captain Krenitzin and Lieutenant Levasheff to the Fox Islands, in 1768, 1769, by order of the Empress of Russia— they sail from Kamtchatka—arrive at Beering's and Copper Islands—reach the Fox Islands—Krenitzin winters at Alaxa—Levasheff upon Unalashka—productions of Unalashka—description of the inhabitants of the Fox Islands—their manners and customs, &c.

ON the 23d of July Captain Krenitzin sailed in the Galliot St. Catherine from the mouth of the Kamtchatka river towards America: he was accompanied by Lieutenant Levasheff, in the Hooker St. Paul. Their instructions were regulated by information derived from Beering's expedition in 1741. Shaping their course accordingly, they found themselves more to the North than they expected; and were told by the Russian traders and hunters, that a similar * mistake was com-

Krenitzin and Levasheff sail from the Mouth of the Kamtchatka River, 1768.

---

* This passage is obscurely expressed. Its meaning may be ascertained by comparing Krenitzin's chart with that of Beering's voyage prefixed to Muller's account of the Russian Discoveries. The route of Krenitzin's vessel was considerably to the North of the course held by Beering and Tschirikoff, and consequently he sailed through the middle of what they had supposed to be a continent, and which he found to be an open sea. See Robertson's History of America, p. 461; and p. 26, of this work.

mitted

mitted in the chart of that expedition. Thefe traders, who for fome years paft were accuftomed to ramble to the diftant iflands in queft of furs, faid that they were fituated much more to the South, and farther Eaft, than **They reach Beering's Ifland;** was imagined. On the 27th they faw Commodore's or Beering's Ifland, which is low and rocky, efpecially to the S. W. On this fide they obferved a fmall harbour, diftinguifhed by two hillocks like boats, and not far from it they found a frefh-water lake.

and Copper Ifland. To the S. E. lies another ifland, called by the Ruffians Mednoi Oftroff, or Copper Ifland, from a great quantity of copper found upon its N. E. coaft, the only fide which is known to the Ruffians. It is wafhed up by the fea, and covers the fhore in fuch abundance, that many fhips may load with it. Perhaps an India trader might make a profitable voyage from thence to China, where this metal is in high demand. This copper is moftly in a metallic or malleable ftate, and many pieces feem as if they had formerly been in fufion. The ifland is not high, but has many hillocks, each of which has the appearance of having formerly been the funnel of a volcano. We may here, once for all, obferve, that all the iflands reprefented in this chart * abound with fuch funnels, called in Ruffian Sopka, in fo much that no ifland, however fmall, was found without one; and

* Namely, the chart prefixed to this journal.

many

many of them confifted of nothing elfe. In fhort, the chain of Iflands here laid down may, without any violent ftretch of imagination, be confidered as thrown up by fome late volcanos. The apparent novelty of every thing feems to juftify this conjecture: nor can any objection be derived from the vegetable productions with which thefe iflands abound; for the fummer after the lower diftrict of Zutphen in Holland was gained from the fea, it was covered over with wild muftard. All thefe lands are fubject to violent and frequent earthquakes, and abound in fulphur. The writer of the journal was not able to inform us whether any lava was found upon them; but he fpeaks of a party-coloured ftone as heavy as iron. From this account it is by no means improbable, that the copper above-mentioned has been melted in fome eruption.

After leaving Copper Ifland, no land was feen from either of the fhips (which had parted company in a fog) till, on the S. E. quarter of their track, was difcovered the chain of iflands or head-lands laid down in the chart. Thefe in general appeared low, the fhore bad, without creeks, and the water between them very fhallow. During their courfe outwards, as well as during their return, they had frequent fogs. It appears from the journal, as well as from the relation of the hunters, that

[marginal note: Arrive at the Fox Iflands.]

that it is very uncommon to have clear weather for five days together, even during fummer.

The St. Catherine wintered in the ftraits of Alaxa, where they hauled her into fhoal water. The inftructions given to the captain fet forth, that a private fhip had in 1762 found there a commodious haven; but he looked for it in vain. The entrance of this ftrait from the N. E. was extremely difficult on account of flats, and ftrong currents both flood and ebb: the entrance however from the S. E. was afterwards found to be much eafier with not lefs than 5½ fathoms water. Upon furvey-ing this ftrait, and the coaft of Alaxa, many fun-nels were obferved in the low grounds clofe to the fhore, and the foil produced few plants. May not this allow one to fuppofe that the coaft had fuffered confiderable changes fince the year 1762? Few of the iflands produce wood, and that only in the vallies by the rivulets. Unalga and Alaxa contain the moft; they abound with frefh water ftreams, and even rivers; from which we may infer that they are extenfive. The foil is in general boggy, and covered with mofs; but Alaxa has more foil, and produces much grafs.

The St. Paul wintered in Unalafhka. This wintering place was obferved to lie in 53° 29′ North latitude, and its longitude from the mouth of Kamtchatka river,

com-

computed by the ſhip's journal, was 27° 05' Eaſt *.   Unalaſhka is about fifty miles long from N. E. to S. W.
and has on the N. E. ſide three bays.   One of them,
called Udagha, ſtretches thirty miles E. N. E. and
W. S. W. nearly through the middle of the iſland.
Another called Igunok, lying N. N. E. and S. S. W.
is a pretty good harbour, with three and a half fathom
water at high tide, and ſandy ground.   It is well ſhel-
tered from the North ſwell at its entrance by rocks,
ſome of which are under water.   The tide flows here
five feet at full and change, and the ſhore is in general
bold and rocky, except in the bay, at the mouth of a
ſmall river.   There are two burning mountains on this
iſland, one called Ayaghiſh, and the other (by the Ruſſians) the Roaring Mountain.   Near the former is a
very copious hot ſpring.   The land is in general rocky,
with loamy and clayey grounds; but the graſs is extremely coarſe, and unfit for paſture.   Hardly any wood
is to be found on it.   Its plants are dwarf cherry († Xy- Productions of
Unalaſhka.
loſteum of Tournefort), wortle berry (Vaccinium Uliginoſum of Linnæus), raſberry, ſarana and ſhikſhu of
Kamtchatka and kutage, larch, white poplar, pine, and

* According to the general map of Ruſſia, the moutn or the Kamtchatka river is in 178° 25' from Fero.   Unalaſhka therefore, according
to this eſtimation, is 205° 30' from Fero, or 187° 55' 15" from Greenwich.

† The Lonicera Pyrenaica of Linnæus.   It is not a dwarf cherry,
but a ſpecies of honeyſuckle.

                                                          birch.

birch *.   The land animals are foxes of different colours, mice, and weafels; there are alfo beavers †, fea
cats, and fea lions, as at Kamtchatka.   Among their fifh
we may reckon cod, perch, pilchards, fmelts, roach,
needle fifh, terpugh, and tchavitcha.   The birds are
eagles, partridges, ducks, teals, urili, ari, and gadi.
The animals, for whofe Ruffian names I can find no
tranflations, are (excepting the Ari) defcribed in Krafhi-
ninikoff's Hiftory of Kamtchatka, or in Steller's relation
contained in the fecond volume of the Memoirs of the
Academy of St. Peterfburg.

Account of the
Inhabitants of
the Fox
Iflands.

The inhabitants of Alaxa, Umnak, Unalafhka, and
the neighbouring iflands, are of a middle ftature, tawny
brown colour, and black hair.   In fummer they wear
coats (parki ‡) made of bird fkins, over which, in bad
weather, and in their boats, they throw cloaks, called
kamli, made of thin whale guts.   On their heads they
wear wooden caps, ornamented with duck's feathers,

---

* All the other journalifts uniformly defcribe Unalafhka as containing
nothing but underwood; we muft therefore fuppofe that the trees here
mentioned were very low and fmall; and this agrees with what goes before,
" hardly any wood is to be found on it."

† By beavers the journalifts certainly mean fea-otters, called by the
Ruffians fea-beavers. See p. 12.

‡ Parki in Ruffian fignifies a fhirt, the coats of thefe iflanders being
made like fhirts.

3

and the ears of the sea-animal, called Scivutcha or sea-lion ; they also adorn these caps with beads of different colours, and with little figures of bone or stone. In the partition of the nostrils they place a pin, about four inches long, made of bone, or of the stalk of a certain black plant ; from the ends of this pin or bodkin they hang, in fine weather and on festivals, rows of beads, one below the other. They thrust beads, and bits of pebble cut like teeth, into holes made in the under-lips. They also wear strings of beads in their ears, with bits of amber, which the inhabitants of the other islands procure from Alaxa, in exchange for arrows and kamli.

They cut their hair before just above the eyes, and some shave the top of their heads like monks. Behind the hair is loose. The dress of the women scarcely differs from that of the men, excepting that it is made of fish-skins. They sew with bone needles, and thread made of fish guts, fastening their work to the ground before them with bodkins. They go with the head uncovered, and the hair cut like that of the men before, but tied up behind in a high knot. They paint their cheeks with strokes of blue and red, and wear nose-pins, beads, and ear-rings like the men ; they hang beads round their neck, and checkered strings round their arms and legs.

L l   In

In their perfons we fhould reckon them extremely nafty. They eat the vermin with which their bodies are covered, and fwallow the mucus from the nofe. Having wafhed themfelves, according to cuftom, firft with urine, and then with water, they fuck their hands dry. When they are fick, they lie three or four days without food ; and if bleeding is neceffary, they open a vein with lancets made of flint, and fuck the blood.

Their principal nourifhment is fifh and whale fat, which they commonly eat raw. They alfo feed upon fea-wrack and roots, particularly the faran, a fpecies of lily ; they eat an herb, called kutage, on account of its bitternefs, only with fifh or fat. They fometimes kindle fire by catching a fpark among dry leaves and powder of fulphur : but the moft common method is by rubbing two pieces of wood together, in the manner practifed at Kamtchatka*, and which Vakfel, Beering's lieutenant, found to be in ufe in that part of North America which he faw in 1741. They are very fond of Ruffian oil and butter, but not of bread. They could not be pre-

---

* The inftrument made ufe of by the Kamtchadals, to procure fire, is a board with feveral holes in it, and a ftick ; the latter is put into the holes, and turned about fwiftly, until the wood within the holes begins to burn, and the fparks fall upon the tinder placed in fuch a manner as to receive them.

vailed

vailed upon to tafte any fugar until the commander
fhewed the example; finding it fweet, they put it up
to carry it home to their wives.

The houfes of thefe iflanders are huts built precifely
in the manner of thofe in Kamtchatka, with the entry
through a hole in the middle of the roof. In one of
thefe huts live feveral families, to the amount of thirty
or forty perfons. They keep themfelves warm by
means of whale fat burnt in fhells, which they place
between their legs. The women fit apart from the
men.

Six or feven of thefe huts or yourts make a village,
of which there are fixteen in Unalafhka. The iflands
feem in general to be well inhabited, as may be conjectured from the great number of boats which are feen
continually plying along the fhore. There are upwards
of a thoufand inhabitants on Unalafhka, and they fay
that it was formerly much more populous. They have
fuffered greatly by their difputes with the Ruffians, and
by a famine in the year 1762; but moft of all from
a change in their way of life. No longer contented
with their original fimplicity, they long for Ruffian
luxuries: in order therefore to obtain a few delicacies,
which are prefently confumed, they dedicate the greateft
part of their time to hunting, for the purpofe of pro-

L l 2   curing

curing furs for the Ruffians: by thefe means, they neglect to lay up a provifion of fifh and roots; and fuffer their children frequently to die of hunger.

Their principal food is fifh, which they catch with bone hooks. Their boats, in which they row to a great diftance from land, are made, like thofe of the Innuet or Efquimaux, of thin flips of wood and fkins: thefe fkins cover the top as well as the fides of the boat, and are drawn tight round the waift of the rower. The oar is a paddle, broad at both ends. Some of their boats hold two perfons; one of whom rows, and the other fifhes: but this kind of boats feem appropriated to their chiefs. They have alfo large boats capable of holding forty men. They kill birds and beafts with darts made of bone, or of wood tipped with fharpened ftone: they ufe thefe kind of darts in war, which break with the blow given by them, and leave the point in the wound.

The manners and character of thefe people are what we fhould expect from their neceffitous fituation, extremely rude and favage. The inhabitants however of Unalafhka are fomewhat lefs barbarous in their manners and behaviour to each other, and alfo more civil to ftrangers than the natives of the other iflands; but

even

even the former are engaged in frequent and bloody quarrels, and commit murder without the leaft compunction. Their difpofition engages them in continual wars, in which they always endeavour to gain their point by ftratagem. The inhabitants of Unimak are formidable to all the reft; they frequently invade the other iflands, and carry off women, the chief object of their wars. Alaxa is moft fubject to thefe incurfions, probably becaufe it is more populous and extenfive. They all agree in hating the Ruffians, whom they confider as general invaders, and therefore kill them whereever they can. The people of Unalafhka however are more friendly; for Lieutenant Levafheff, being informed that there was a Ruffian veffel in the ftraits of Alaxa, prevailed on fome Unalafhkans to carry a letter, which they undertook, notwithftanding the danger they were expofed to from the inhabitants of the intervening iflands.

The journalift fays, that thefe people have no kind of religion, nor any notion of a God. We obferve however among them fufficient marks of fuch a religion as might be expected from people in their fituation. For the journalift informs us, that they have fortunetellers employed by them at their feftivals. Thefe perfons pretend to foretel events by the information of the Kugans or Dæmons. In their divinations they put on
wooden

wooden mafks, made in the form in which they fay the Kugan appeared to them; they then dance with violent motions, beating at the fame time drums covered with fifh fkins. The inhabitants alfo wear little figures on their caps, and place others round their huts, to keep off the devils. Thefe are fufficient marks of a favage religion.

It is common for them to have two, three, or four wives, and fome have alfo an object of unnatural affection, who is dreffed like the women. The wives do not all live together, but, like the Kamtchadals, in different yourts. It is not unufual for the men to exchange their wives, and even fell them, in time of dearth, for a bladder of fat; the hufband afterwards endeavours to get back his wife, if fhe is a favourite, and if unfuccefsful he fometimes kills himfelf. When ftrangers arrive at a village, it is always cuftomary for the women to go out to meet them, while the men remain at home: this is confidered as a pledge of friendfhip and fecurity. When a man dies in the hut belonging to his wife, fhe retires into a dark hole, where fhe remains forty days. The hufband pays the fame compliment to his favourite wife upon her death. When both parents die, the children are left to fhift for themfelves. The Ruffians found many in this fituation, and fome were brought for fale.

In

In each village there is a fort of chief called Tookoo: he decides differences by arbitration, and the neighbours enforce the fentence. When he goes out to fea he is exempt from working, and has a fervant, called Kalè, for the purpofe of rowing the canoe ; this is the only mark of his dignity: at all other times he labours like the reft. The office is not hereditary ; but is generally conferred on him who is moft remarkable for his perfonal qualities ; or who poffeffes a great influence by the number of his friends. Hence it frequently happens, that the perfon who has the largeft family is chofen.

During their feftivals, which are held after the fifhing feafon ends in April, the men and women fing fongs ; the women dance fometimes fingly, and fometimes in pairs, waving in their hands blown bladders ; they begin with gentle movements, which become at laft extremely violent.

The inhabitants of Unalafhka are called Kogholaghi. Thofe of Akutan, and farther Eaft to Unimak, are called Kighigufi ; and thofe of Unimak and Alaxa are called Kataghayekiki. They cannot tell whence they have thefe names, and now begin to call themfelves by the general name of Aleyut, given them by the Ruffians,

4   and

and borrowed from fome of the *Kuril iflands.   Upon
being afked concerning their origin, they faid that they
had always inhabited thefe iflands, and knew nothing of
any other country beyond them.   All that could be ga-
thered from them was, that the greateft numbers came
from Alaxa, and that they did not know whether that
land had any bounds.   The Ruffians furveyed this ifland
very far to the N. E. in boats, being out about a fort-
night, and fet up a crofs at the end of their furvey.   The
boats of the iflanders are like thofe of the Americans.   It
appears however from their cuftoms and way of life, fo
far as thefe are not neceffarily prefcribed to them by
their fituation, that they are of Kamtchadal original.
Their huts, their manner of kindling fire, and their objects of unnatural affections, lead to this conjecture.   Add
to this, the almoft continual Wefterly winds, which muft
render the paffage Weftward extremely difficult.   Beering
and Tchirikoff could never obtain Eafterly winds but by
going to the Southward.

The Ruffians have for fome years paft been accuftomed
to go to thefe iflands in queft of furs, of which they
have impofed a tax on the inhabitants.   The manner of
carrying on this trade is as follows.   The Ruffian traders
go in Autumn to Beering's and Copper Ifland, and there
winter: they then employ themfelves in catching the

* I cannot find, that any of the Kuril Ifles are called Aleyut in the
catalogue of thofe iflands given by Mr. Muller, S. R. G. III. p. 86—92.
Neither are any of them laid down under that name in the Ruffian charts.

fea-cat, and afterwards the Scivutcha, or fea-lion. The flefh of the latter is prepared for food, and it is very delicate. They carry the fkins of thefe fea-animals to the Eaftern iflands. Next fummer they go Eaftward, to the Fox-iflands; and again lay their fhips up for the winter. They then endeavour to procure, either by perfuafion or force, the children of the inhabitants, particularly of the Tookoos, as hoftages. This being accomplifhed, they deliver to the inhabitants fox-traps, and alfo fkins for their boats, for which they oblige them to bring furs and provifions during the winter. After obtaining from them a certain quantity of furs, by way of tax, for which they give them quittances; the Ruffians pay for the reft in beads, falfe pearls, goat's wool, copper kettles, hatchets, &c. In the fpring they get back their traps, and deliver up their hoftages. They dare not hunt alone, nor in fmall numbers, on account of the hatred of the natives. Thefe people could not, for fome time, comprehend for what purpofe the Ruffians impofed a tribute of fkins, which were not to be their own property, but belonged to an abfent perfon; for their Tookoos have no revenue. Nor could they be made to believe, that there were any more Ruffians than thofe who came among them; for in their own country all the men of an ifland go out together. At prefent they comprehend fomething of Kamtchatka, by means of the Kamtchadals and Koriacs who come with the Ruffians; and on their arrival love

M m to

to affociate with people whofe manner of life refembles their own.

Krenitzin and Levafheff returned from this expedition into the mouth of Kamtchatka river in autumn 1769.

The chart which accompanies this journal was com- pofed by the pilot Jacob Yakoff, under the infpection of the commanders * Krenitzin and Levafheff. The track of the St. Paul is marked both in going out and return- ing. The harbour of the St. Paul in the ifland Una- lafhka, and the ftraits of Alaxa, are laid down from obfervations made during the winter 1768; and the iflands connected by bearings and diftances taken during a cruife of the St. Paul twice repeated.

In this chart the variation is faid to be

In Lat.	Long.		Points
54° 40′.	204.		2 Eaft.
52 20	201		$1\frac{1}{2}$
52 50	198		$1\frac{1}{2}$
53 20	192	30	1
53 40	188		1
54 50	182	30	$0\frac{3}{4}$
55 00	180	30	$0\frac{3}{4}$

But the arrows in the compafs imply that the variation is *Weft*; probably the miftake is in the arrows.

* Krenitzin was drowned foon after his return to Kamtchatka in a canoe belonging to the natives.

N°

N° II.

oncerning the longitude of Kamtchatka, *and of the Eaſtern extremity of* Aſia, *as laid down by the* Ruſſian *Geographers.*

THE important queſtion concerning the longitude Longitude of the extreme Parts of Aſia; of the extreme parts of Aſia has been ſo differently ſtated by the moſt celebrated geographers, that it may not be amiſs to refer the curious reader to the principal treatiſes upon that ſubject. The proofs by which Mr. Muller and the Ruſſian geographers place the by Mr. Muller and the Ruſſian Geographers; longitude of the Eaſtern extremity of Aſia beyond 200 degrees from the firſt meridian of Fero, or 180° 6′ 15″ from Paris, are drawn from the obſervations of the ſatellites of Jupiter, made by Kraſſilnikoff at Kamtchatka, and in different parts of Siberia, and from the expeditions of the Ruſſians by land and ſea towards Tſchukotſkoi Noſs.

Mr. Engel calls in queſtion the exactneſs of theſe by Mr. Engel. obſervations, and takes off twenty-nine degrees from the

longitude

longitude of Kamtchatka, as laid down by the Ruffians. To this purpofe he has given to the public,

1. Memoires et obfervations geographiques et critiques fur la fituation des Pays Septentrionaux de l'Afie et de l'Amerique.   A Laufanne, 1765.

2. Geographifche und Critifche Nachricht ueber die Lage der noerdlichen Gegenden von Afien und America. Mittau, 1772.

by Mr. Vau-
gondy. It appears to Monfieur de Vaugondy, that there are not fufficient grounds for fo extraordinary a diminution: accordingly he fhortens the continent of Afia only eleven degrees of longitude; and upon this fubject he has given the two following treatifes:

1. Lettre au fujet d'une carte fyftematique des Pays Septentrionaux de l'Afie et de l'Amerique.   Paris, 1768.

2. Nouveau fyfteme geographique, par lequel on concilie les anciennes connoiffances fur les Pays au Nord Oueft de l'Amerique.   Paris, 1774.

Monf. Buache
fupports the
Syftem of the
Ruffians
againft Engel
and Vaugondy. In oppofition to thefe authors, Monfieur Buache has publifhed an excellent treatife, entitled Memoires fur les Pays de l'Afie et de l'Amerique.   Paris, 1775.

In

In this memoir he diffents from the opinions of Meffrs Engel and Vaugondy; and defends the fyftem of the Ruffian geographers in the following manner. Monfieur Maraldi, after comparing the obfervations of the fatellites of Jupiter, taken at Kamtchatka by Kraf-filnikoff, with the tables, has determined the longitude of Ochotfk, Bolcherefk, and the port of St Peter and Paul, from the firft meridian of Paris as follows:

	h	′	″
* Longitude of Ochotfk	9	23	30
of Bolcherefk	10	17	17
of the Port	10	25	5

Latitude of Ochotfk 59° 22′, of Bolcherefk 52° 55′, of the Port 53° 1′.

The

* Kraffilnikoff compared his obfervations with correfponding ones taken at Peterfburg, which gave refults as follow:

From comparing an obfervation of an eclipfe of the firft fatellite, taken at Ochotfk the 17th of January, 1743, with an obfervation of an eclipfe of the fame fatellite taken at Peterfburg on the 15th of January in the fame year, the difference of longitude between Petersburg and Ochotfk appeared to be 7ʰ 31′ 29″; from a comparifon of two other fimilar obfervations the difference of longitude was 7ʰ 31′ 34″, a mean of which (rejecting the ¼ fecond) is 7ʰ 31′ 31″, being the true difference between the meridians of Petersburg and Ochotfk according to thefe obfervations. By adding the difference of the longitude between Petersburg and Paris, which is 1ʰ 52′ 25″, we have the longitude of Ochotfk from Paris 7ʰ 23′ 56″, which differs only 26″ from the refult of Monf. Maraldi. Nov. Comm. Pet. III. p. 470.

In

APPENDIX I.

The comparifon of the following refults, deduced from correfponding obfervations * of the eclipfes of Jupiter's fatellites taken at Bolcherefk and at the port of Peter and Paul by Kraffilnikoff, and at Pekin by the Jefuit miffionaries, will fhew from their near agreement the care and attention which muft have been given to the obfervations; and from hence there is reafon to fuppofe, that the fufpicions of inaccuracy imputed to Kraffilnikoff are ill founded.

1741, Old Stile.

	h	′	″	
Jan. 27, Em. 1 Sat.	12	9	25	at the port of St. Peter and Paul.
	9	20	35	at Pekin.
Difference of the meridian at Pekin and the Port	2	48	50	

	h	′	″	
Jan. 30, Imm. 111 Sat.	12	5	30	at the Port.
	9	16	30	at Pekin.
	2	49	0	

In the fame manner the longitude of Bolcherefk appears from the correfponding obfervations taken at that place and at Petersburg to be 10ʰ 20′ 22″, differing from Mr. Maraldi about 2′ 5″. Nov. Com. p. 469.

But the longitude of the port of St. Peter and Paul, eftimated in the fame manner from correfponding obfervations, differs from the longitude as computed by Monf. Maraldi no more than 20 feconds; p. 469.

* Obf. Aft. Ecc. Sat. Jovis, &c. Nov. Com. Petr. vol. III. p. 452, &c. Obf. Aft. Pekini factæ. Ant. Hallerftein—Curante Max. Hell. Vindibonæ, 1768.

Feb.

	h	′	″	
Feb. 5, 1 Sat.	8	33	26	at the Port.
	5	43	45	at Pekin.
	2	49	41	

	h	′	″
Feb. 12, Em. 1 Sat.	10	28	49
	7	39	29
	2	49	20

And the longitude from Paris to Pekin being	7	36	23
The difference of the meridians of Paris and the Port will be	10	25	36

Which differs only 31 feconds from the determination of Mr. Maraldi.

1741. Old Style.

	h	′	″	
March 23, Em. 11 Sat.	10	55	2	at Bolcherefk.
	8	14	0	at Pekin.
	2	41	2	

	h	′	″	
Dec. 31, Im. 1 Sat.	10	51	58	at Bolcherefk.
	8	9	45	at Pekin.

Difference of the meridian at Pekin and Bolcherefk	2	42	13

	h	′	″
By taking the medium the difference of the longitude between Bolcherefk and Pekin will be found to be	2	41	37
Between Bolcherefk and Paris	10	18	0

Which differs only one minute and one fecond from the determination of Mr. Maraldi.

In

In order to call in queſtion the concluſions drawn from the obſervations of Kraſſilnikoff, Monſieur de Vaugondy pretends that the inſtruments and pendulums, which he made uſe of at Kamtchatka, were much damaged by the length of the journey; and that the perſon who was ſent to repair them was an unſkilful workman. But this opinion ſeems to have been advanced without ſufficient foundation. Indeed Kraſſilnikoff* himſelf allows that his pendulum occaſionally ſtopt, even when neceſſary to aſcertain the true time of the obſervation. He admits therefore that the obſervations which he took under theſe diſadvantages (when he could not correct them by preceding or ſubſequent obſervations of the ſun or ſtars) are not to be depended upon, and has accordingly diſtinguiſhed them by an aſteriſk; there are however a number of others, which were not liable to any exception of this kind; and the obſervations already mentioned in this number are compriſed under this claſs.

If the arguments which have been already produced ſhould not appear ſufficiently ſatisfactory, we have the further teſtimony of Mr. Muller, who was in thoſe parts at the ſame time with Kraſſilnikoff, and who is the only competent judge of this matter now alive. For that re-

* Nov. Com. Pet. III. p. 444.

ſpectable

fpectable author has given me the moft pofitive affur-
ances, that the inftruments were not damaged in fuch a
manner as to affect the accuracy of the obfervations when
in the hands of a fkilful obferver.

That the longitude of Kamtchatka is laid down with Accuracy of the Ruffian Geographers.
fufficient accuracy by the Ruffian geographers, will ap--
pear by comparing it with the longitude of Yakutfk; for
as the latter has been clearly eftablifhed by a variety of
obfervations, taken at different times and by different
perfons, if there is any error in placing Kamtchatka fo
far to the Eaft, it will be found in the longitude between
Yakutfk and Bolcherefk. A fhort comparifon therefore
of fome of the different obfervations made at Yakutfk
will help to fettle the longitude of Kamtchatka, and
will ftill farther confirm the character of a fkilful obferver, which has been given to Kraffilnikoff.

Kraffilnikoff in returning from Kamtchatka obferved
at Yakutfk feveral eclipfes of the fatellites of Jupiter,
of which the following are mentioned by him as the
moft exact.

1744, Old Style.

h ′ ″

* Feb. 7. Imm. 1. Sat. 11 18 35 fomewhat doubtful.
22. Imm. 11. Sat. 10 31 11 ⎫
29. Imm. 11. Sat. 13 6 54 ⎬ all exact.
Mar. 1. Imm. 1. Sat. 11 23 0 ⎭
Apr. 9. Em. 1. Sat. 12 23 50

* Nov. Comm. Petr. T. III. p. 460.

N n

The

The same eclipses, as calculated by the tables of Mr. Wargentin, for the Meridian of Paris, are as follow:

			h	'	"		h	'	"
Feb.	7.	Imm.	1. 2	49	0	Difference of	8	29	35
	27.	Imm.	11. 2	3	10	the meridians	8	28	1
	29.	Imm.	11. 4	38	17	of Paris ——	8	28	37
Mar.	1.	Imm.	1. 3	3	37	and Yakutſk	8	29	23
Apr.	9.	Em.	1. 3	54	12		8	29	46
						The mean of which is	8	29	5

The obſervations of Mr. Iſlenieff *, made at Yakutſk in the year 1769, to which place he was ſent to obſerve the tranſit of Venus, have received the ſanction of the Imperial Academy. The longitude which he fixes for Yakutſk is 8^h 29' 34". this correſponds, to a ſufficient degree of exactneſs, with the longitude inferred from the obſervations of Kraſſilnikoff.

Thus the longitude of Yakutſk from Paris being 8^h 29° 4". or in degrees 127 16 0. and of Bolche-reſk 10 17 17, or in degrees 150° 19' 15. the difference of the longitude of theſe two places, from aſtronomical obſervations, amounts to 1 48 8. or in degrees 27° 3' 0". The latitude of Bolchereſk is 52° 55' 0". and that of Yakutſk 62° 1' 50". and the difference of

* For Iſlenieff's obſervations at Yakutſk, ſee Nov. Com. Tom. XIV. Part III. p. 268 to 321.

their

their longitude being from the preceding determination 27 3 0. the direct diſtance between the places meaſured on a great circle of the earth will appear by trigonometry to be 16° 57'. or about 1773 verſts, reckoning 104½ verſts to a degree. This diſtance conſiſts partly of ſea, and partly of land; and a conſtant intercourſe is kept up between the two places by means of Ochotſk, which lies between them. The diſtance by ſea from Bolcherefk to Ochotſk is eſtimated by ſhips reckonings to be 1254 verſts, and the diſtance by land from Ochotſk to Yakutſk is 927 verſts, making altogether 2181. The direct diſtance deduced by trigonometry (on a ſuppoſition that the difference of longitude between Bolcherefk and Yakutſk is 27° 3'.) is 1773, falling ſhort of 2181 by 408. a difference naturally to be expected from conſidering, that neither roads by land, or the courſe of ſhips at ſea, are ever performed preciſely on a great circle of the earth, which is the ſhorteſt line that can be drawn on the earth's ſurface between two places.

By this agreement between the diſtance thus eſtimated, and that deduced by computation, on ſuppoſing the difference of longitude between Yakutſk and Bolcherefk to be 27° 3'. it ſeems very improbable, that there ſhould be an error of many degrees in the aſtronomical determination.

Since

Since then the longitude between Fero and Peterfburg is acknowledged to be 48°—that between Peterfburg and Yakutfk 99° 21'—and as the diftance in longitude between Yakutfk and Bolcherefk cannot be materially lefs than 27° 3'. it follows that the longitude of
Bolcherefk from Fero cannot be much lefs than 174° 24'.
Where then fhall we find place for fo great an error as
27 degrees, which, according to Mr. Engel, or even of
11°. which, according to Monf. Vaugondy, is imputed
to the Ruffian geographers in fixing the longitude of
Kamtchatka ?

		From the ifle of Fero		
Longitude of Yakutfk	—	147	0	0
of Ochotfk	—	160	7	0
of Bolcherefk	—	174	13	0
of the Port of St. Peter and Paul	176	10	0

Longitude of
the Extreme
Parts of Afia
determined by
the Ruffians.
As no aftronomical obfervations have been made further to the Eaft than the Port of St. Peter and Paul, it is
impoffible to fix, with any degree of certainty, the longitude of the North-Eaftern promontory of Afia. It appears however from Beering's and Synd's coafting voyages
towards Tfchukotfkoi Nofs, and from other expeditions
to thofe parts by land and fea, that the coaft of Afia in
lat. 64. ftretches at leaft 23° 2 30. from the Port, or
to about 200° longitude from the ifle of Fero.

N° III.

Nº III.

Summary of the proofs tending to shew, that Beering *and* Tschirikoff *either reached* America *in* 1741, *or came very near it.*

THE coast which Beering reached, and called Cape St. Elias, lay, according to his estimation, in 58° 28′ N. latitude, and in longitude 236° from Fero: the coast touched at by Tschirikoff was situated in lat. 56° long. 241° *.

Steller, who accompanied Beering in his expedition towards America, endeavours to prove, that they discovered that continent by the following arguments †: The coasts were bold, presenting continual chains of high mountains, some of which were so elevated, that their tops were covered with snow, their sides were cloathed

Arguments advanced by Steller to prove that Beering and Tschirikoff discovered America.

* The reader will find the narrative of this voyage made by Beering and Tschirikoff in Müller's account of the Russian Discoveries, S. R. G. III. p. 193, &c.

† See Krashininikoff's account of Kamtchatka, Chap. X. French Translation ; Chap. IV. English translation.

from

from the bottom to the top with large tracts of thick
and fine wood *.

Steller went aſhore, where he remained only a few
hours; during which time he obſerved ſeveral ſpecies of
birds which are not known in Siberia: amongſt theſe was
the bird deſcribed by † Cateſby, under the name of Blue
Jay; and which has never yet been found in any country
but North America. The ſoil was very different from
that of the neighbouring iſlands, and at Kamtchatka:
and he collected ſeveral plants, which are deemed by
botaniſts peculiar to America.

The following liſt of theſe plants was communicated
to me by Mr. Pallas: I inſert them however without pre-

---

* The recent navigations in thoſe ſeas ſtrongly confirm this argument.
For in general all the New-diſcovered Iſlands are quite deſtitute of trees;
even the largeſt produce nothing but underwood, one of the moſt Eaſ-
terly Kadyak alone excepted, upon which ſmall willows and alders were
obſerved growing in vallies at ſome diſtance from the coaſt. See
p. 118.

† See Cateſby's Natural Hiſtory of Florida, Carolina, &c. This bird
is called by Linnæus Corvus Chriſtatus. I have ſeen in Mr. Pennant's
MS account of the hiſtory of the animals, birds, &c. of N. America,
and the Northern hemiſphere, as high as lat. 60, an exact deſcription of
this bird. Whenever that ingenious author, to whom we are indebted
for many elegant and intereſting publications, gives this part of his labours to the world, the zoology of theſe countries will be fully and accurately conſidered.

fuming

fuming to decide, whether they are the exclufive growth of North America : the determination of this point is the province of botany.

Trillium Erectum.

Fumaria Cucullaria.

A fpecies of Dracontium, with leaves like the Canna Indica.

Uvularia Perfoliata.

Heuchera Americana.

Mimulus Luteus, a Peruvian plant.

A fpecies of Rubus, probably a variety of the Rubus Idæus, but with larger berries, and a large lacinated red calyx.

None of thefe plants are found in Kamtchatka, or in any of the neighbouring iflands *.

* According to Mr. Pallas, the plants of the New-difcovered Iflands are moftly alpine, like thofe of Siberia ; this he attributes to the fhortnefs and coldnefs of the fummer, occafioned by the frequency of the North winds. His words are : " Quoique les hivers de ces ifles foient affez temperés par l'air de la mer, de façon que les neiges ne couvrent jamais la terre que par intervalles, la plupart des plantes y font alpines, comme en Siberie, par la raifon que l'eté y eft tout auffi courte et froide, à caufe des vents de nord qui y regnent." This paffage is taken from a MS treatife in the French language, relative to the New-difcovered Iflands, communicated to me by my very learned and ingenious friend Mr. Pallas, profeffor of natural hiftory at St. Peterfburg ; from which I have been enabled to collect a confiderable degree of information. This treatife was fent to Monf. Buffon ; and that celebrated naturalift has made great ufe of it in the fifth volume of his Supplement à l'Hiftoire Naturelle.

Though

Though thefe circumftances fhould not be confidered as affording decifive proofs, that Beering reached America; yet they will furely be admitted as ftrong prefumptions, that he very nearly approached that continent *.

* The reader will recollect in this place, that the natives of the contiguous iflands touched at by Beering and Tfchirikoff " prefented to " the Ruffians the calumet, or pipe of peace, which is a fymbol of " friendfhip univerfal among the people of North America, and an " ufage of arbitrary inftitution peculiar to them." See Robertfon's Hift. Am. vol. I. p. 276.   S. R. G. III. p. 214.

N° IV.

N° IV.

List of the principal charts representing the Russian discoveries.

THE following is an authentic list of the principal charts of the Russian discoveries hitherto published. It is accompanied with a few explanatory remarks.

1. Carte des nouvelles decouvertes au nord de la mer du sud, tant à l'Est de la Siberie et du Kamtchatka, qu'à l'Ouest de la Nouvelle France dressée sur les memoires de Mr. de l'Isle, par Philippe Buache, 1750. A memoir relative to this chart was soon afterwards published, with the following title, Explication de la carte des nouvelles decouvertes au Nord de la mer du sud par Mr. de l'Isle; Paris, 1752, 4to.

This map is alluded to, p. 26 of this work.

2. Carte des nouvelles decouvertes entre la partie orientale de l'Asie et l'Occidentale de l'Amerique, avec des vues sur la grande terre réconnue, par les Russes, en 1741, par Phil. Buache, 1752.

3. Nouvelle carte des decouvertes faites par des vaisseaux Russiens aux côtes inconnues de l'Amerique septentrionale avec les pais adjacens, dressée sur les memoires

O o   authentiques

authentiques de ceux qui ont affifté à ces dècouvertes, et
fur d'autres connoiffances ; dont on rend raifon dans un
memoire feparé : à St. Peterfburg, à l'Academie Imperiale
des fciences, 1754. 1758.

This map was publifhed under the infpection of Mr.
Muller, and is ftill prefixed to his account of the Ruffian
difcoveries*. The part which exhibits the New-difcovered
Ifles and the coaft of America was chiefly taken from
the chart of Beering's expedition.   Accordingly that continent is reprefented as advancing, between 50 and 60
degrees of latitude, to within a fmall diftance of Kamtchatka.   Nor could there be any reafon to fufpect, that
fuch experienced failors as Beering and Tfchirikoff had
miftaken a chain of iflands for promontories belonging to
America; until fubfequent navigators had actually failed
through that very part which was fuppofed to be a
continent.

4. A fecond chart publifhed by the Academy, but not
under the infpection of Mr. Muller, bears the fame title
as the former.

Nouvelle carte des dècouvertes faites par des vaiffeaux
Ruffiens aux côtes inconnues de l'Amerique, &c. 1773.

* This map was publifhed by Jefferys under the following title : " A
" Map of the Difcoveries made by the Ruffians on the North Weft
" coaft of America, publifhed by the Royal Academy of Sciences at
" Peterfburg.   Republifhed by Thomas Jefferys, Geographer to his
" Majefty, 1761."

It

It is for the moſt part a copy of a manuſcript chart
known in Ruſſia by the name of the chart of the Promyſchlenics, or merchant adventurers, and which was
ſketched from the mere reports of perſons who had ſailed
to the New-diſcovered Iſlands. As to the ſize and poſition of the New-diſcovered Iſlands, this chart of the
Academy is extremely erroneous: it is however free
from the above-mentioned miſtake, which runs through
all the former charts, namely, the repreſenting of the
coaſt of America, between 50 and 60 degrees of latitude, as contiguous to Kamtchatka. It likewiſe re-
moves that part of the ſame continent lying in latitude
66, from 210° longitude to 224°, and in its ſtead lays
down a large iſland, which ſtretches between latitude
64° and 71° 30′, from 207° longitude to 218°, to
within a ſmall diſtance of both continents. But whether this latter alteration be equally juſtifiable or not,
is a queſtion, the deciſion of which muſt be left to future navigators *.

5. Carte

* Mr. Muller has long ago acknowledged, in the moſt candid and
public manner, the incorrectneſs of the former chart, as far as it relates
to the part which repreſents America as contiguous to Kamtchatka:
but he ſtill maintains his opinion concerning the actual vicinity of the
two continents in an higher latitude. The following quotation is taken
from a letter written by Mr. Muller in 1774, of which I have a copy
in my poſſeſſion. " Poſterity muſt judge if the new chart of the Aca-
" demy is to be preferred to the former one for removing the conti-

" nent

5. Carte du nouvel Archipel du Nord decouvert par les Ruſſes dans la mer de Kamtchatka et d'Anadir.

This chart is prefixed to Mr. Stæhlin's account of the New Northern Archipelago. In the Engliſh tranſlation it is called, A Map of the New Northern Archipelago, diſcovered by the Ruſſians in the ſeas of Kamtchatka and Anadyr. It differs from the laſt-mentioned chart only in the ſize and poſition of a few of the iſlands, and in the addition of five or ſix new ones, and is equally incorrect. The New-diſcovered Iſlands are claſſed in this chart into three groups, which are called the Iſles of Anadyr*, the Olutorian† Iſles, and the Aleütian Iſles. The two laſt-mentioned charts are alluded to, p. 26 of this work.

6. An

" nent of America (which is repreſented as lying near the coaſt of
" Tſchutſki) to a greater diſtance. Synd, who is more to be truſted
" than the Promyſchlenics, perſiſts in the old ſyſtem. He places Ame-
" rica as near as before to Tſchukotſkoi Noſs, but knows nothing of a
" large iſland called Alaſhka, which takes up the place of the conti-
" nent, and which ought to be laid down much more to the South or
" South Eaſt."

* Monſieur Buffon has adopted the appellation and erroneous repreſentation of the iſles of Anadyr in his Carte de deux regions Polaires,
lately publiſhed. See Supplement à l'Hiſt. Nat. vol. V. p. 615.

† The Olutorian Iſles are ſo named from the ſmall river of Olutora,
which flows into the ſea at Kamtchatka, about latitude 61°. The following

6. An excellent map of the Empire of Ruffia, publifhed by the geographical department of the Academy
of Sciences at St. Peterfburg in 1776, comprehends the
greateft part of the New-difcovered Iflands. A reduced
copy of this chart being prefixed to this work, I fhall
only mention the authorities from whence the com-
pilers have laid down the New-difcovered Iflands.
The Aleütian ifles are partly taken from Beering's
chart, partly from *Otcheredin's, whofe voyage is related
in the eleventh chapter, and partly from other MS.

lowing remarks upon this group of iflands are taken from Mr. Muller's
letter mentioned in the note, p. 283. " This appellation of Olutorian
" Ifles is not in ufe at Kamtchatka. Thefe iflands, called upon this
" chart Olutorians, lie according to the chart of the Promyfchlenics,
" and the chart of the Academy, very remote from the river Olutora :
" and it feems as if they were advanced upon this chart nearer to
" Kamtchatka only in favour of the name. They cannot be fituated fo
" near that coaft, becaufe they were neither feen by Beering in 1728,
nor by the Promyfchlenics, Novikoff and Bacchoff, when they failed in
" 1728 from the Anadyr to Beering's Ifland." See p. 42.

* I have a MS. copy of Otcheredin's chart in my poffeffion ; but as
the Fox Iflands, in the general Map of Ruffia, are copied from thence,
the reader will find them laid down upon the reduced map prefixed to
this work. The anonymous author of the account of the Ruffian Difcoveries, of whofe work I have given a tranflation in Part I. feems to
have followed, in moft particulars, Otcheredin's chart and journal for
the longitude, latitude, fize, and pofition of the New-difcovered Iflands.
For this reafon, I fhould have had his chart engraved if the Fox Iflands
upon the general map had not been taken from thence : there feemed
no occafion therefore for encreafing the expence of this work, already
too great from the number of charts, by the addition of another not
abfolutely neceffary.

2   charts

charts of different navigators.   The iflands near the
coaft of the Tfchutfki are copied from Synd's chart.
The Fox Hlands are laid down from the chart of Otcheredin.   The reader will perceive, that the pofition of
the Fox Iflands, upon this general map of Ruffia, is
materially different from that affigned to them in the
chart of Krenitzin's and Levafheff's voyage.   In the
former they are reprefented as ftretching between
56° 61′ North latitude, and 210° and 230° longitude
from the ifle of Fero : in the latter they are fituated
between 51° 40′ and 55° 20′ latitude, and 199° 30′ and
207° 30′ longitude.   According to the moft recent accounts received from Peterfburg, the pofition given to
them upon this general map is confiderably too much
to the North and Eaft ; confequently that affigned to
them upon Krenitzin's chart is probably the moft to be
depended upon.

7. Carte des découvertes Ruffes dans la mer orientale et en Amerique, pour fervir à l'Effai* fur le commerce

* The twelfth chapter of this Effay relates to the difcoveries and
commerce of the Ruffians in the Eaftern Ocean. The account of the
Ruffian difcoveries is a tranflation of Mr. Stæhlin's Defcription of the
New Northern Archipelago. In addition, he has fubjoined an account
of Kamtchatka, and a fhort fketch of the Ruffian commerce to the New-
difcovered Iflands, and to America. If we may believe the author of
this Effay, the Ruffians have not only difcovered America, but they alfo
every year form occafional fettlements upon that continent, fimilar to
thofe of the Europeans in Newfoundland. His words are : " Il eft donc
                                                          certain,

merce de Ruffie, 1778, Amfterdam. It is natural to expect, that a chart fo recently publifhed fhould be fuperior to all the preceding ones ; whereas, on the contrary, it is by far the moft incorrect reprefentation of the New-difcovered Iflands which has yet appeared.

certain, que les Ruffes ont découvert le continent de l'Amérique ; mais on peut affurer qu'ils n'y ont encore aucun port, aucun comptoir. Il en eft des établiffements de cette nation dans la grande terre, comme de ceux des nations Européennes dans l'ifle de Terre Neuve. Ses vaiffeaux ou frégates arrivent en Amérique ; leurs equipages et les Cofaques chaffeurs s'établiffent fur la côte ; les uns fe retranchent, et les autres y font la chaffe et la pêche du chien marin et du narval. Ils reviennent enfuite au Kamtchatka, après avoir été relevés par d'autres frégates fur les mêmes parages, ou à des diftances plus ou moins eloignés, &c. &c." See Effai fur le commerce de la Ruffie, p. 292, 293. Thus the public is impofed upon by fictious and exaggerated accounts.

N° V.

N° V.

Position of the Andreanoffsky Isles *ascertained—Number of the* Aleütian Isles.

WHEN the anonymous author published his account of the Russian Discoveries in 1766, the position of the Andreanoffsky Isles was not ascertained. It was generally supposed, that they formed part of that cluster of islands, which Synd* fell in with in his voyage towards Tschukotskoï Nofs; and Buffon† represents them to be the same with those laid down in Stæhlin's chart, under the name of Anadirsky Isles. The anonymous author, in the passage here referred to, supposes them to be N. E. of the Aleütian Isles; " at the distance " of 600 or 800 versts; that their direction is probably " East and West, and that some of them may unite " with that part of the Fox Islands which are most " contiguous to the opposite continent." This conjecture was advanced upon a supposition that the Andreanoffsky Isles lay near the coast of the Tschutski;

* See N° IX. of this Appendix.

† Isles Anadyr ou Andrien. Supp. vol. V. p. 591.

and

and that fome of the Fox Iflands were fituated in latitude 61, as they are laid down upon the general map
of Ruffia. But according to fubfequent information
the Andreanoffsky Ifles lie between the Aleütian and the Pofition of the Andreanoffsky Ifles.
Fox Iflands, and complete the connection between
Kamtchatka and America *· Their chain is fuppofed to
begin in about latitude 53, near the moft Eafterly of the
Aleütian Ifles, and to extend in a fcattered feries towards
the Fox Iflands. The moft North Eafterly of thefe
iflands are faid to be fo near the moft Southerly of the
Fox Iflands, that they feem occafionally to have been
taken for them. An inftance of this occurs in p. 61
and 62 of this work; where Atchu and Amlak are
reckoned among the Fox Iflands. It is however more
probable, that they are part of the group called by the
Aleütian chief Negho †, and known to the Ruffians
under the name of Andreanoffsky Iflands, becaufe they
were fuppofed to have been firft difcovered by Andrean
Tolftyk, whofe voyage is related in the feventh chapter of the Firft Part.

I take this opportunity of adding, that the anonymous Number of the Aleütian Ifles.
author, in defcribing the Aleütian Ifles, both in the
firft and laft chapter of the account of the Ruffian

* P. 58. Some of the remoter iflands are faid to be E. S. E. of the
Aleütian Ifles; thefe muft be either part of the Andreanoffsky Ifles, or
the moft Southerly of the Fox Iflands.

† See N° VIII. of this Appendix.

difco-

discoveries, mentions only three; namely, Attak, Semitfhi, Shemiya.   But the Aleütian Ifles confift of a much larger number; and their chain includes all the iflands comprehended by the iflander in the two groups of Khao and Safignan*.   Many of them are laid down upon the general map of Ruffia; and fome of them are occafionally alluded to in the journals of the Ruffian voyages †.

* See N° VIII.
† See p. 30, and particularly p. 46, where fome of thefe iflands are mentioned under the names of Ibiya, Kifka, and Olas.

N° VI.

N° VI.

Conjectures concerning the proximity of the Fox Islands *to the continent of* America.

THE anonymous author, in the course of his account of the Russian discoveries, endeavoured to prove, by many circumstances drawn from natural history, that the Fox Islands must lie near the continent of America: hence he grounds his conjecture, that "the time is not far distant when some of the Russian navigators will fall-in with that coast."

The small willows and alders which, according to Glottoff, were found growing upon Kadyak, do not appear to have been sufficient either in size or quantity to ascertain, with any degree of certainty, the close vicinity of that island to America. River-otters, wolves, bears, and wild boars, which were observed upon the same island, will perhaps be thought to afford a stronger presumption in favour of a neighbouring continent; martens were also caught there, an animal which is not known in the Eastern parts of Siberia, nor found upon any of the other islands. All the above-mentioned animals, martens alone excepted, were seen upon Alaksu, which is situated more to the North East than Kadyak,

Proofs of the Vicinity of the Fox Islands to America.

P p 2   and

and alfo rein-deers and wild dogs. To thefe proofs drawn from natural hiftory, we muft add the reports of a mountainous country covered with forefts, and of a great promontory called Atachtak, lying ftill more to the N. E. which were prevalent among the inhabitants of Alakfu and Kadyak.

Although thefe circumftances have been already mentioned *, yet I have thought proper to recapitulate them here, in order to lay before the reader in one point of view the feveral proofs advanced by the anonymous author, which feem to fhew, that the Fox Iflands are fituated near America. Many of them afford, beyond a doubt, evident figns of a lefs open fea; and give certain marks of a nearer approach towards the oppofite continent. But how far that diftance may be fuppofed, muft be left to the judgment of the reader; and remains to be afcertained by fubfequent navigators. All that we know for certain is, that, as far as any Ruffian veffels have hitherto failed, a chain of iflands has been difcovered lying E. or N. E. by E. from Kamtchatka, and ftretching towards America. Part of this chain has only been touched at; the reft is unknown; and all beyond is uncertainty and conjecture.

* See p. 68 and 69—116—118—170.

N° VII.

N° VII.

Of the Tſchutſki—*Reports of the vicinity of* America *to their coaſt, firſt propagated by them, ſeem to be confirmed by late accounts from thoſe parts.*

THE Tſchutſki, it is well known, inhabit the North The Tſchutſki. Eaſtern part of Siberia; their country is a ſmall tract of land, bounded on the North by the Frozen Sea, on the Eaſt by the Eaſtern Ocean; on the South it borders upon the river Anadyr, and on that of Kovyma to the Weſt. The N. E. cape of this country is called Tſchu-kotſkoi-Noſs, or the promontory of the Tſchutſki. Its inhabitants are the only people of Siberia who have not yet been ſubdued by the Ruſſians.

The anonymous author agrees with Mr. Muller in ſuppoſing, that America advances to within a ſmall diſtance of the coaſt of the Tſchutſki; which he ſays " is confirmed by the lateſt accounts procured from theſe parts."

The firſt intelligence concerning the ſuppoſed vicinity between Aſia and America was derived from the reports

2   of

of the Tſchutſki in their intercourſe with the Ruſſians. Vague and uncertain accounts, drawn from a barbarous people, cannot deſerve implicit credit; but as they have been uniformly and invariably propagated by the inhabitants of thoſe regions from the middle of the laſt century to the preſent time, they muſt merit at leaſt the attention of every curious enquirer.

The Reports concerning the Proximity of America to their Coaſt.

Theſe reports were firſt related in Muller's account of the Ruſſian diſcoveries, and have been lately thought worthy of notice by Dr. Robertſon *, in his Hiſtory of America. Their probability ſeems ſtill further increaſed by the following circumſtances. One Pleniſner, a native of Courland, was appointed commander of Ochotſk, in the year 1760, with an expreſs order from the court to proceed as far as † Anadirſk, and to procure all poſſible intelligence concerning the North Eaſtern part of Siberia, and the oppoſite continent. In conſequence of this order Pleniſner repaired to Anadirſk, and proceeded likewiſe to Kovimſkoi Oſtrog: the former of theſe Ruſſian ſettlements is ſituated near the Southern, the latter near the Weſtern limits of the Tſchutſki. Not content however with collecting all the information in his power from the neighbouring Koriacs, who have frequent intercourſe

* Hiſt. of America, vol. I. p. 274—277.
† Anadirſk has been lately deſtroyed by the Ruſſians themſelves.

with

with the Tfchutfki; he alfo fent one Daurkin into their country. This perfon was a native Tfchutfki, who had been taken prifoner, and bred up by the Ruffians: he continued two years with his countrymen; and made feveral expeditions with them to the neighbouring iflands, which lie off the Eaftern coaft of Siberia.

The fum of the intelligence brought back by this Daurkin was as follows: that Tfchukotfkoi-Nofs is a very narrow peninfula; that the Tfchutfki carry on a trade of barter with the inhabitants of America; that they employ fix days in paffing the ftrait which feparates the two continents: they direct their courfe from ifland to ifland, and the diftance from the one to the other is fo fmall, that they are able to pafs every night afhore. More to the North he defcribes the two continents as approaching ftill nearer to each other, with only two iflands lying between them.

This intelligence remarkably coincided with the accounts collected by Plenifner himfelf among the Koriacs. Plenifner returned to Peterfburg in 1776, and brought with him feveral * maps and charts of the North Eaftern parts

* The moft important of thefe maps comprehends the country of the Tfchutfki, together with the nations which border immediately upon them. This map was chiefly taken during a fecond expedition made by major Pauloffsky

parts of Siberia, which were afterwards made ufe of in the compilation of the general map of Ruffia, publifhed by the academy in 1776 *. By thefe means the country of the Tfchutfki has been laid down with a greater degree of accuracy than heretofore. Thefe are probably the late accounts from thofe parts which the anonymous author alludes to.

Pauloffsky againft the Tfchutfki; and his march into tnat country is traced upon it. The firft expedition of that Ruffian officer, in which he penetrated as far as Tfchukotfkoi-Nofs, is related by Mr. Muller, S. R. G. III. p. 134—138. We have no account of this fecond expedition, during which he had feveral fkirmifhes with the Tfchutfki, and came off victorious; but upon his return was furprifed and killed by them. This expedition was made about the year 1750.

* The circumftances mentioned in the text were communicated to me during my continuance at Peterfburg by feveral perfons of credit, who had frequently converfed with Plenifner fince his return to the capital, where he died in the latter end of the year 1778.

N° VIII.

N° VIII.

List of the New-discovered Islands, procured from an Aleütian chief—Catalogue of islands called by different names in the Account of the Russian Discoveries.

THE subsequent list of the New-discovered Islands was procured from an Aleütian chief brought to Petersburg in 1771, and examined at the desire of the Empress by Mr. Muller, who divides them into four principal groups. He regulates this division partly by a similarity of the language spoken by the inhabitants, and partly by vicinity of situation.

Mr. Muller divides the New-discovered Islands into four Groups.

The first group*, called by the islander Safignan, comprehends, 1. Beering's Island. 2. Copper Island. 3. Otma. 4. Samya, or Shemiya. 5. Anakta.

First Group called Safignan.

The second group is called Khao, and comprises eight islands: 1. Immak. 2. Kifka. 3. Tchetchina. 4. Ava. 5. Kavia. 6. Tschagulak. 7. Ulagama. 8. Amitschidga.

Khao, the second Group.

* These two first groups probably belong to the Aleütian Isles.

Q q   The

The third general name is Negho, and comprehends
the iflands known by the Ruffians under the name of
Andreanoffskye Oftrova : fixteen were mentioned by the
iflander, under the following names :

1. Amatkinak. 2. Ulak. 3. Unalga. 4. Navotfha.
5. Uliga. 6. Anagin. 7. Kagulak. 8. Illafk, or
Illak. 9. Takavanga, upon which is a volcano. 10. Kanaga, which has alfo a volcano. 11. Leg. 12. Shet-
fhuna. 13. Tagaloon : near the coaft of the three
laft mentioned iflands feveral fmall rocky ifles are fituated. 14. An ifland without a name, called by the
Ruffians Goreloi *. 15. Atchu. 16. Amla.

The fourth group is denominated Kavalang, and
comprehends fixteen iflands : thefe are called by the Ruffians Lyffie Oftrova, or the Fox Iflands.

1. Amuchta. 2. Tfchigama. 3. Tfchegula. 4. Unif-
tra. 5. Ulaga. 6. Tana-gulana. 7. Kagamin. 8. Kigalga. 9. Schelmaga. 10. Umnak. 11. Aghun-Alafh-
ka. 12. Unimga. At a fmall diftance from Unimga,
towards the North, ftretches a promontory called by the
iflanders the Land of Black Foxes, with a fmall river
called Alafhka, which empties itfelf oppofite to the laft-

* Goreloi is fuppofed by the Ruffian navigators to be the fame ifland
as Atchu, and is reckcned by them among the Fox Iflands. See Part I.
p. 61. and Nº V. of this Appendix.

mentioned

mentioned ifland into a gulf proper for a haven. The extent of this land is not known. To the South Eaft of this promontory lie four little iflands. 13. Uligan. 14. Antun-duffume. 15. Semidit. 16. Senagak.

Many of thefe names are not found either in the journals or charts: while others are wanting in this lift which are mentioned in both journals and charts. Nor is this to be wondered at; for the names of the iflands have been certainly altered and corrupted by the Ruffian navigators. Sometimes the fame name has been applied to different iflands by the different journalifts; at other times the fame ifland has been called by different names. Several inftances of thefe changes feem to occur in the account of the Ruffian Difcoveries: namely,

Iflands called by different Names in the Ruffian Journals.

Att, Attak, and Ataku.

Shemiya and Sabiya.

Atchu, Atchak, Atach, Goreloi or Burned Ifland.

Amlak, Amleg.

Ayagh, Kayachu.

Alakfu, Alagfhak, Alachfhak.

Aghunalafhka, Unalafhka.

N° IX.

Voyage of Lieutenant Synd *to the North East of* Siberia—
*He discovers a cluster of islands, and a promontory,
which he supposes to belong to the continent of* America,
lying near the coast of the Tschutski.

IN 1764 lieutenant Synd sailed from Ochotsk, upon a
voyage of discovery towards the continent of America.
He was ordered to take a different course from that held
by the late Russian vessels, which lay due East from the
coast of Kamtchatka. As he steered therefore his course
more to the North East than any of the preceding navigators, and as it appears from all the voyages related in
the first part of this work*, that the vicinity of America
is to be sought for in that quarter alone, any accurate
account of this expedition would not fail of being highly
interesting. It is therefore a great mortification to me,
that, while I raise the reader's curiosity, I am not able
fully to satisfy it. The following intelligence concerning this voyage is all which I was able to procure. It is
accompanied with an authentic chart.

* See p. 27.

2

CHART of SYND's VOYAGE
towards Tschukotskoi Noss.

P.Oljutorskoi

Aparhxan R.

Drakin P.

I.Karaginskoi

P.Ukinskoi

Vernonotskoi P.

P.Kinmit

P.Stolberet

P.Kinnikhatskoi

P.Tschastprinskoi

P.Kronozkoi

Beering's Island

Iljin

Shupghskoi

Kamtchatka

Tinilsk

Vka R.

Kamtchatka R.

K A M T C H A T K A

Haifatovk

Beloshei

Bay of St Peter St Paul

Alaik

I.Shushu

I.Pusinni

I.Gtlanit

60

55

Longitude East from Ochotsk.

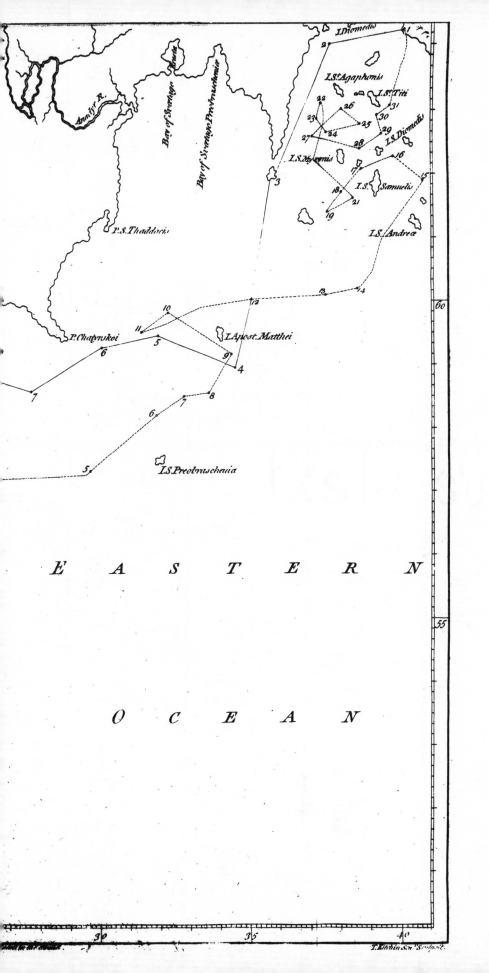

I. Diomedis

2

I. St Agaphonis

I. St Titi

22
26
31

23
25
30

27
24
28
I. S. Diomedis

I. S. Myronis
29

16

18
I. S. Samuelis

21
19
15

Anadyr R.

Bay of Sceretsa South

Bay of Sceretsa Provincialmea

3

P. S. Thaddæi

I. S. Andreæ

13
14

60

10
12

P. Chapnikoi

11

5
I. Apost. Matthei

6
9
4

7
8

6
7

5

I. S. Preobraschenia

5

E   A   S   T   E   R   N

55

O   C   E   A   N

30
35
40

T. Kitchin Sen. Sculp. et.

In 1764 Synd put to sea from the port of Ochotſk, but did not paſs (we know not by what accident) the Southern Cape of Kamtchatka and Shuſhu, the firſt Kuril Iſle, before 1766. He then ſteered his courſe North at no great diſtance from the coaſt of the peninſula, but made very little progreſs that year, for he wintered South of the river Uka.

The following year he ſailed from Ukinſki Point due Eaſt and North Eaſt, until he fell in with a cluſter of iſlands* ſtretching between 61 and 62 degrees of latitude, and 195° and 202° longitude. Theſe iſlands lie South Eaſt and Eaſt of the coaſt of the Tſchutſki; and ſeveral of them are ſituated very near the ſhore. Beſides theſe ſmall iſlands, he diſcovered alſo a mountainous coaſt lying within one degree of the coaſt of the Tſchutſki, between 64 and 66 North latitude; its moſt Weſtern extremity was ſituated in longitude 38° 15′ from Ochotſk, or 199° 1′ from Fero. This land is laid down in his chart as part of the continent of America; but we cannot determine upon what proofs he grounds this repreſentation, until a more circumſtantial account of his voyage is communicated to the public.

* Theſe are certainly ſome of the iſlands which the Tſchutſki reſort to in their way to what they call the continent of America.

Synd

Synd feems to have made but a fhort ftay afhore. Inftead of endeavouring to furvey its coafts, or of fteering
more to the Eaft, he almoft inftantly fhaped his courfe
due Weft towards the courfe of the Tfchutfki, then
turned directly South and South Weft, until he came
oppofite to Chatyrfkoi Nofs. From that point he continued to coaft the peninfula of Kamtchatka, doubled the
cape, and reached Ochotfk in 1768.

N° X.

Specimen of the Aleütian language.

Sun	Agaiya	One	Tagatak
Moon	Tughilag	Two	Alag
Wind	Katſhik	Three	Kankoos
Water	Tana	Four	Setſchi
Fire	Kighenag	Five	Tſhaw
Earth hut	Oollae	Six	Atoo
Chief	Toigon	Seven	Ooloo
Man	Taiyaga	Eight	Kapoé
Wood	Yaga	Nine	Shifet
Shield	Kuyak	Ten	Aſok.
Sea-otter	Tſcholota		
Name of the nation.	Kanagiſt		

It is very remarkable, that none of theſe words bear the leaſt reſemblance to thoſe of the ſame ſignification, which are found in the different dialeɛts ſpoken by the Koriaks, Kamtchadals, and the inhabitants of the Kuril Iſles.

N° XI.

Nº XI.

Attempts of the Ruffians *to difcover a North Eaft paffage—*
Voyages from Archangel *towards the* Lena—*From the*
Lena *towards* Kamtchatka—*Extract from* Muller's *ac-*
count of Defchneff's *voyage round* Tfchukotfkoi Nofs—
Narrative of a voyage made by Shalauroff *from the* Lena
to Shelatfkoi Nofs.

THE only communication hitherto known between
the Atlantic and Pacific Ocean, or between Europe
and the Eaft Indies, is made either by failing round the
Cape of Good Hope, or by doubling Cape Horn. But as
both thefe navigations are very long and dangerous, the
great object of feveral late European voyages has been
turned towards the difcovery of a North Eaft or a North
Weft paffage. As this work is entirely confined to the
Ruffian navigations, any difquifition concerning the
North Weft paffage is totally foreign to the purpofe; and
for the fame reafon, in what relates to the North Eaft, thefe
refearches extend only to the attempts of the Ruffians for
the difcovery of that paffage.

The advocates for the North Eaft paffage have divided
that navigation into three principal parts; and by endeavouring to fhew that thefe three parts have been

paffed

paffed at different times, they conclude from thence, that the whole when taken collectively is practicable.

Thefe three parts are, 1. from Archangel to the Lena; 2. from the Lena to Kamtchatka; 3. from Kamtchatka to Japan. With refpect to the latter, the connection between the feas of Kamtchatka and Japan firft appeared from fome Japanefe veffels, which were wrecked upon the coaft of Kamtchatka in the beginning of this century; and this communication has been unqueftionably proved from feveral voyages made by the Ruffians from Kamtchatka to Japan *.

No one ever afferted that the firft part from Archangel to the Lena was ever performed in one voyage; but feveral perfons having advanced that this navigation has been made by the Ruffians at different times, it becomes neceffary to examine the accounts of the Ruffian voyages in thofe feas.

In 1734 lieutenant Morovieff failed from Archangel toward the river Oby; and got no farther the firft year than the mouth of the Petfchora. The next fummer he paffed through the ftraits of Weygatz into the fea of Kara; and coafted along the Eaftern fide of that fea, as high as latitude 72° 30', but did not double the promontory which feparates the fea of Kara from the Bay of

Voyages from Archangel to the Yenisei.

* S. R. G. III. p. 78, and p. 166, &c.

Oby. In 1738, the lieutenants Malgyin and Skurakoff doubled that promontory with great difficulty, and entered the bay of Oby. During these expeditions the navigators met with great dangers and impediments from the ice. Several unsuccessful attempts were made to pass from the bay of Oby to the Yenisèi, which was at last effected in 1738 by two vessels commanded by lieutenants Offzin and Koskeleff. The same year the pilot Feodor Menin sailed from the Yenisèi towards the Lena : he steered North as high as lat. 72°. 15'. and when he came to the mouth of the Piasida he was stopped by the ice ; and finding it impossible to force a passage, he returned to the Yenisèi *.

Unsuccessful Attempt to pass from the Yenisèi to the Lena.

Voyage of Prontshistsheff from the Lena towards the Yenisèi.

July, 1735, lieutenant Prontshistsheff sailed from Yakutsk up the Lena to its mouth, in order to pass from thence by sea to the Yenisèi. The Western mouths of the Lena were so choaked up with ice, that he was obliged to pass through the most Easterly one ; and was prevented by contrary winds from getting out until the 13th of August. Having steered North West along the islands which lie scattered before the mouths of the Lena, he found himself in lat. 70° 4'. He saw much ice to the North and North East; and observed ice-mountains from twenty-four to sixty feet in height. He steered betwixt the ice, which in no place left a free channel of

* P. 145 to 149.

greater

greater breadth than an hundred or two hundred yards. The veffel being much damaged, on the 1ft of September he ran up the mouth of the Olenek, which, according to his eftimation, lies in 72° 30', near which place he paffed the winter *.

He got out of the Olenek the beginning of Auguft in the following year; and arrived on the third at the mouth of the Anabara, which he found to lie in lat. 73° 1'. There he continued until the 10th, while fome of the crew went up the country in fearch of fome mines. On the 10th he proceeded on his voyage: before he reached the mouth of the Chatanga he was fo entirely furrounded and hemmed in with ice, that it was not without great difficulty and danger he was able to get loofe. He then obferved a large field of ice ftretching into the fea, on which account he was obliged to continue near the fhore, and to run up the Chatanga. The mouth of this river was in lat. 74° 9'. From thence he bent his courfe moftly Northward along the fhore, until he reached the mouth of the Taimura on the 18th. He then proceeded further, and followed the coaft towards the Piafida. Near the fhore were feveral fmall iflands, between which and the land the ice was immovably fixed. He then directed his courfe toward the fea, in order to pafs round the

* Gmelin Reife, II. 425 to 427.

R r 2

chain

chain of iflands.   At firft he found the fea more free
to the North of the iflands, while he obferved much ice
lying between them.   He came at length to the laft ifland,
fituated in lat. 77° 25'.   Between this ifland and the
fhore, as well as on the other fide of the ifland which lay
moft to the North, the ice was firm and immovable.   He
attempted however to fteer ftill more to the North; and
having advanced about fix miles, he was prevented by
a thick fog from proceeding: this fog being difperfed,
he faw on each fide, and before him, nothing but ice;

Prevented by a Chain of Iflands and the Ice from getting to the Yenifei. that towards the fea was not fixed; but the accumulated
maffes were all fo clofe, that the fmalleft veffel could not
have worked its way through.   Still attempting however
to pafs to the North; he was forced by the ice N. E.
Apprehenfive of being hemmed in, he returned to the
Taimura; and from thence got, with much difficulty
and danger, to the Olenek, on the 29th of Auguft.

This narrative of Prontfhiftfheff's expedition is extracted from the account of profeffor * Gmelin: according to Mr. Muller †, who has given a curfory relation
of the fame voyage, Prontfhiftfheff did not quite reach the
mouth of the Taimura; for he there found the chain of
iflands ftretching from the continent far into the fea.
The channels between the iflands were fo choaked up

* Gmelin Reife, vol. II. p. 427 to p. 434.
† S. R. G. III. p. 149, 150.

with

with ice, that it was impoffible to force a paffage : after
fteering as high as lat. 77° 25′, he found fuch a plain
of fixed ice before him, that he had no profpect of
getting any farther. Accordingly he returned to the
Olenek.

Another attempt was made to pafs from the Lena to
the Yenisèi in 1739, by Chariton Laptieff, with equal
bad fuccefs ; and he relates, that between the rivers
Piafida and Taimura a promontory ftretches into the
fea which he could not double, the fea being entirely
frozen up before he could pafs round *.

From all thefe circumftances we muft collect, that the
whole fpace between Archangel and the Lena has never
yet been navigated; for in going Eaft from the Yenisèi
the Ruffians could get no farther than the mouth of the
Piafida ; and, in coming Weft from the Lena, they were
ftopped, according to Gmelin, North of the Piafida ;
and, according to Muller, Eaft of the Taimura.

Cape between the Rivers Chatanga and Piafida never yet doubled.

The Ruffians, who fail almoft annually from Archangel, and other towns, to Nova Zemla, for the purpofe of catching fea-horfes, feals, and white bears, make

---

* Gmelin Reife, p. 440. Mr. Muller fays only, that Laptieff met
with the fame obftacles which forced Prontfhiftfheff to return. S. R. G.
III. p. 150.

4

to

to the Weſtern Coaſt; and no Ruſſian veſſel has ever paſſed round its North Eaſtern extremity *.

The

* Although this work is confined to the Ruſſian Diſcoveries, yet as the N. E. paſſage is a ſubject of ſuch intereſting curioſity, it might ſeem an omiſſion in not mentioning, that ſeveral Engliſh and Dutch veſſels have paſſed through the Straits of Weygatz into the ſea of Kara; they all met with great obſtructions from the ice, and had much difficulty in getting through. See Hiſtoire Gen. Des Voyages, tome XV. paſſim.

In 1696 Heemſkirk and Barentz, after having ſailed along the Weſtern coaſt of Nova Zemla, doubled the North Eaſtern cape lying in latitude 77° 20′, and got no lower along the Eaſtern coaſt than 76°, where they wintered.

See an account of this remarkable voyage in Girard Le Ver's Vraye Deſcription des Trois Voyages De Mer, p. 13 to 45; and Hiſt. Gen. des Voy. tom. XV. p. 111 to 139.

No veſſel of any nation has ever paſſed round that Cape, which extends to the North of the Piaſida, and is laid down in the Ruſſian charts in about 78° latitude. We have already ſeen that no Ruſſian veſſel has ever got from the Piaſida to the Chatanga, or from the Chatanga to the Piaſida; and yet ſome authors have poſitively aſſerted, that this promontory has been ſailed round. In order therefore to elude the Ruſſian accounts, which clearly aſſert the contrary, it is pretended, that Gmelin and Muller have purpoſely concealed ſome parts of the Ruſſian journals, and have impoſed upon the world by a miſrepreſentation of facts. But without entering into any diſpute on this head, I can venture to affirm, that no ſufficient proof has been as yet advanced in ſupport of this aſſertion; and therefore, until ſome poſitive information ſhall be produced, we cannot deny plain facts, or prefer hearſay evidence to circumſtantial and well-atteſted accounts.

Mr. Engel has a remarkable paſſage in his Eſſai ſur une route par la Nord Eſt, which it may be proper to conſider in this place, becauſe he aſſerts in the moſt poſitive manner, that two Dutch veſſels formerly paſſed three hundred leagues to the North Eaſt of Nova Zemla; from thence

The navigation from the Lena to Kamtchatka now remains to be confidered.   If we may believe fome authors,
this

thence he infers that they muft have doubled the above-mentioned Cape,
which extends to the North of the Piafida, and have got at leaft as far
Eaft as the mouth of the Olenek. His words are, L'Illuftre Societé Roy-
ale, fous l'an 1675, rapporte ce voyage, et dit, que peu d'années aupara-
vant une Societé de merchands d'Amfterdam avoit fait une tentative pour
chercher le paffage du Nord Eft, et équippa deux vaiffeaux les quels etant
paffé au feptante neuf ou huitantieme degrè de latitude, avoient pouffè fe-
lon Wood, jufqu' à trois cent lieues à l'Eft de la Nouvelle Zemble, &c. &c.
Upon this fact he founds his proof that the navigation from Archangel
to the Lena has been performed. Par confequent cette partie de la route
a ètè faite.   He refts the truth of this account on the authority of the
Philofophical Tranfactions, and of Captain Wood, who failed upon a
voyage for the difcovery of the North Eaft paffage in 1676. The latter,
in the relation of his voyage, enumerates feveral arguments which induced him to believe the practicability of the North Eaft paffage.—
" The feventh argument," he fays, " was another narration, printed in
" the Tranfactions, of two fhips of late that had attempted the paffage,
" failed 300 leagues to the Eaftward of Nova Zemla, and had after profe-
" cuted the voyage, had there not a difference arofe betwixt the undertakers
" and the Eaft-India company." We here find that Captain Wood refers to the Philofophical Tranfactions for his authority. The narration
printed in the Tranfactions, and which is alluded to by both Captain
Wood and Mr. Engel, is to be found in Vol. IX. of the Philofophical
Tranfactions, p. 209, for December 1674. It confifts of a very curious
" Narrative of fome obfervations made upon feveral voyages, under-
" taken to find a way for failing about the North to the Eaft-Indies;
" together with inftructions given by the Dutch Eaft-India Company
" for the difcovery of the famous land of Jeffo near Japan." Thefe inftructions were, in 1643, given to Martin Geritfes Vries, captain of the
fhip Caftricum, " who fet out to difcover the unknown Eaftern coaft
" of

this navigation has been open for above a century and
an half; and feveral veffels have at different times
paffed

" of Tartary, the kingdom of Kata, and the Weft coaft of America,
" together with the ifles fituate to the Eaft of Japan, cried up for their
" riches of gold and filver." Thefe inftructions contain no relation of
two Dutch veffels, who paffed 300 leagues Eaft of Nova Zemla.
Mention is made of two Dutch veffels, " who were fent out in the
" year 1639, under the command of Captain Kwaft, to difcover the
" Eaft coaft of the Great Tartary, efpecially the famous gold and filver
" iflands; though, by reafon of feveral unfortunate accidents, they
" both returned re infectâ." Short mention is afterwards made of Captain Kwaft's journal, together with the writings of the merchants who
were with him, as follows : " That in the South Sea, at the 37½ de-
" grees Northern latitude, and about 400 Spanifh, or 343 Dutch miles,
" that is, 28 degrees longitude Eaft of Japan, there lay a very great
" and high ifland, inhabited by a white, handfome, kind and civilized
" people, exceedingly opulent in gold and filver, &c. &c."
   From thefe extracts it appears, that, in the fhort account of the journals of the two Dutch veffels, no longitude is mentioned to the Eaft of
Nova Zemla; but the difcoveries of Kwaft were made in the South
fea, to which place he, as well as Captain Vries afterwards, muft have
failed round the Cape of Good Hope. The author of the narrative
concludes, indeed, that the N. E. paffage is practicable, in the following words : " To promote this paffage out of the Eaft-Indies to the
" North into Europe, it were neceffary to fail from the Eaft-Indies to
" the Weftward of Japan, all along Corea, to fee how the fea-coafts
" tend to the North of the faid Corea, and with what conveniency
" fhips might fail as far as Nova Zemla, and to the North of the fame.
" Where our author faith, that undoubtedly it would be found, that
" having paffed the North corner of Nova Zemla, or, through Wey-
" gatz, the North end of Yelmer land, one might go on South-Eaft-
" ward, and make a fuccefsful voyage." But mere conjectures cannot
be admitted as evidence. As we can find no other information relative

                                                                   to

paſſed round the North Eaſtern extremity of Aſia. But if we conſult the Ruſſian accounts, we ſhall find, that frequent expeditions have been unqueſtionably made from the Lena to the Kovyma; but that the voyage from the Kovyma round Tſchukotſkoi Noſs, into the Eaſtern ocean, has been performed but once. According to Mr. Muller, this formidable cape was doubled in the year 1648. The material incidents of this remarkable voyage are as follow *:

" In 1648 ſeven kotches or veſſels ſailed from the mouth of the river Kovyma†, in order to penetrate into the Eaſtern Ocean. Of theſe, four were never more heard of: the remaining three were commanded by Simon Deſhneff, Geraſim Ankudinoff, two chiefs of the Coſſacs, and Fedot Alexeeff, the head of the Promyſh-lenics. Deſhneff and Ankudinoff quarrelled before their

Narrative of
Deſhneff's
Voyage round
Tſchukotſkoi-
Noſs.

to the fact mentioned by Captain Wood and Mr. Engel, (namely, that two Dutch veſſels have paſſed 300 leagues to the Eaſt of Nova Zemla) we have no reaſon to credit mere aſſertions without proof: we may therefore advance as a fact, that hitherto we have no authentic account, that any veſſel has ever paſſed the cape to the Eaſt of Nova Zemla, which lies North of the river Piaſida. See Relation of Wood's Voyage, &c. in the Account of ſeveral late Voyages and Diſcoveries to the South and North, &c. London, 1694, p. 148. See alſo Engel, Mem. et Obſ. Geo. p. 231—234.

* I ſhould not have ſwelled my book with this extract, if the Engliſh tranſlation of Mr. Muller's work was not extremely erroneous in ſome material paſſages. S. R. G. III. p. 8—20.

† Mr. Muller calls it Kolyma.

departure:

departure : this difpute was owing to the jealoufy of Defhneff, who was unwilling that Ankudinoff fhould fhare with him the honour, as well as the profits, which might refult from the expected difcoveries. Each veffel was probably manned with about thirty perfons ; Ankudinoff's, we certainly know, carried that number. Defhneff promifed before-hand a tribute of feven fables, to be exacted from the inhabitants on the banks of Anadyr ; fo fanguine were his hopes of reaching that river. This indeed he finally effected ; but not fo foon, nor with fo little difficulty, as he had prefumed.

On the 20th of June, 1648, the three veffels failed upon this remarkable expedition from the river Kovyma. Confidering the little knowledge we have of the extreme regions of Afia, it is much to be regretted, that all the incidents of this voyage are not circumftantially related. Defhneff*, in an account of his expedition fent to

Yakutfk,

---

* In order thoroughly to underftand this narrative, it is neceffary to inform the reader, that the voyage made by Defhneff was entirely forgotten until the year 1736, when Mr. Muller found, in the archives of Yakutfk, the original accounts of the Ruffian navigations in the Frozen Ocean.

Thefe papers were extracted, under his infpection, at Yakutfk, and fent to Petersburg ; where they are now preferved in the library belonging to the Imperial Academy of Sciences : they confift of feveral folio volumes. The circumftances relating to Defhneff are contained in the fecond volume. Soliverftoff and Stadukin, having laid claim to the dif-

covery

Yakutſk, ſeems only as it were accidentally to mention his adventures by ſea; he takes no notice of any occurrence

covery of the country on the mouth of the Anadyr, had aſſerted, in conſequence of this claim, that they had arrived there by ſea, after having doubled Tſchukotſkoi Noſs. Deſhneff, in anſwer, ſent ſeveral memorials, petitions, and complaints, againſt Stadukin and Soliverſtoff, to the commander of Yakutſk, in which he ſets forth, that he had the ſole right to that diſcovery, and refutes the arguments advanced by the others. From theſe memorials Mr. Muller has extracted his account of Deſhneff's voyage. When I was at Petersburg, I had an opportunity of ſeeing theſe papers: and as they are written in the Ruſſian language, I prevailed upon my ingenious friend Mr. Pallas to inſpect the part which relates to Deſhneff. Accordingly Mr. Pallas, with his uſual readi-
neſs to oblige, not only compared the memorials with Mr. Muller's ac-
count, but even took the trouble to make ſome extracts from the moſt material parts: theſe extracts are here ſubjoined; becauſe they will not only ſerve to confirm the exactneſs of Mr. Muller, but alſo becauſe they tend to throw ſome light on ſeveral obſcure paſſages. In one of Deſhneff's memorials he ſays, " To go from the river Kovyma to the Anadyr,
" a great promontory muſt be doubled, which ſtretches very far into
" the ſea: it is not that promontory which lies next to the river
" Tſchukotſkia. Stadukin never arrived at this great promontory:
" near it are two iſlands, whoſe inhabitants make holes in their under-
" lips, and inſert therein pieces of the ſea-horſe tuſh, worked into the
" form of teeth. This promontory ſtretches between North and North
" Eaſt: It is known on the Ruſſian ſide by the little river Stanovie,
" which flows into the ſea, near the ſpot where the Tſchutſki have erected
" a heap of whale-bones like a tower. The coaſt from the promon-
" tory turns round towards the Anadyr, and it is poſſible with a good
" wind to ſail from the point to that river in three days and nights: and
" it will take up no more time to go by land to the ſame river, becauſe
" it diſcharges itſelf into a bay." In another memorial Deſhneff ſays,
" that he was ordered to go by ſea from the Indigirka to the Kovyma;
" and

rence until he reached the great promontory of the
Tſchutſki; no obſtructions from the ice are mentioned,
and probably there were none; for he obſerves upon
another occaſion, that the ſea is not every year ſo free

" and from thence with his crew to the Anadyr, which was then newly
" diſcovered.   That the firſt time he ſailed from the Kovyma, he
" was forced by the ice to return to that river; but that next
" year he again ſailed from thence by ſea, and after great danger, miſ-
" fortunes, and with the loſs of part of his ſhipping, arrived at laſt at
" the mouth of the Anadyr.   Stadukin, having in vain attempted to go
" by ſea, afterwards ventured to paſs over the chain of mountains then
" unknown; and reached by that means the Anadyr. Soliverſtoff and
" his party, who quarrelled with Deſhneff, went to the ſame place from
" the Kovyma by land; and the tribute was afterwards ſent to the laſt
" mentioned river acroſs the mountains, which were very dangerous to
" paſs amidſt the tribes of Koriacs and Yukagirs, who had been lately re-
" duced by the Ruſſians."

In another memorial Deſhneff complains bitterly of Soliverſtoff;
and aſſerts, " that one Severka Martemyanoff, who had been gained
" over by Soliverſtoff, was ſent to Yakutſk, with an account that he
" (Soliverſtoff) had diſcovered the coaſts to the North of the Anadyr,
" where large numbers of ſea-horſes are found." Deſhneff hereupon
" ſays, that Soliverſtoff and Stadukin never reached the rocky promon-
" tory, which is inhabited by numerous bodies of the Tſchutſki; over-
" againſt which are iſlands whoſe inhabitants wear artificial teeth thruſt
" through their under lips.   This is not the firſt promontory from the
" river Kovyma, called Svatoi Noſs; but another far more conſiderable,
" and very well known to him (Deſhneff), becauſe the veſſel of Anku-
" nidoff was wrecked there; and becauſe he had there taken priſoners
" ſome of the people, who were rowing in their boats; and ſeen the
" iſlanders with teeth in their lips.   He alſo well knew, that it was ſtill
" far from that promontory to the river Anadyr."

from ice as it was at this time. He commences his narrative with a defcription of the great promontory : " It " is," fays he, " very different from that which is fituated " Weft of the Kovyma, near the river Tfchukotfkia. It " lies between North and North Eaft, and bends, in a " circular direction, towards the Anadyr. It is diftin- " guifhed on the Ruffian (namely, the Weftern) fide, by " a rivulet which falls into the fea, clofe to which the " Tfchutfki have raifed a pile, like a tower, with the " bones of whales. Oppofite the promontory (it is not " faid on which fide) are two iflands, on which he ob- " ferved people of the nation of the Tfchutfki, who had " pieces of the fea-horfe tooth thruft into holes made in " their lips. With a good wind it is poffible to fail from " this promontory to the Anadyr in three days ; and the " journey by land may be performed in the fame fpace " of time, becaufe the Anadyr falls into a bay." An-kudinoff's kotche was wrecked on this promontory, and the crew was diftributed on board the two remaining veffels. On the 20th of September, Defhneff and Fedot Alexeef went on fhore, and had a fkirmifh with the Tfchutfki, in which Alexeef was wounded. The two veffels foon afterwards loft fight of each other, and never again rejoined. Defhneff was driven about by tempef-tuous winds until October, when he was fhipwrecked (as it appears from circumftances) confiderably to the South of the Anadyr, not far from the river Olutora.

What

What became of Fedot Alexeef and his crew will be mentioned hereafter. Defhneff and his companions, who amounted to twenty-five perſons, now ſought for the Anadyr; but being entirely unacquainted with the country, ten weeks elapſed before they reached its banks at a ſmall diſtance from its mouth: here he found neither wood nor inhabitants, &c.

The following year he went further up the river, and built Anadirſkoi Oſtrog: here he was joined by ſome Ruſſians on the 25th of April, 1650, who came by land from the river Kovyma. In 1652, Defhneff having conſtructed a veſſel, ſailed down the Anadyr as far as its mouth, and obſerved on the North ſide a ſand bank, which ſtretched a conſiderable way into the ſea. A ſand bank of this kind is called, in Siberia, Korga. Great numbers of ſea-horſes were found to reſort to the mouth of the Anadyr. Defhneff collected ſeveral of their teeth, and thought himſelf amply compenſated by this acquiſition for the trouble of his expedition. In the following year, Defhneff ordered wood to be felled for the purpoſe of conſtructing a veſſel, in which he propoſed ſending the tribute which he had collected by ſea to Yakutſk *. But this deſign was laid aſide from the

* That is, by ſea, from the mouth of the Anadyr, round Tſchukotſkoi Noſs to the river Lena, and then up that river to Yakutſk.

want

want of other materials. It was alfo reported, that the fea about Tchukotfkoi Nofs was not every year free from ice.

Another expedition was made in 1654 to the Korga, for the purpofe of collecting fea-horfe teeth. A Coffac, named Yufko Soliverftoff, was one of the party, the fame who not long before had accompanied the Coffac Michael Stadukin, upon a voyage of difcovery in the Frozen Sea. This perfon was fent from Yakutsk to collect fea-horfe teeth, for the benefit of the crown. In his inftructions mention is made of the river Yentfhendon, which falls into the bay of Penfhinfk, and of the Anadyr; and he was ordered to exact a tribute from the inhabitants dwelling near thefe rivers; for the adventures of Defhneff were not as yet known at Yakutsk. This was the occafion of new difcontents. Soliverftoff claimed to himfelf the difcovery of the Korga, as if he had failed to that place in his voyage with Stadukin in 1649. Defhneff, however, proved that Soliverftoff had not even reached Tfchukotskoi Nofs, which he defcribes as nothing but bare rock, and it was but too well known to him, becaufe the veffel of Ankudinoff was fhipwrecked there. " Tfchukotskoi Nofs," adds Defhneff, " is not the firft promontory * which prefents itfelf
" under

* We may collect from Defhneff's reafoning, that Soliverftoff, in endeavouring to prove that he had failed round the Eaftern extremity of Afia,

" under the name of Svatoi Noſs. It is known by the
" two iſlands ſituated oppoſite to it, whoſe inhabitants
" (as is before-mentioned) place pieces of the ſea-horſe
" tuſh into holes made in their lips. Deſhneff alone
" had ſeen theſe people, which neither Stadukin nor
" Soliverſtoff had pretended to have done: and the
" Korga, or ſand-bank, at the mouth of the river Ana-
" dyr, was at ſome diſtance from theſe iſlands."

While Deſhneff was ſurveying the ſea-coaſt, he ſaw
in an habitation belonging to ſome Koriacs a woman of
Yakutsk, who, as he recollected, belonged to Fedot
Alexeef: Upon his enquiry concerning the fate of her
maſter, ſhe replied, " that Fedot and Geraſim (Ankudi-
" noff) had died of the ſcurvy; that part of the crew had
" been ſlain; that a few had eſcaped in ſmall veſſels,
" and have never ſince been heard of." Traces of the
latter were afterwards found in the peninſula of Kamt-

Aſia, had miſtaken a promontory called Svatoi Noſs for Tſchukotſkoi
Noſs: for otherwiſe, why ſhould Deſhneff, in his refutation of Soli-
verſtoff, begin by aſſerting, that Svatoi Noſs was not Tſchukotſkoi Noſs.
The only cape laid down in the Ruſſian maps, under the name of Svatoi
Noſs, is ſituated 25 degrees to the Weſt of the Kovyma: but we cannot
poſſibly ſuppoſe this to be the promontory here alluded to; becauſe, in
ſailing from the Kovyma towards the Anadyr, " the firſt promontory
" which preſents itſelf" muſt neceſſarily be Eaſt of the Kovyma. Svatoi
Noſs, in the Ruſſian language, ſignifies Sacred Promontory; and the
Ruſſians occaſionally apply it to any cape which it is difficult to double.
It therefore moſt probably here relates to the firſt cape, which Soliverſtoff reached after he had ſailed from Kovyma.

chatka;

chatka; to which place they probably arrived with a favourite wind, by following the coaft, and running up the Kamtchatka river.

When Volodimir Atlaffoff, in 1697, firft entered upon the reduction of Kamtchatka, he found that the inhabitants had already fome knowledge of the Ruffians. A common tradition ftill prevails amongft them, that, long before the expedition of Atlaffoff, one * Fedotoff (who was probably the fon of Fedot Alexeeff) and his companions had refided amongft them, and had intermarried with the natives. They ftill fhew the fpot where the Ruffian habitations ftood; namely, at the mouth of the fmall river Nikul, which falls into the Kamtchatka river, and is called by the Ruffians Fedotika. Upon Atlaffoff's arrival none of the firft Ruffians remained. They are faid to have been held in great veneration, and almoft deified by the inhabitants, who at firft imagined that no human power could hurt them, until they quarreled amongft themfelves, and the blood was feen to flow fròm the wounds which they gave each other: and upon a feparation taking place between the Ruffians, part of them had been killed by the Koriacs, as they were going to the fea of Penfhinfk, and the remainder by the Kamtchadals. The river Fedotika falls into the Southern fide of the Kamtchatka river about an hundred and eighty verfts

* Fedotoff, in the Ruffian language, fignifies the fon of Fedot.

T t   below

below Upper Kamtchatkoi Oftrog. At the time of the firft expedition to Kamtchatka, in 1697, the remains of two villages ftill fubfifted, which had probably been inhabited by Fedotoff and his companions,: and no one knew which way they came into the peninfula, until it was difcovered from the archives of Yakutfk in 1636."

* No other navigator, fubfequent to Defhneff, has ever pretended to have paffed the North Eaftern extremity of Afia,

---

* Mr. Engel indeed pretends that lieutenant Laptieff, in 1739, doubled Tfchukotfkoi-Nofs, becaufe Gmelin fays, that " he paffed from the " Kovyma to Anadirfk partly by water and partly by land." For Mr. Engel afferts the impoffibility of getting from the Kovyma to Anadirfk, partly by land and partly by water, without going from the Kovyma to the mouth of the Anadyr by fea, and from thence to Anadirfk by land. But Mr. Muller (who has given a more particular account of the conclufion of this expedition) informs us, that Laptieff and his crew, after having wintered near the Indigirka, paffed from its mouth in fmall boats to the Kovyma; and as it was dangerous, on account of the Tfchutski, to follow the coaft any farther, either by land or water, he went through the interior part of the country to Anadirsk, and from thence to the mouth of the Anadyr. Gmelin Reife, vol. II. p. 440. S. R. G. III. p. 157.

Mention is alfo made by Gmelin of a man who paffed in a fmall boat from the Kovyma round Tfcukotskoi-Nofs into the fea of Kamtchatka; and Mr. Engel has not omitted to bring this paffage in fupport of his fyftem, with this difference, that he refers to the authority of Muller, inftead of Gmelin, for the truth of the fact. But as we have no account of this expedition, and as the manner in which it is mentioned by Gmelin implies that he had it merely from tradition, we cannot lay any ftrefs upon fuch vague and uncertain reports. The paffage is as follows: " Es find " fo gar Spuren vorhanden, dafs ein Kerl mit einem Schifflein, das nicht " viel groeffer als ein Schifferkahn gevefen, von Kolyma bis Tfchukotskoi-
" Nofs

NORTHERN O

Mouths
of the
Lena

Lena River

Yana River

Swatoi Noss

I. Diomed

Chroma R.

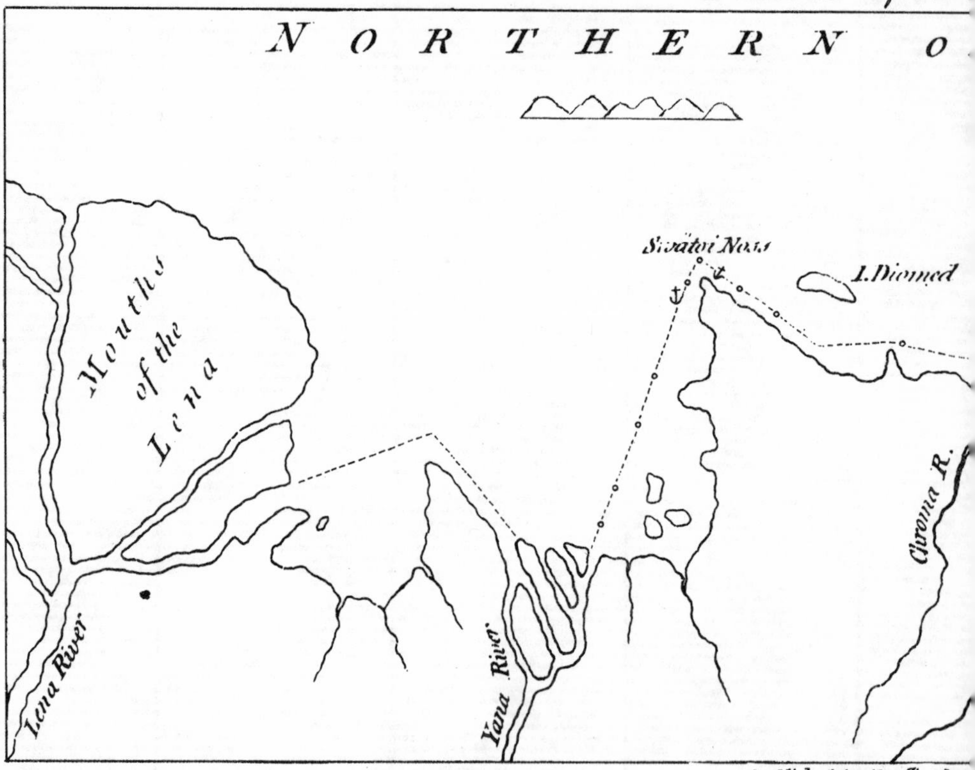

Published April 13.th 1780

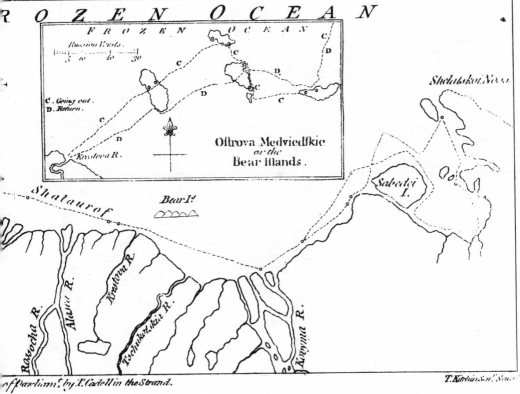

F R O Z E N   O C E A N

F R O Z E N   O C E A N

Russian Versts.
5   10   20   30

C . Going out .
D . Return .

C
C
C
C
D
D
C
C
C
D
D
D
C

Ostrova Medviedskie
or the
Bear Islands .

Shelatskoi Nos

Sabadei
I.

Shatauros

Bear I.

Kovleva R.

Rossocha R.

Alasei R.

Kovleva R.

Tschukotskii R.

Kovyma R.

T. Kitchin Sc.t Sou.t

Afia, notwithſtanding all the attempts which have been made to accompliſh this paſſage, as well from * Kamt-chatka as from the Frozen Ocean.

The following narrative of a late voyage, performed by one Shalauroff, from the Lena towards Tſchukotſkoi-Noſs, will ſhew the great impediments which obſtruct a coaſting navigation in the Frozen Sea, even at the moſt favourable ſeaſon of the year.

Shalauroff, a Ruſſian merchant of Yakutſk, having conſtructed a ſhitik at his own expence, went down the Lena in 1761 †.   He was accompanied by an exiled mid-ſhipman, whom he had found at Yakutſk, and to whom

Voyage of Shalauroff.

───────────

" Noſs vorbey, und bis nach Kamtſchatka gekommen ſey." Gmelin Reiſe II. p. 437. Mem. et Obſ. Geog. &c. p. 10.

* Beering, in his voyage from Kamtchatka, in 1628, towards Tſchu-kotſkoi-Noſs, ſailed along the coaſt of the Tſchutski as high as lat. 67°. 18′. and obſerving the coaſt take a Weſterly direction, he too haſtily concluded, that he had paſſed the North Eaſtern extremity. Apprehenſive, if he had attempted to proceed, of being locked in by the ice, he returned to Kamtchatka. If he had followed the ſhore, he would have found that what he took for the Northern ocean was nothing more than a deep bay; and that the coaſt of the Tſchutski, which he conſidered as turning uni-formly to the Weſt, took again a Northerly direction. S. R. G. III. p. 117.

† According to another MS. account of Shalauroff's voyage, which I have in my poſſeſſion, he is ſaid to have ſet out upon this expedition in 1760; and was prevented by the continued drifts of floating ice, which the Northerly winds drove towards the ſhore, from penetrating that year any further than the mouth of the Yana, where he wintered. In 1761, he put to ſea on the 29th of July, paſſed Svatoi-Noſs, &c. &c.

T t 2   we

we are indebted for the chart of this expedition. Shalauroff got out of the Southern mouth of the Lena in
July, but was so much embarraſſed by the ice, that he ran
the veſſel into the mouth of the Yana, where he was detained by the ice until the 29th of Auguſt, when he again
ſet ſail. Being prevented by the ice from keeping the
open ſea, he coaſted the ſhore; and, having doubled
Svatoi-Nofs on the 6th of September, diſcovered at a ſmall
diſtance out at Sea, to the North, a mountainous land,
which is probably ſome unknown iſland in the Frozen Sea.
He was employed from the 7th to the 15th in getting
through the ſtrait between Diomed's iſland and the coaſt
of Siberia; which he effected, not without great difficulty.
From the 16th he had a free ſea and a fair S. W. wind,
which carried them in 24 hours beyond the mouth of the
Indigirka. The favourable breeze continuing, he paſſed
on the 18th the Alaſca. Soon afterwards, the veſſel
approaching too near the ſhore was entangled amongſt
vaſt floating maſſes of ice, between ſome iſlands * and
the

* Theſe iſlands are Medviedkie Oſtrova, or the Bear Iſlands; they
are alſo called Kreſſſtoffskie Oſtrova, becauſe they lie oppoſite the mouth
of the ſmall river Kreſtova. For a long time vague reports were propagated that the continent of America ſtretched along the Frozen Ocean,
very near the coaſts of Siberia; and ſome perſons pretended to have diſcovered its ſhore not far from the rivers Kovyma and Kreſtova. But the
falſity of theſe reports was proved by an expedition made in 1764, by
ſome Ruſſian officers ſent by Denys Ivanovitch Tſchitcherin, governor of
Tobolsk.

the main land. And now the late feafon of the year obliged Shalauroff to look out for a wintering place; he accordingly ran the veffel into one of the mouths of the river Kovyma, where fhe was laid up. The crew immediately conftructed an hut, which they fecured with a rampart of frozen fnow, and a battery of the fmall guns. The wild rein-deer reforted to this place in large herds, and were fhot in great plenty from the enclofure. Before the fetting-in of winter, various fpecies of falmon and trout came up the river in fhoals: thefe fifh afforded the crew a plentiful fubfiftence, and preferved them from the fcurvy *.

Winters at the Mouth of the Kovyma.

The mouth of the Kovyma was not freed from ice before the 21ft of July, 1762, when Shalauroff again

Departure from thence in July.

Tobolsk. Thefe officers went in winter, when the fea was frozen, in fledges drawn by dogs, from the mouth of the Kreftova. They found nothing but five fmall rocky iflands, fince called the Bear Iflands, which were quite uninhabited; but fome traces were found of former inhabitants, namely, the ruins of huts. They obferved alfo on one of the iflands a kind of wooden ftage built of drift-wood, which feemed as if it had been intended for defence. As far as they durft venture out over the Frozen Sea, no land could be feen, but high mountains of ice obftructed their paffage, and forced them to return. See the map of this expedition upon the chart of Shalauroff's voage.

* Raw fifh are confidered in thofe Northern countries as a prefervative againft the fcurvy.

put

put to fea, and fteered until the 28th N. E. by N. E.
$\frac{1}{4}$ E. Here he obferved the variation of the compafs
afhore, and found it to be 11° 15″ Eaft. The 28th a
contrary wind, which was followed by a calm, obliged
him to come to an anchor, and kept him ftationary
until the 10th of Auguft, when a favourable breeze
fpringing up, he fet fail; he then endeavoured to fteer
at fome diftance from fhore, holding a more Eafterly
courfe, and N. E. by E. But the veffel was impeded by
large bodies of floating ice, and a ftrong current, which
feemed to bear Weftward at the rate of a verft an hour.
Thefe circumftances very much retarded his courfe. On
the 18th, the weather being thick and foggy, he found
himfelf unexpectedly near the coaft with a number of
ice iflands before him, which on the 19th entirely furrounded and hemmed in the veffel. He continued in
that fituation, and in a continual fog, until the 23d,
when he got clear, and endevoured by fteering N. E.
to regain the open fea, which was much lefs clogged
with ice than near the fhore. He was forced, however, by contrary winds, S. E. and E. among large
maffes of floating ice. This drift of ice being paffed,
he again ftood to the N. E. in order to double She-
latfkoi-Nofs*; but before he could reach the iflands

* He does not feem to have been deterred from proceeding by any
fuppofed difficulty in paffing Shelatskoi-Nofs, but to have veered about
merely on account of the late feafon of the year. Shelatskoi-Nofs is fo
called from the Shelagen, a tribe of the Tfchutski, and has been fuppofed to be the fame as Tfchukotskoi-Nofs. S. R. G. III. p. 52.

lying

lying near it, he was so retarded by contrary winds, that he was obliged, on account of the advanced season, to search for a wintering place. He accordingly sailed South towards an open bay, which lies on the West side of Shelatskoi-Nofs, and which no navigator had explored before him. He steered into it on the 25th, and got upon a shoal between a small island, and a point of land which juts from the Eastern coast of this bay. Having got clear with much difficulty, he continued for a short time a S. E. course, then turned S. W. He then landed in order to discover a spot proper for their winter residence; and found two small rivulets, but neither trees nor drift wood. The vessel was towed along the Southerly side of the bay as far as the island Sabedèi. On the 5th of September, he saw some huts of the Tschutski close to the narrow channel between Sabadèi and the main land; but the inhabitants fled on his approach.

Not being able to double Shelatskoi Nofs, returns towards the Kovyma.

Not having met with with a proper situation, he stood out to sea, and got round the island Sabadèi on the 8th, when he fastened the vessel to a large body of ice, and was carried along by a current towards W. S. W. at the rate of five versts an hour. On the 10th, he saw far to the N. E. by N. a mountain, and steered the 11th and 12th towards his former wintering place in the river Kovyma. Shalauroff proposed to have made

Winters a second Time at the Kovyma, and returns to the Lena.

the

the following year another attempt to double Shelatſkoi-
Noſs; but want of proviſion, and the mutiny of the
crew, forced him to return to the Lena in 1763. It
is worth remarking, that during his whole voyage he
found the currents ſetting in almoſt uniformly from
the Eaſt. Two remarkable rocks were obſerved by
Shalauroff near the point where the coaſt turns to
the N. E. towards the channel which ſeparates the
iſland Sabadèi from the continent; theſe rocks may
ſerve to direct future navigators: one is called Saetſhie
Kamen, or Hare's Rock, and riſes like a crooked horn;
the other Baranèi Kamen, or Sheep's Rock; it is in
the ſhape of a pear, narrower at the bottom than at top,
and riſes twenty-nine yards above high-water mark.

Second Expe-
dition of Sha-
lauroff.

Shalauroff, who concluded from his own experience,
that the attempt to double Tſchukotſkoi-Noſs, though
difficult, was by no means impracticable, was not diſ-
couraged by his former want of ſuccefs from engaging
a ſecond time in the ſame enterprize; he accordingly
fitted out the ſame ſhitik, and in 1764 departed as before from the river Lena. We have no poſitive accounts of this ſecond voyage: for neither Shalauroff or
any of his crew have ever returned. The following
circumſtances lead us to conclude, that both he and
his crew were killed near the Anadyr by the Tſchutſki,
about the third year after their departure from the Lena.

4   About

About that time the Koriacs of the Anadyr refufed to take from the Ruffians the provifion of flour, which they are accuftomed to purchafe every year.   Enquiry being made by the governor of Anadirfk, he found that they had been amply fupplied with that commodity by the Tfchutfki.   The latter had procured it from the plunder of Shalauroff's veffel, the crew of which appeared to have perifhed near the Anadyr.   From thefe facts, which have been fince confirmed by repeated intelligence from the Koriacs and Tfchutfki, it has been afferted, that Shalauroff had doubled the N. E. cape of Afia.   But this affertion amounts only to conjecture; for the arrival of the crew at the mouth of the Anadyr affords no decifive proof that they had paffed round the Eaftern extremity of Afia; for they might have penetrated to that river by land, from the Weftern fide of Tfchukotfkoi-Nofs.

No Account of this Expedi-. tion, he and his Crew being killed by the Tfchutfki.

In reviewing thefe feveral accounts of the Ruffian voyages in the Frozen Sea, as far as they relate to a North Eaft paffage, we may obferve, that the cape which ftretches to the North of the Piafida has never been doubled; and that the exiftence of a paffage round Tfchukotfkoi-Nofs refts upon the fingle authority of Defhneff.   Admitting however a practicable navigation round thefe two promontories, yet when we confider the difficulties and dangers which the Ruffians en-

U u   countered

bability, that this is the plant which produces the true rhubarb. But this inference does not appear to be absolutely conclusive; for the same trials have been repeated, and with similar succefs, upon the roots of the R. Rhaponticum and R. Rhabarbarum.

R. Rhaponti-
cum.

The leaves of the R. Rhaponticum are round, and fometimes broader than they are long. This fpecies is found abundantly in the loamy and dry deferts between the Volga and the Yaik*, towards the Cafpian Sea. It was probably from this fort that the name Rha, which is the Tartarian appellation of the river Volga, was firft applied by the Arabian phyficians to the feveral fpecies of rheum. The roots however which grow in thefe warm plains are rather too aftringent; and therefore ought not to be ufed in cafes where opening medicines are required. The Calmucs call it Badfhona, or a ftomachic. The young fhoots of this plant, which appear in March or April, are deemed a good antifcorbutic; and are ufed as fuch by the Ruffians. The R. Rhaponticum is not to be found to the Weft of the Volga. The feeds of this fpecies produced at Peterfburg plants of a much greater fize than the wild ones: the leaves were large, and of a roundifh cordated figure.

* The Yaik, now called the Ural, falls into the Cafpian Sea, about four degrees to the Eaft of the Volga.

The

The R. Rhabarbarum grows in the crevices of bare _{R. Rhabar-barum.} rocky mountains, and alfo upon gravelly foils: it is more particularly found in the high vallies of the romantic country fituated beyond Lake Baikal. Its buds do not fhoot before the end of April; and it continues in flower during the whole month of May. The ftalks of the leaves are eaten raw by the Tartars: they produce upon moft perfons, who are unaccuftomed to them, a kind of fpafmodic contraction of the throat, which goes off in a few hours; it returns however at every meal, until they become habituated to this kind of diet. The Ruffians make ufe of the leaves in their hodge-podge: accordingly, foups of this fort affect ftrangers in the manner above mentioned. In Siberia the ftalk is fometimes preferved as a fweetmeat; and a cuftom prevails among the Germans of introducing at their tables the buds of this plant, as well as of the Rheum Palmatum, inftead of cauli-flower.

The R. Rhaponticum which commonly grows near the torrents has, as well as the R. Rhabarbarum of Siberia, the upper part of its roots generally rotten, from too much moifture: accordingly, a very fmall portion of the lower extremity is fit for ufe. The Ruffian College of Phyficians order, for the ufe of their military hofpital, large quantities of thefe roots to be dug up in Siberia, which are prefcribed under the name of rhapontic. But the perfons employed in digging and pre-

X x   paring

barb; and his defcription of that plant anfwered to the figure of the Rheum Rhaponticum. The truth of this defcription was ftill further confirmed by fome Mongol travellers who had been in the neighbourhood of the Koko-Nor and Thibet; and had obferved the rhubarb growing wild upon thofe mountains.

The experiments alfo made by Zuchert and others, upon the roots of the R. Rhabarbarum and R. Rhaponticum fufficiently prove, that this valuable drug was procured from thofe roots in great perfection. But as the feeds of the Rheum Palmatum were received from the father of the abovementioned Bucharian merchant as taken from the plant which furnifhes the true rhubarb, we have reafon to conjecture, that thefe three fpecies, viz. R. Palmatum, R. Rhaponticum, and R. Rhabarbarum, when found in a drier and milder alpine climate, and in proper fituations, are indifcriminately drawn up; whenever the fize of the plant feems to promife a fine root. And perhaps the remarkable difference of the rhubarb, imported to Kiachta, is occafioned by this indifcriminate method of collecting them. Moft certain it is, that thefe plants grow wild upon the mountains, without the leaft cultivation; and thofe are efteemed the beft which are found near the Koko-Nor, and about the fources of the river Koango.

The true Rhubarb probably procured from different Species of Rheum.

Formerly

Formerly the exportation of rhubarb was confined to the crown of Ruffia: and no perfons but thofe employed by government were allowed the permiffion of fending it to foreign countries; this monopoly however has been taken off by the prefent emprefs, and the free exportation of it from St. Peterfburg granted to all perfons upon paying the duty. It is fold in the firft inftance by the College of Commerce for the profit of the Sovereign; and is preferved in their magazines at St. Peterfburg. The current price is fettled every year by the College of Commerce.

It is received from the Bucharian merchants at Kiachta in exchange for furs; and the prime coft is rated at 16 roubles per pood. By adding the pay of the commiffioners who purchafe it, and of the apothecary who examines it, and allowing for other neceffary expences, the value of a pood at Kiachta amounts to 25 roubles; add to this the carriage from the frontiers to St. Peterfburg, and it is calculated that the price of a pood ftands the crown at 30 roubles. The largeft exportation of rhubarb ever known from Ruffia, was made in the year 1765. when 1350 pood were exported, at 65 roubles per pood.

Price of Rhubarb in Ruffia.

E X-

TABLE of LONGITUDE and LATITUDE.

FOR the convenience of the Reader, the following Table exhibits in one point of view the longitude and latitude of the principal places mentioned in this performance. Their longitudes are eſtimated from the firſt meridian of the Iſle of Fero, and from that of the Royal Obſervatory at Greenwich. The longitude of Greenwich from Fero is computed at 17° 34′ 45″. The longitude of the places marked * has been taken from aſtronomical obſervations.

Table of Longitude and Latitude.

	Latitude. D.	M.	S.	Longitude. Fero. D.	M.	S.	Greenwich. D.	M.
* Petersburg —	59	56	23	48	0	0	30	25 †
* Moſcow —	55	45	45	55	6	30	37	31
* Archangel —	64	33	24	56	15	0	38	40
* Tobolſk —	58	12	22	85	40	0	68	26
* Tomſk —	56	30	0	102	50	0	85	15
* Irkutſk —	52	18	15	122	13	0	104	38
* Selenginſk —	51	6	0	124	18	30	106	44
Kiachta —	35	0	0	124	18	0	106	43
* Yakutſk —	62	1	50	147	0	0	129	25
* Ochotſk —	59	22	0	160	7	0	142	32
* Bolchereſk —	52	55	0	174	13	0	156	38
* Port of St. Peter and Paul	35	1	0	176	10	0	158	36
Eaſtern Extremity of Siberia	66	0	0	200	0	0	182	25
Unalaſhka { According to the general map of Ruſſia	58	0	0	223	0	0	205	25
According to the chart of Krenitzin and Levaſheff	53	30	0	205	30	0	187	55

† I have omitted the ſeconds in the longitude from Greenwich.

INDEX.

I N D E X.

A.

AGIAK, an interpreter, p. 133.

Aguladock, a leader of the Unalaſh-
kans, taken priſoner by Solovioff,
139.

Agulok, a dwelling-place on Unalaſhka, 137.

Aiſchin-Giord, chief of the Manſhurs
at the beginning of the 17th
century, 198.

Aktunak, an iſland to the Eaſt of
Kadyak, 108.

Akun (one of the Fox Iſlands), 159.

Akutan (one of the Fox Iſlands),
159.

Alakſu, or *Alachſhak*, one of the
moſt remote Eaſtern iſlands, 65.
Cuſtoms of the inhabitants, 68.
Animals found on that iſland, *ib.*
Conjectured to be not far from
the continent of America, 69.

Alaxa (one of the Fox Iſlands), 254.

Albaſin, and the other Ruſſian forts
on the Amoor, deſtroyed by the
Chineſe, 198. The Ruſſians taken there refuſe to return from
Pekin, 208.

Aleütian Iſſes diſcovered, 21. 29.
their ſituation and names, 24.
Names of perſons there, bear a
ſurpriſing reſemblance to thoſe of
the Greenlanders, 40. Inhabitants deſcribed, 41. 46. Account
of thoſe iſlands, 45. 55. The
manners and cuſtoms of the inhabitants reſemble thoſe of the Fox
Iſlands, 173. Are entirely ſubject
to Ruſſia, 174. Their number,
289. Specimen of the Aleütian
language, 303. See *Fox Iſlands,
Ibiya, Novodtſikoff, Tſiuproff.*

Alexeeff (Feodot). See *Deſhneff*.

Aleyut. See *Fox Iſlands*.

Alloi (a prince of the Calmucs), his
ſuperſtitious regard for the memory of Yermac, 194.

Amaganak, a toigon of Unalaſhka,
143.

America, moſt probable courſe for
diſcovering the neareſt coaſt of
that continent, pointed out, 27.
See *Iſlands, Deliſle, Alakſu,
Kadyak, Fox Iſlands, Steller.*

Amlak, one of the Andreanoſſkye
Iſlands, 76.

Y y

Ana-

Z z

Tien,

W.

INDEX.

W.

Wheels, a carriage with four wheels a mark of high diftinction among the Chinefe, 218.

White month, explained, 228.

Women, none allowed to live at Maimatfchin, and why, 231.

Wfevidoff (Andrew), his voyage to the New-difcovered Iflands, 38.

Y.

Yakoff (Jacob), compofed the chart of Krenitzin and Levafheff's voyage, 266.

Yediger (a Tartar chief), pays tribute to the Ruffians, 179. See *Kutchum Chan*.

Tenifei, a river of Siberia, 305, & feq.

Terken, a town of Little Bucharia, 333.

Yermac, being driven from the Cafpian Sea, retires to Orel, 181, where he winters, and determines to invade Siberia, 182. To which he is inftigated by Strogo-noff, 183. Marches towards Siberia, and returns to Orel, 184. Sets out on a fecond expedition, and arrives at Tchingi, 185. Defeats Kutchum Chan at Tfchuvatch, 186. Marches to Sibir, and feats himfelf on the throne, 187. Cedes his conqueft to the Tzar of Mufcovy, 189. Who fends him a reinforcement, under the command of prince Bolkofky, 190. Is furprifed by Kutchum Chan, 191. And drowned, 192. Veneration paid to his memory, 193. See *Altai*, *Ruffians*, *Siberia*, *Ivan Vaffelivitch* II.

Yefimoff (Sava), one of Yermac's followers, an accurate hiftorian of thofe times, 192.

Yugoff (Emilian), his voyage, 38. Dies on Copper Ifland, 39.

Z.

Zuchert. See *Rhubarb*.

Zuruchaitu. Defcription of, 244. Its trade very inconfiderable, 245. See *Kiachta*.

FINIS.

SUPPLEMENT

TO THE

RUSSIAN DISCOVERIES.

A

COMPARATIVE VIEW

OF THE

RUSSIAN DISCOVERIES

WITH THOSE MADE BY

CAPTAINS COOK AND CLERKE;

AND A SKETCH OF

WHAT REMAINS TO BE ASCERTAINED BY
FUTURE NAVIGATORS.

BY WILLIAM COXE, A.M. F.R.S.

One of the Senior Fellows of King's College, Cambridge; Member of
the Imperial Œconomical Society at St. Peterſburgh, of the Royal
Academy of Sciences at Copenhagen; and Chaplain to his Grace the
Duke of MARLBOROUGH.

LONDON,
PRINTED BY J. NICHOLS,
FOR T. CADELL, IN THE STRAND.
MDCCLXXXVII.

T O

PETER SIMON PALLAS, M. D. F. R. S.

COUNSELLOR OF THE BOARD OF MINES TO THE

EMPRESS OF RUSSIA, MEMBER OF THE IMPERIAL

ACADEMY OF SCIENCES AT ST. PETERSBURGH, &c. &c.

THE FOLLOWING ATTEMPT TO COMPARE

THE DISCOVERIES OF A NATION,

WHOSE CIVIL, TOPOGRAPHICAL, AND

NATURAL HISTORY

HE HAS SO AMPLY ELUCIDATED, IS INSCRIBED

BY

HIS FAITHFUL AND OBEDIENT

HUMBLE SERVANT,

WILLIAM COXE.

Cambridge,
April 25, 1787.

ADVERTISEMENT.

THE author would have arranged, at a more early period, the following Comparative View, which seems necessarily connected with his former publication on the Russian Discoveries; if he had not been absent from England when Cook's Voyage first made its appearance; and if continued travels and avocations had not prevented him from consulting those books, charts, and manuscripts, which the examination of so intricate a subject required.

Mr. Pallas has lately favoured the public, in his *Neue Nordische Beytraege*, with several curious particulars concerning the Tchutfki, the two islands lying between East Cape and Cape Prince of Wales, and relative to the New-discovered islands. An extract of some of these particulars is given by Mr. Pennant in his Introduction to the Arctic Zoology, and more amply in his Supplement to that interesting work, in which the reader will find an excellent map of those parts, which are mentioned in this Comparative View.

OCTAVO EDITION.

Just published,

Elegantly printed in Four Volumes Octavo, illustrated with Maps, Plans, and other Plates, Price 1l. 10s. bound,

The Third Edition of

TRAVELS into Poland, Russia, Sweden, and Denmark, Interspersed with Historical Relations and Political Inquiries.

By WILLIAM COXE, A. M. F. R. S.

One of the Senior Fellows of King's College Cambridge, Chaplain to his Grace the Duke of Marlborough, Member of the Imperial Oeconomical Society of St. Petersburgh, and of the Royal Academy of Sciences at Copenhagen.

Printed for T. Cadell, in the Strand.

By whom will speedily be published,

An Octavo Edition of Mr. Coxe's Account of the Russian Discoveries between Asia and America; in which will be added a Comparative View of the Russian Discoveries with those made by Captains Cook and Clerke, &c. &c.

C H A P I.

A comparative View of the Ruffian *Difcoveries, with thofe made by* Cook *and* Clerke. 1. *On the Coaft of* Afia. 2. *On that of* America. 3. *With refpect to the New-difcovered Iflands.*

AS my account of the Ruffian Difcoveries, printed in 1780, contained the principal intelligence at that time known; and as, fince its publication, a new light has been thrown upon that important fubject by Cook and Clerke, I fhall, in this chapter, compare the difcoveries of the Ruffians with the fubfequent obfervations of the Englifh navigators. 1. On the coaft of Afia, 2. on that of America; and 3. with refpect to the New-difcovered Iflands.

The accuracy of Krafilnikof's obfervations, at the Port of St. Peter and St. Paul, has been confirmed by Captain Cook. The latter places that harbour in lat. 53′ 1″, long. 158′ 36″ eaft * ; the former in lat. 53′ 0″ 38″, long. 176′ 10″ from Fero, or 158′ 35″ from Greenwich. The difference is only 22 feconds in the latitude, and 7 minutes in the longitude. Hence the affertion of Vaugondy, that the Ruffians had advanced the peninfula of Kamtchatka eleven degrees too much to the eaft, and of Engel, who fuppofed that error to be no lefs than 29 degrees, is evidently confuted; and the juftnefs of the aftronomical obfervations, made by the Ruffian geographers,

---

* It is neceffary to apprife the reader, that, in this Supplement, whenever the longitude given by Cook is mentioned, it is taken from the meridian of Greenwich. The reader is alfo defired to confult the maps and charts which accompany Cook's Voyage to the Pacific Ocean.

B which

which I attempted to prove in the fecond number of the Appendix to the Ruffian Difcoveries, is now incontrovertibly afcertained.

Though we cannot expect nearly the fame accuracy in the longitude of thofe places, which have not been laid down by aftronomical obfervations; yet we fhall find, perhaps, that the errors of the Ruffians, even under fuch difadvantages, have not always been fo great, as might reafonably be fuppofed. Thus while the latitude of Kamtchatka Nofs, and of Kronotfkoi Nofs the moft north-eafterly point in the peninfula of Kamtchatka, agrees with the latitude of thofe places, given by Captain Cook, their longitude is laid down 2' 46" too much to the weft; and the fame error feems to prevail in the bearings of the Kamtchatka Coaft, as traced on the Ruffian charts.

Towards the north, the deficiency in the longitude is far more confiderable. The promontory of St. Thaddæus, the moft north eafterly point in the country of the Koriacs, lies, according to Cook, in lat. 62' 50", long. 180'; and is fituated, on the general map of Ruffia, in lat. 63, long. 190, from Fero, or 172' 25" from Greenwich; which gives a difference of only 50' in the latitude, but of 7' 35" in the longitude.

The next point of land obferved by the Englifh navigators, was that promontory called by Beering Tchukotfkoi Nofs, a name adopted by Captain Cook, but which is denominated by moft of the Ruffian geographers Anadirfkoi Nofs, from its pofition on the Bay of the Anadyr. The application of the term Tchukotfkoi Nofs to this promontory, may, perhaps, occafion fome confufion to future navigators and geographers, as that appellation has been ufually given, and ought therefore to be appropriated to the eaftern extremity of Afia, the Eaft Cape of Cook.

From Anadirfkoi Nofs, placed by the Englifh in lat. 64' 13", under the name of Tchukotfkoi Nofs, to Cape Serdze Kamen, in

lat.

lat. 67. the utmoſt extent of Beering's navigation to the north, Captain Cook, with great candour, does juſtice to the memory of Beering, by obſerving, that " he has here delineated the " coaſt very well, and fixed the latitude and longitude of the " places better than could be expected from the methods he " had to go by *."

Within this ſpace our great navigator has corrected the errors of the Ruſſian charts, and aſcertained the poſition of the real Tchukotſkoi Noſs, which Muller had erroneouſly conjectured to lie above the 70th degree of latitude. He calls this great promontory of the Tchutſki Eaſt Cape, proves it to be the moſt eaſtern extremity of Aſia, and fixes its latitude in 66′ 6″, and long. 190′ 22″. Thus he has unqueſtionably ſhewn, that the Ruſſians did not err in aſſerting, that the north eaſtern extremity of Aſia ſtretched beyond the 200th degree of longitude from the Iſle of Fero, or 182′ from Greenwich.

The earlieſt and moſt important of the Ruſſian voyages in theſe parts, as it firſt aſcertained the ſeparation of the two continents, is that remarkable expedition of Deſhnef, in which, according to Muller, he ſailed from the mouth of the Kovyma, doubled Tchukotſkoi Noſs, or the Eaſt Cape of Cook, and was

* Cook's Voyage, vol. II. p. 474. The reader is deſired to correct a paſſage in the note, p. 323, of my Ruſſian Diſcoveries; in which I aſſerted, upon the authority of Muller, that Beering, in his expedition to the northern coaſts of Aſia, did not double the north eaſtern promontory of that continent, properly called Tchulotskoi Noſs. Whereas it appears, from a comparative view of Beering's and Cook's diſcoveries, that the former actually paſſed that celebrated point ; and, that Cape Serdze Kamen, the utmoſt extent of his voyage, is ſituated to the north and not, according to Muller, to the ſouth of the ſaid promontory. Captain Cook, who alone could aſcertain theſe points, and whoſe judgment muſt be conſidered as deciſive, informs us, that Muller's account of Beering's expedition, and that part of the chart prefixed to his Ruſſian Diſcoveries, which refers to that expedition, are leſs accurate than the relation of the ſame voyage, and the annexed map publiſhed by Dr. Campbell in the ſecond edition of Harris's Collection of Voyages.

ſhip-

fhipwrecked in the Sea of Kamtchatka. An account of this expedition is given in my Ruffian Difcoveries *. But as, from
want of circumftantial evidence, many perfons ftill doubt, whether Defhnef failed round this celebrated promontory; it may
not, perhaps, be unintérefting to ftate a few particulars in
Cook's narrative, which may feem to corroborate the authenticity of Defhnef's voyage.

Defhnef's defcription of the North Eaftern Cape correfponds
in feveral material circumftances with that of the fame promontory given by Cook. According to Defhnef it " *confifts almoft*
" *entirely of rocks* +." Cook fays, that " it fhews a fteep *rocky*
" cliff next the fea; and at the very point are *fome rocks like fpires.*
" The land about this promontory is compofed of hills and vallies:
" the former terminate at the fea in *fteep rocky points*, and the lat-
" ter in low fhores. The hills feemed to be *naked rocks* ‡."

Defhnef adds, that, on the coaft near the promontory, the
natives had reared a *pile like a tower, with the bones of whales.*
Cook likewife noticed thefe piles as very common on the coaft
of the Tfchutfki. " Over the dwelling ftands a kind of fentry
box, *comtofed of the large bones of large fifh* ;" and again, " near
the dwellings were erected ftages of *bones*, fuch as before defcribed §." Cook alfo agrees with Defhnef in placing two fmall
iflands directly oppofite to the promontory; and Captain King ||
confirms another affertion of the Ruffian navigator, that the
paffage from the fame promontory to the mouth of the Anadyr
may, with a fair wind, be performed in feventy-two hours **.

* See p. 314.
+ " Aus lauter Felfen beftunde." S. R. G. III. p. 17.
‡ Cook's Voyage, Vol. II. p. 472.
§ Vol. II. p. 451, 472. || Vol. III. p. 264.
** The reader will find thefe two laft-mentioned points more fully difcuffed by
Captain King, Vol. III. p. 264.

To

To thofe perfons who object to Defhnef's narrative, becaufe
Cook and Clerke were, in two fucceffive years, prevented by the
ice from penetrating into the frozen ocean; it may be replied,
that Defhnef paffed in a fmall veffel, which might more eafily
be worked through than the Englifh fhips; and that the year, in
which Defhnef failed round, is reprefented as more free from
ice than ufual. The feafon alfo, in which Defhnef probably
doubled the great Siberian promontory, was more favourable to
navigation in the Frozen Sea, than the times of the year employed by the Englifh. For although he failed on the firft of
July *, yet he does not appear to have arrived in the Eaftern
Ocean until the latter end of September. Soon after Ankunidof's
veffel was fhipwrecked on Tchukotfkoi Nofs, Defhnef mentions,
that he landed on the firft of October †, and fkirmifhed with the
Tchutfki. It follows therefore, from the length of the interval
between the day of his departure from the mouth of the Kovyma
to his arrival in the Eaftern Ocean, that he probably waited for
an opportunity of getting through the ice, which he at length
effected. Whereas Cook quitted that dreary region on the 29th
of Auguft; and Clerke, fo early as the month of July. The
middle and the latter end of September are generally efteemed the
moft proper periods for navigating the Frozen Ocean.

The fole aim of Defhnef being to fail from the Kovyma to the
Anadyr, it was not incompatible with his plan to continue on the
coaft, and to perfevere in expecting a favourable occafion for
executing his purpofe, without expofing himfelf to thofe difficulties and dangers, which feamen from more diftant quarters
muft neceffarily experience. On the contrary, the grand defign
of the Englifh navigators being to afcertain the practicability of a
North Eaftern paffage, and having incontrovertibly determined

* June 20, O. S.   † Sept. 20, O. S.

4   that

that important queftion in the negative, they accomplifhed the primary object of their expedition. They could not therefore, confiftently with their views and inftructions, by delaying their departure from thofe frozen regions, hazard the danger of being hemmed in by the ice, in order merely to fhow the poffibility of getting round to the Kovyma.

Should all thefe circumftances be confidered as proofs, that Defhnef performed this much-difputed voyage; yet, as he neither made any aftronomical obfervations, nor traced a chart of the coaft, his expedition, though it decided the long-agitated difpute concerning the feparation of the two continents, did not, however, contribute to an accurate knowledge of the north-eaftern extremity of Afia, for which we are indebted to Cook alone.

2. The difcoveries of the Ruffians on the Continent of America come next under confideration. Several of thofe coafts, vifited by the Ruffians, which they fuppofed, though on very uncertain grounds, to be parts of America, and which they had imperfectly defcribed, have been afcertained by Cook to belong to that Continent.

Thus Cook * difcovered a great mountain on the Coaft of America, in latitude 58′ 53″, longitude 220′ 52″, which he allows to be the fame as Beering's Mount St. Elias, lying, according to his eftimation, in latitude 58′ 28″, longitude 236′, from Fero, or 218′ 25″ from Greenwich. The difference in latitude is merely 28 feconds, and of longitude only 2′ 27″; and the defcriptions of it, given by Cook and Beering, exactly agree.

Cook † likewife explored the fame Continent, fituated in latitude 54′ 43″ and 55′ 20″, in longitude 224′ 44″, which makes it probable, that the land vifited by Tchirikof, and placed by

* Vol. II. p. 346.   † Ib. p. 343.

him

him in latitude 56′, longitude 241′ from Fero, or 223′ 25″ from Greenwich, was really a part of America.

Alaxa, called fometimes Alaxfu, Alachfhak and Alafhka, reached by many Ruffians *, particularly by Krenitzin and Levatchef, and fuppofed to be a great ifland in the vicinity of America, was found by Cook to be a promontory of that Continent. Its fouth-weftern point, reprefented on Krenitzin's chart, in latitude 54′ 42″, longitude 206′ 50″, from Fero, or 189′ 15″ from Greenwich, is laid down by Cook in latitude 54′ 10″, longitude 195′, which gives only a difference of 32 minutes in latitude, and 5′ 45″ in longitude.

That promontory lying oppofite to the country of the Tchutfki, which, according to Muller †, was firft feen by Gvofdef in 1730, and the moft weftern point of which is reprefented on the chart that accompanies his Ruffian Difcoveries, as lying in the 66th degree of latitude, and in the 211th of longitude from the Ifle of Fero, or 193′ 25″ from Greenwich. This point of land is probably the fame as that touched at by Synd, and placed by him in latitude 64′ 40″, and longitude 38′ 15″ from Okotfk; or 181° 25′ from Greenwich.

This promontory, named Cape Prince of Wales, Cook found to be the moft weftern point of America hitherto explored, lying in latitude 65′ 46′, in longitude 191′ 45″, which gives a difference of latitude from Muller of only 14 minutes, from Synd of 1′ 20″; and of longitude from Muller of only 1′ 40″, but from Synd of 10 degrees. It is diftant from the eaftern cape of Siberia only thirteen leagues. Thus Cook has the glory of afcertaining the vicinity of the two continents, which had only

* See Ruf. Dif. p. 65. 68, 69. 254.   † S. R. G. III. p. 131.

been

been conjectured from the reports of the Tchutfki, and from the imperfect obfervations of the Ruffian navigators.

It reflects the higheft honour even on the British name, that our great navigator extended his difcoveries much further in one expedition, and at fo great a diftance from the point of his departure, than the Ruffians accomplifhed in a long feries of years, and in parts belonging or contiguous to their own empire. But although we afcribe this tribute of applaufe to the man whofe claim is indifputably founded; yet we ought not to with-hold that portion of praife due to the Ruffians, for having firft navigated thofe feas, and made thofe difcoveries which the Englifh have confirmed and greatly exceeded.

It muft indeed be confeffed, that Cook cenfures with juftice Staehlin's chart of the New Archipelago *; and ftrongly con-demns it as an impofition on the public; fuch fictions in a work fo refpectably vouched, as the moft accurate reprefentation of the New-difcovered Iflands, being calculated only to miflead future navigators. In fact, Muller alfo, and the beft-informed Ruffians, had previoufly pronounced Mr. Staehling's account, and the annexed map, to be extremely erroneous †.

But our great navigator feems to have been too rigid in cenfuring Muller for placing Tchukotfkoi Nofs in too high a latitude; and for " his very imperfect knowledge of the geo-" graphy of thefe parts ‡." He did not fufficiently appre-ciate the merits of an author, who, though he unavoid-ably erred in fome particulars, yet deferves great appro-bation for his fagacity in uniformly fupporting the exiftence

* Vol. II. p. 475. 486. 506. particularly.
† Ruf. Dif. p. 28. 283, 284.
‡ Vol. II. 470, 471. See alfo p. 503

of

of Beering's Straits, and the vicinity of the two continents; when those opinions had been treated as chimerical. If Cook had been able to read Muller's account of the Russian Discoveries in the original German, and not in inaccurate translations *; if he had fairly weighed the extreme difficulty of drawing intelligence from imperfect journals of ignorant adventurers, from vague accounts, or uncertain tradition; if he had distinguished what Muller advances as conjectural †, from what he lays down as fact; if he had known that Muller had candidly acknowledged and rectified several mistakes; if he had compared his trifling sources of information with his own positive proofs; he would not have been offended by those inaccuracies, which must necessarily arise from such complicated and multifarious questions: he would probably have been less severe in his judgement of a writer, who first excited the curiosity of the public towards those discoveries, which occasioned his own glorious expedition, under the auspices of the sovereign who now sits upon the British throne.

3 . The new-discovered islands between Asia and America form the third part of the present inquiry.

As my former account of the Russian Discoveries renders it unnecessary to particularize all the islands visited by the Russians, and laid down in their charts, I shall only select the principal islands which were either ascertained, or appear to have been observed by the English navigators.

Kadyak, one of the most distant islands reached by the Rus-

* The English translation of that work is the most inaccurate.

† Mr. Muller's map of the north eastern coast of Siberia is allowed, by Captain King, " to bear a considerable resemblance to the survey of the English navigators, " as far as the latter extended ‡ ;" and it is to be observed, that the great promontory, which Muller lays down in latitude 75. as Tchukotskoi Nos, is represented in his map as very uncertain; and as a country, the extent of which is wholly unknown. *Pays des Tschutski dont on ne connoit pas l'etendue.*

‡ Vol. III. p. 263.

C

fians, is fully defcribed from Glottof's journal in the tenth chapter of my Ruffian Difcoveries. It is placed by Glottof in the 230th degree of longitude from Fero, or 212' 25" from Greenwich; and is fuppofed to be not far diftant from the coaft of a wide extended woody continent, or from that part of America which Beering formerly touched at. This conjecture is confirmed by Cook, who mentions it as contiguous to America, and forming one of an extenfive group, which he imagines to comprife thofe called by Beering Shumagin's Iflands *. Its true pofition is determined by Cook to be in latitude 55' 18", and longitude 199. The difference of longitude will not appear fo remarkably erroneous, when it is confidered that Glottof's account was computed merely from fhips reckonings, and that of Cook is founded on aftronomical obfervations.

This group is part of that chain, called the Fox Iflands; the longitude of which is very erroneoufly given upon all the Ruffian maps, and the latitude faithfully reprefented only on Krenitzin's chart; as will be more fully fhewn in the comparative account of Unalafka.

The next ifland which Cook accurately defcribes is that named Halibut, probably the fame as the ifland called Sannaga by Soloviof, in his journal, a manufcript extract of which I have in my poffeffion. This ifland, termed Senagak by the Aleutian chief †, is flightly mentioned in my account of the Ruffian Difcoveries ‡, but is not laid down in any of their charts under that name; it will probably appear to be Halibut's Ifland, by a comparative examination of the two defcriptions given by Cook and Soloviof.

* Vol. II. p. 413.   † Ruff. Dif. p. 296.
‡ It is not improbable, that this ifland is the fame as Kita Managan, which is reprefented on Krenitzin's chart, as lying near to Alaxa, and which has nearly the fame pofition as Halibut's Ifland in Cook's chart.

Halibut's

" Halibut's Ifland lies near to the promontory of Alaſka,
" is feven or eight leagues in circuit, and, except the *head, which*
" *is a round hill, the land of it is very low and barren.* There are
" feveral fmall iflands near it of a fimilar appearance ; but there
" feemed to be a paffage between them and the main, two or
" three leagues broad *."

Soloviof +, who anchored in a bay of Sannaga, Auguſt 19,
1771, thus defcribes it :

" Sannaga is fituated not far from Unimak and Alaxa, and is
" feparated from the latter by a channel of about twenty leagues.
" It appeared to be about eight leagues in length, and about a
" league and three quarters in breadth. On the northern fide of
" the weſtern point is a *fmall peak, joined to a low ridge of hills*
" *extending* to the eaſt and weſt, about a verſt, or three quarters
" of a mile. *Except this rifing ground, the whole ifland is low and*
" *marſhy.* It is watered by many fprings and lakes, containing
" fiſh fimilar to thofe of Okotſk. *The ifland produces neither*
" *trees nor berries.* It is furrounded by many fmall iflands. It
" is feparated from a little ifland fituated near its fouthern point
" by a ſtrait, about a league broad, which is fometimes dry. In
" reconnoitring this iſland, Solovief obferved feveral deferted
" huts, but met with no inhabitants."

Unalaſka or Oonalaſka, the largeſt ifland, next to Umnak, in
the whole chain of the Fox Iflands, and which has been frequently vifited and defcribed by the Ruffians, was alfo particularly obferved by Cook, who anchored in a fine bay on the
north fide, called by the natives Sanganovodha, and of which he

---

* Vol. II. p. 416.

+ I have only printed a fmall part of his journal, as it contains no material in-
formation, in additional to thofe journals already publiſhed in my Account of the
Ruffian Difcoveries. Soloviof failed from Okotſk on this expedition to the Fox
Iflands on the 6th of September, 1770 ; and returned on the 16th of July, 1775.

has

has given a chart. Unalaſka is placed by Cook in latitude 53′ 55″, longitude 193′ 30″; by Krenitzin in latitude 53′ 30″, longitude 205′ 30″ from Fero; or 187′ 55″ from Greenwich; on the general map of Ruſſia in latitude 58′, longitude 225′ from Fero; or 205′ 25″ from Greenwich. Thus it appears, that in latitude Krenitzin only differs from Cook 25 minutes; and in longitude 5′ 35″; whereas the general map of Ruſſia varies 4′ 5″ even in latitude, and in longitude 11′ 55″. The ſame error alſo prevails in the poſition of Unimak, Umnak, Amughta, and the other iſles adjacent to Unalaſka, the ſituations of which are corrected and determined by Cook *. Here it may be remarked, that the relative poſition of that part of the Fox Iſlands, which ſtretches ſouth-eaſt from the head-land Alaxa, is well laid down in Krenitzin's chart; and that in all reſpects it deſerves the preference over the repreſentation of thoſe iſlands on the general Map of Ruſſia.

The deſcription of Unalaſka and of the contiguous iſlands, their extent, productions, and the manners of the natives, as given by Cook, correſponds entirely with the account of the ſame iſlands in the Ruſſian Diſcoveries; and ſerves to prove, that the journals, from which my account was drawn, are in theſe reſpects faithful and accurate. No iſlands in the chain of the Fox Iſlands were obſerved by Cook to the weſt of Amughta: a few ſcattered Iſlands are indeed repreſented on the chart which accompanies his journal, not from his own obſervation, but from a map communicated by a Ruſſian, named Iſmailof, which I ſhall hereafter conſider †.

Whether the iſland, called by Cook Gore's Iſland, lying in latitude 60′ 10″, in longitude 187′, may be conſidered

* See Cook's Voyage, Vol. II.
† Vol. II. p. 497, &c. See alſo Vol. III. p. 193, 194.

as

as the ifland of St. Matthew, placed on Synd's chart in latitude 59' 30", longitude 34' 10" from Okotfk; or 176' 42" from Greenwich; is a conjecture which may deferve inquiry. The difference of latitude is only 40 minutes; and the deficiency in the longitude of 10' 18" nearly coincides with Synd's error of longitude obfervable in other inftances, while the general outline of its coaft, its relative fize and bearings to the head-lands of the two continents, fufficiently agree in the two charts.

The exiftence of the ifland St. Laurence, obferved by Beering near the Coaft of Siberia, was alfo confirmed by Cook; and it is not without probability, that thofe called Clerke's, Anderfon's, and King's Iflands, may perhaps form part of that group obferved by Synd, and reprefented, on his chart, as lying near the head-lands of the Tchutfki.

The moft eaftern part of Copper Ifland is laid down, in the Ruffian charts, in latitude 55', longitude 184' from Fero; or 166' 25" from Greenwich; and, after the obfervations of the Englifh, is determined to lie in latitude 54' 28", longitude 167' 52", which gives a difference of but 32' in the latitude, and of only 1' 27" in the longitude.

CHAP.

CHAP. II.

Sketch of what remains to be ascertained.—1. *On the coast of* Asia. —2. *On that of* America.—3. *And in relation to the New-discovered Islands.*—*Expedition of Captain* Billings.

HAVING now reviewed and compared the Russian Discoveries with those made by Cook and Clerke, it is the design of this second chapter to lay before the reader what remains to be ascertained in those remote quarters of the globe. In treating this subject, I shall follow the same order which I adopted in the first; and endeavour to explain the *desiderata* towards completing the geography, 1. of the Asiatic coast; 2. of the American Continent; 3. of the New-discovered Islands.

1. What principally remains to be examined on the Asiatic coast, is that region of Siberia stretching from Cape North in latitude 68′ 56″, longitude 180′ 51″, the utmost extent of Cook's discoveries, to the mouth of the Kovyma in the Frozen Ocean.

Cook conjectures, and the conjectures of so great a man deserve to be weighed with the utmost attention, that the northern coast of Asia, from the Indigirka eastwards, has been laid down by the Russian geographers more than two degrees too much to the northward: and Captain King no less ingeniously conceives, that nearly the same error of longitude prevails in the bearings of the Asiatic coast in the Frozen Ocean, which is proved to

3   exist

exift in the eaftern coaft of Siberia *. If therefore it fhould be deemed probable, that the Kovyma is reprefented too much to the north and weft, the diftance between the mouth of that river and Cape North muft be confiderably lefs than is ufually imagined +.

It now remains to determine the unknown coaft between Cape North and Shelatfkoi Nofs, the moft eaftern point traced by the Ruffians in the Frozen Ocean, to take a more accurate delineation of the fhore between Shelatfkoi Nofs and the Kovyma than has been effected by Shalaurof ‡, and to fix, by aftronomical obfervations, the longitude and latitude of the mouth of the Kovyma.

2. The principal objects of examination on the American coaft are the following parts of that continent, which Cook was prevented from exploring. That fpace reaching from Woody Point in latitude 50′ 1″, and longitude 229′ 26″, to latitude 53′ 22″, longitude 225′ 14″, comprizes 3′ 22″ of latitude, and 4′ 12″ of longitude; and is the more remarkable, as it contains the place where geographers have afcribed the ftrait of Admiral de Fonte. "And although there is little reafon to give credit," as Cook expreffes himfelf, "to fuch vague and improbable "ftories, as carry their own confutation § ;" yet it is to be regretted, that he was prevented from entirely difproving thofe pretended difcoveries which fome perfons ftill confider as authentic.

The fhore between Shoal-Nefs, in latitude 60′, longitude 198′ 10″, and Point Shallow Water, in latitude 63′, longitude 198′, is alfo entirely undefcribed ; and what renders this coaft an in-

* See thefe queftions fully and ably difcuffed by Captain King, Vol. III.
+ Cook's Voyage, Vol. II. p. 263—270.
‡ See Shalaurof's Voyage and Chart in my Ruffian Difcoveries.
§ Vol. II. p. 343.

terefting

terefting fubject of inquiry, is the inference of Captain **Cook**, that here runs a confiderable river from the continent into the fea *.

Perhaps it would well deferve the attention of fome future navigator, to explore Cook's river ftill further than the Englifh navigator was able to penetrate : he traced it as high as latitude 61' 30", longitude 210', feventy leagues or more from its mouth, without feeing the leaft appearance of its fource. Perhaps this great river, which, to ufe Cook's expreffion +, " promifes to vie with the moft confiderable ones already " known to be capable of extenfive inland navigation," may nearly join thofe waters and lakes which Hearne difcovered in his curious expedition from Hudfon's Bay to the Arapathefcow Indians, recorded in Dr. Douglas's learned Introduction to Cook's Voyage ‡ ; and may thus help to eftablifh an inland communication between the Pacific and Atlantic Oceans.

To the north of Beering's Straits, the land of America from Point § Mufgrave in latitude 67' 45", longitude 194' 51", to Icy Cape, in latitude 70' 29", longitude 198' 20", where Cook was totally ftopped by the ice, was not, excepting a fmall portion near Cape Lifburne, and another to the fouth of that promontory, obferved either by Cook or Clerke; and its true bearings muft be afcertained by future navigators.

But the moft important point of further inquiry is to trace the direction of the American continent from Icy Cape, whether it again trends to the north weft, and, according to the reports of the Tchutfki, approaches the coafts of Northern Siberia, or verges directly to the eaft towards Baffin's Bay.

* Vol. II. p. 491.   + Ib. p. 396.
‡ P. xlvii.   § Vol. II. p. 454. 461.

The

The execution of such an undertaking, in such distant regions, and in so high a latitude, must necessarily be attended
with extreme difficulty and hazard.   For the points of distance
between Icy Cape and the north western extremity of Buffin's
Bay, include a space of no less than seventy-one degrees longitude : of which nearly the central point has been explored by
Hearne alone *.

It must be neverthelefs admitted, that such inquiries, however
interefting to increafe our knowledge of the globe, do not tend to
throw any new light on the practicability of a north-eaft paffage;
which has been difproved by the obftacles and difficulties en-
countered by the Ruffians in navigating the Frozen Ocean +, and
more particularly by the undoubted teftimony of Cook himfelf.

3. The new-difcovered iflands remain to be confidered.
We have already remarked, that, as Cook obferved only a few of
thofe numerous iflands which lie fcattered in the Eaftern Ocean
between Afia and America, the pofition and defcription of the
remainder are to be drawn from the Ruffian accounts.   It cannot
be denied that the Ruffians have frequently corrupted their names,
increafed their number, and miftaken their fituation.   It is probable,
indeed, that Synd may have augmented the number of iflands
which lie near the coafts of the Tchutfki ; that St. Theodore, Imyak,
and Tzetchina, which are laid down among the Aleutian Ifles in
the general map of Ruffia, do not exift ; and that the Andreanofſki
Ifles, which are confidered as a feparate group, form the moft
wefterly part of that extenfive chain termed the Fox Iflands, of
which Unalafhka, fo amply defcribed by Cook and the Ruffians,
is nearly the center.

It may be urged, however, that, if the inaccuracy of the Ruffian
charts, in general, be admitted, and their accounts are juftly

* See Introduction to Cook's Voyage.
+ See Ruffian Difcoveries, p. 330.

D   deemed

deemed imperfect, what advantages can be derived from their publication?

To this it may be replied, that confiderable information may be obtained even from imperfect accounts, and that many points have, in effect, been afcertained, as the reader has already perceived in this Comparative View. We find even Cook himfelf anxious to procure intelligence from a Ruffian named Ifmailof, from whom he received a chart of the Ruffian Difcoveries. This chart, however, was not founded on the obfervations of a fingle navigator, but feems to have been a compilation from different charts and journals, and, confequently, extremely erroneous.

Nor does it appear that Ifmailof either poffeffed, or had feen, Krenitzin's chart of the Fox Iflands, which, according to the obfervations of the Englifh, is proved to be the moft accurate reprefentation of the Fox Iflands given by the Ruffians. The correction of this erroneous chart from Ifmailof's own experience, and additional remarks, muft have been ftill doubtful. For, as Captain Cook could not fpeak the Ruffian language, and as he had no Ruffian interpreter on board, the imperfect knowledge of this illiterate man was rendered ftill more imperfect by the only mode of communication they could adopt, that of converfing by figns.

And yet, under all thefe difadvantages, Cook gained fome information relative to the pofition and number of the iflands which he had not explored; an information which he has thought worthy to be laid before the public.

He particularly informs us, that " a paffage was marked in " Ifmailof's chart, communicating with Briftol Bay, which " covers about fifteen leagues on the coaft, that I had fuppofed " to belong to the continent, into an ifland diftinguifhed by the " name of Oonemak. This paffage might eafily efcape us, as

" we

" we were informed that it is very narrow, fhallow, and only to
" be navigated through with boats, or very fmall veffels *."

The exiftence of this ftrait, which Cook has adopted in his
chart, from Ifmailof's obfervations, might likewife have been
collected from Krenitzin's chart, and the feveral journals in my
Account of the Ruffian Difcoveries, wherein Unimak or Oonemak is fhewn to be an ifland feparated from Alaxa, fince proved
to be the continent of America, by a narrow ftrait.

It muft not be thought furprifing, that a collection of
voyages, performed by ignorant traders merely for the fake of
obtaining furs, and not with a view of difcovery, fhould be de-
fective in determining the pofition and number of fo many iflands.
We ought rather to wonder that the defcriptions, in general, are
tolerably accurate, and afford that degree of information which
they are found to contain. Nor muft it be forgotten that Beering's
and Krenitzin's expedition, which alone were undertaken by Imperial authority, reflect confiderable honour on the Ruffian
name.

The particulars, which remain to be afcertained with refpect to
the new-difcovered iflands, are, to remove the uncertainty arifing
from the confufion of names, to determine the true number,
and to fix the longitude and latitude. And when it is confidered
that the fea, unexplored by Cook, includes a fpace of at leaft
ten degrees of latitude, and twenty of longitude, much, in
this inftance, remains to be effected by the labours of future adventurers.

Thefe are the principal objects of examination on the coafts of
Afia and America, and in refpect to the new-difcovered iflands.
In order to forward thefe great ends, the Emprefs of Ruffia,

* Vol. II. p. 505.

D 2

with

with that boundlefs liberality and enlightened fpirit which characterifes her actions, has planned and commanded a voyage of difcovery. The care of this expedition, which was agitated and determined during my fecond vifit to Peterfburgh in 1785, is committed to Captain Billings, an Englifh naval officer in the Ruffian fervice, who is well qualified to conduct fuch an undertaking, as he accompanied Captain Cook in his laft celebrated voyage to the Pacific Ocean. I fhall briefly ftate the plan and purport of this expedition.

According to its firft object, Captain Billings is to proceed by Irkutfk, Yakutfk, and Okotfk to Kovimfkoi Oftrog: having traced the courfe of the Kovyma, and fettled by aftronomical obfervations the exact pofition of its mouth, he will endeavour to delineate the coafts extending from that point to Cape North, the utmoft period of Cook's navigation on the north eaftern fhores of Siberia. For this purpofe he will embark in fuch veffels as are ufually employed for coafting voyages in the Frozen Ocean; fix the longitude and latitude of the principal parts by aftronomical obfervations; form exact charts of the bays and inlets which he may have occafion to explore; and caufe views to be taken of the bearings, head-lands, and remarkable objects on the coaft. If he fhould be prevented by the ice, or any other obftacle, from getting round by fea to Tchukotfkoi-Nofs, he muft difembark, and endeavour to proceed by land or over the ice, furveying the coaft and diftrict of the Tchutfki and obtaining an accurate knowledge of their manners, population, and country. In both cafes, and in all inftances, he is enjoined to abftain from the leaft degree of violence; is directed to ufe every effort towards conciliating the affection of the natives; to obtain information and affiftance by the gentleft treatment, and a proper diftribution of prefents; and to confirm them in their

de-

dependence and favourable opinion of the Ruffian government, to which they have recently fubmitted.

While he continues in thefe parts, he will not neglect an opportunity of exploring the iflands and coafts of America, that may be fituated in the Frozen Ocean, or to the north of Beering's ftraits.

Having attempted to execute thefe defigns, he is to return to Okotfk, where two fhips of a proper burden for a voyage of difcovery, will be prepared for his further embarkation.

He is then to fail and follow the numerous chain of iflands which extend to the continent of America; determining their refpective longitudes and latitudes by a feries of aftronomical obfervations; taking an exact chart of their pofitions, and particularly noticing thofe roads and harbours which appear to be moft fecure. He is alfo to extend his refearches towards fuch parts of the American coaft, which bad weather and other impediments prevented preceding navigators from furveying. And in cafe his former attempts to determine the coaft of the Tchutfki from the mouth of the Kovyma to Cape North, and to gain an accurate information of the country, fhould be ineffectual; he is again ordered to fail towards Tchukotfkoi-Nofs, and endeavour to penetrate by fea from Beering's Straits to the mouth of the Kovyma, and to make thofe obfervations, and obtain that intelligence of thofe regions, which he could not procure on the former occafion.

Six years will be requifite for the accomplifhment of thefe various purpofes. In order to enfure its fuccefs, every poffible encouragement, in regard to promotion and rank, as the refpective objects are fulfilled, is given to the commander and his followers. No expence has been fpared towards pro-

4

curing

curing such an apparatus and inftruments as are neeeffary for this expedition.

For the purpofe alfo of elucidating the natural hiftory of thofe diftant regions, at prefent fo imperfectly known, the commander is accompanied by Monfieur Patrin, an eminent French natu-ralift, fome time refident at Irkutfk, who is furnifhed with fuch excellent inftructions as are moft calculated to forward the ob-ject of his miffion.

Captain Billings fet out from St. Peterfburgh on this expedi-tion in the latter end of 1785. He arrived at Irkutfk in March, 1786; and at Okotfk in July of the fame year, from whence he propofed inftantly to take his departure for the Kovyma. It is not indeed improbable, that, before the prefent period, he may have afcertained the longitude and latitude of the mouth of the Kovyma; and thus have determined one important fact, relative to the precife diftance between the Kovyma and Cape North. The length of time requifite for the conveying of intelligence from thofe diftant regions to St. Peterfburgh, and the difficulty of obtaining certain information from that capital, renders it impoffible to gratify the further curiofity of the reader.

POST-

———

POSTSCRIPT.

THE reader is requested to correct the longitude of Kamtchatka, mentioned p. 5 of my Russian Discoveries, as lying between 173 and 182 degrees from the isle of Fero; or 155 and 165 from Greenwich. Whereas, by the observations of the English, it is situated between 155 and 169 from Greenwich; or 172 and 186 from Fero; the Russian geographers having laid down the north-eastern part of the peninsula near three degrees too much to the west.

———

ERRATA.

P. 242. l. 11. for 1.313.621, &c. read 1.383.621.
P. 344. latitude of Port of St. Peter and Paul, for 35, read 53.

The Hiſtory of England, from the invaſion of Julius Cæſar to the Revolution. A new Edition, printed on a fine paper, with many Corrections and Additions; and a complete Index, 8 vols. Royal Paper, 7l. 7s.

⁎ Another Edition on ſmall Paper, 4l. 10s.

Another Edition in 8 vols. 8vo. 2l. 8s.

The Hiſtory of Scotland, during the Reigns of Queen Mary and of King James VI. till his acceſſion to the Crown of England; with a Review of the Scottiſh Hiſtory, previous to that period; and an Appendix, containing Original Papers: 2 vols. By William Robertſon, D. D. the 5th Edition, 1l. 10s.

Another Edition in 2 vols. 8vo. 10s.

The Hiſtory of the Reign of the Emperor Charles V. with a View of the Progreſs of Society in Europe, from the Subverſion of the Roman Empire to the Beginning of the ſixteenth Century. By William Robertſon, D. D. Embelliſhed with 4 plates, elegantly engraved; 3 Vols. 3l. 3s.

Another Edition in 4 Vols. 8vo. 1l. 4s.

The Hiſtory of America, Vol. I. and II. By the ſame Author. Illuſtrated with Maps. 2l. 2s.

Another Edition in 3 vols. 8vo. 18s.

The Hiſtory of the Reign of Philip the Second, King of Spain. By Robert Watſon, LL. D. Profeſſor of Philoſophy and Rhetoric at the Univerſity of St. Andrew. 2d Edition; 2 vols. 2l. 2s.

Another Edition in 3 Vols. 8vo. 18s.

The Hiſtory of the Decline and Fall of the Roman Empire. By Edward Gibbon, Eſq; Vol. I. from the Reign of Trajan, to that of Conſtantine; the 3d Edition. 1l. 4s.

An Acount of the Voyages undertaken by Order of his preſent Majeſty for making Diſcoveries in the Southern Hemiſphere, and ſucceſſively performed by Commodore Byron, Capt. Wallis, and Capt. Carteret, in the Dolphin, and Swallow, and the Endeavour; drawn up from the Journals which were kept by the ſeveral Commanders, and from the Papers of Joſeph Banks, Eſq; and Dr. Solander. By John Hawkeſworth, LL. D. Illuſtrated with Cuts and a great Variety of Charts and

Maps

BOOKS printed for T. CADELL.

Maps (in all 52 Plates) relative to the Countries now first difcovered, or hitherto but imperfectly known. Price 3 l. 12 s.

An Account of a Voyage towards the South Pole, and round the World: performed in his Majefty's Ships the Refolution and Adventure, in 1772, 1773, 1774, and 1775. Written by James Cooke, Commander of the Refolution. In which is included, Captain Furneaux's Narrative of his Proceedings in the Adventure, during the Separation of the Ships. Elegantly printed in 2 Vols. Royal. Illuftrated with Maps and Charts, and a Variety of Portraits of Perfons and Views of Places, drawn during the Voyage by Mr. Hodges, and engraved by the moft eminent Mafters. 2 l. 12 s.

Lord Anfon's Voyage round the World, 1 l. 1 s.

A Philofophical and Political Hiftory of the Settlements and Trade of the Europeans in the Eaft and Weft Indies, tranflated from the French of the Abbé Reynal. By J. Juftamond, M. A. A new Edition, carefully revifed, in 5 Vols. 8vo. and illuftrated with Maps, 1 l. 10 s.

A Tour through Sicily and Malta. In a Series of Letters to William Beckford, Efq; of Somerly in Suffolk, from P. Brydone, F.R.S. 2 Vols. illuftrated with a Map. 3d Edition. 12 s.

A View of Society and Manners in France, Switzerland, and Germany, with Anecdotes relating to fome eminent Characters. By John Moore, M. D. 2 Vols. 3d Edit. 12 s.

Ruffia; or a Complete Hiftorical Account of all the Nations which compofe that Empire, 2 Vols. 12 s.—The Third and Fourth Volumes (which will conclude the Work) are in the Prefs.

A Tour through fome of the Northern Parts of Europe, particularly Copenhagen, Stockholm, and Peterfburgh, in a Series of Letters, by N. Wraxall, jun. 3d Edition. 6 s.

A Journal to the Weftern Ifles of Scotland. By the Author of the Rambler. 6 s.

Letters from an Englifh Traveller (Martin Sherlock, Efq;) Tranflated from the French Original, printed at Geneva and at Paris, with Notes. A new Edition, revifed and corrected, fmall 8vo. Price 2 s. 6 d.